EYE OF THE CHICKENHAWK

Simon Dovey

Copyright © 2023 Simon Dovey

All rights reserved.

ISBN: 9780645953800

"There is always a rash of kidnapping and abductions of schoolchildren in the football months. Preteens of both sexes are traditionally seized and grabbed off the streets by gangs of organized perverts who traditionally give them as Christmas gifts to each other to be personal sex slaves and playthings. Most of these things are obviously Wrong and Evil and Ugly — but at least they are Traditional."
— Hunter Thompson, Loathsome Secrets of a Star-Crossed Child in the Final Days of the American Century

The Snuff film
The Snuff Film 4

The Dean Corll Murders - Houston Texas '73
The Dean Corll Murders 13
John Norman Connection 17
DOMLyric 22
Roy Ames Connection 26

The John Gacy Murders - Chicago Illinois 1972-78
Phillip Paske & The Delta Project 34
John Wayne Gacy 40
John Norman Connection 45
Table 51
Hermes 53

North Fox Island - Michigan '76
Hermes & The Delta Project 57
Francis Shelden & North Fox Island 59
Gerald Richards Network Diagram 66
Father Bud's Boys Farm 67

Troop 137 & Adelphi Tours ... 68

Francis Shelden Arrest Warrant ... 77

Oakland County Child Murders - MIchigan 1976-77(Cold Case:2004-2009)

North Fox Island Connection ... 83

Francis Shelden Snuff Film Connection ... 96

Chris Busch & General Motors ... 102

Spartacus International - UK, Amsterdam, Germany, Australia '79-95

Francis Shelden & John Stamford ... 111

Clarence Henry Osborne Connection ... 115

The Elm Guest House - UK 1982, 1990(Cold Case: 2012-2015)

Elm Guest House & Westminster Pedophile Dossier ... 121

Carol Kasir Inquest & Mary Moss Files ... 124

Sidney Cooke & Operation Midland ... 129

Jason Swift Snuff Film & Amsterdam Connection ... 136

Operation Framework - Amsterdam 1992-93

Warwick Spinks & Amsterdam Snuff films ... 140

Chris Denning, Operation Yewtree & the BBC ... 145

Warwick Spinks, Alan Williams & TAG Films 157

The HIK Report, Rolodex Affair & Joris Demmink - Amsterdam 1994, 1998

The HIK Report & Lothar Glandorf 162

The Rolodex Affair & Joris Demmink 165

Apollo Bulletin Board - Zandvoort 1998

Gerrit Ulrich & Robbie Van Der Plancken 174

The Manuel Schadwald Snuff Film 179

The X-Dossier - Belgium 1996-97

Marc Dutroux Kidnappings 193

MIchel Nihoul Connection 196

The X-Dossier 203

The CRIES Connection 218

Spartacus & Abrasax Connection 226

The X-Witnesses 231

Dutroux & Hypnosis 239

Epilogue: The Finders - Washington D.C 1987

The Finders & The Odyssey Network 247

Author's Note

This is independant research. This is an advantage in two respects. First, researchers with institutional accreditation are restricted in their inquiries by taboo. That is — the fear of losing credibility through expressing unacceptable ideas, or even facts. I am unrestricted in this regard. Secondly, because I lack credibility the burden of proof falls more heavily upon me as I cannot take certain liberties in reaching conclusions. My book reflects the reality of this and in my opinion having no credibility is an asset so long as one is aware of it and strives to demonstrate it through the substance of what they present. As a result, almost every paragraph in this book is footnoted with the sources from which it was derived. This is not to achieve any kind of academic veneer. I am not an academic and this is not an academic book. Academics cannot research the subject dealt with here because it is taboo for them to do so.

Information in this book has been sourced from other books, newspapers of record and tabloids, law enforcement reports, government records, NGO reports, court filings, and online articles. Regarding this last item, many urls provided have since become dead or will become dead in the future. They can be accessed using website archival tools.

By far the most useful resource has been the compilations of research materials compiled and made available by various semi-anonymous individuals, who have discovered, paid for, and compiled much of the primary source evidence on online forums, databases, articles, and blogs. Where appropriate these have been cited as secondary sources in the footnotes. Given the largely anonymous nature of online information, attribution of credit for who discovered what first becomes difficult. As such, the following online resources haven't been cited but can be credited for compiling much of the primary source information cited in this book, and along with it much of the legwork in research.

- Cavdef.org
- Spotlightonabuse.wordpress.com
- theneedleblog.wordpress.com
- catherinebroad.blog

One last note. Pedophilia was often conflated with homosexuality by news and law enforcement agencies in the 1970s and 1980s. Many of the sources used, such as police reports and newspaper articles, characterise crimes such as the rape, torture, and murder of children as homosexual ones. The men involved in such crimes, in many instances, did not have sex with other men at the peer level. Some were married to women. The homophobic slant given in police reports and news articles at the time these crimes were committed does not preclude these as evidence of the crimes themselves. They are the only pieces of evidence we have.

Network Continuity Map

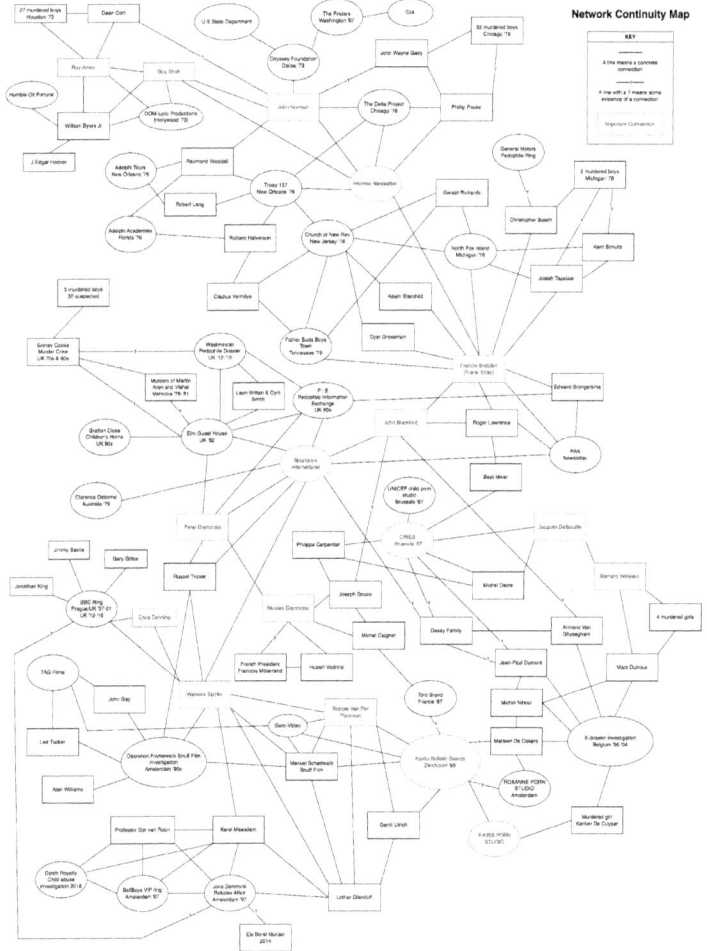

The Snuff Film

If art is a peek inside the psyche of society at any given moment, the snuff film is sure to mark the end of it. The definition here is specific. It is not just a film produced to capture a live murder on film, but one produced for the express purpose of pleasing an audience. Live murder films produced and circulated by drug cartels or terrorist groups are not snuff films but propaganda, as they are not intended to be enjoyed.

One would imagine the desire to film a real murder had existed long before the means to do so became widespread around the turn of the 20th century. As image capture technology became more widely available in the early decades of that century, it's hard to imagine somebody somewhere didn't make the very first snuff film.

Yet the usual culprits still to this day, for some strange reason, assert such a thing is an urban myth. As one fact-checker put it in 2021, *"All the fretting about it aside, not so much as one snuff film has been found. Time and again, what is originally decried in the press as a film of a murder turns out, upon further investigation, to be a fake. Police on three continents routinely investigate films brought to them, and so far this has always been their verdict. No snuff films. Some clever fakes, yes. But no real product."*[1]

As nice as that would be, in reality snuff films were confirmed by law enforcement authorities before the turn of the 20th century. In 1999 it was reported:

> "Two Germans have been jailed for life after becoming the first people in Europe to be convicted of murder while producing a 'snuff movie,' a film in which real victims are tortured and killed. A court in the town of Hagan heard how Ernst Dieter Korzen, 37, and Stefan Michael Mahn, 30, filmed themselves sexually assaulting and torturing a 21-year-old woman in 1997 to produce the snuff movies which they expected to sell for more than $25,000. The victim died before the production was complete and the pair kidnapped a second woman to finish the video. But she escaped and the men were arrested…Wolfgang Rahmer, the chief prosecutor, told the court 'From my experience this represents a new depth in perversion. You see the victim begging for her life, pain being inflicted and massive sexual torture'… According to Andre Rogge, a private detective in Belgium, the cruel fantasies of such movie makers even extend to children. Rogge specializes in seeking missing children and fears many are victims of the snuff film industry. He said the German case was not isolated, but involved an international network."
> — 'Snuff movie makers get life', The Windsor Star, Ontario Canada, April 13 1999

These fears were confirmed the following year when Italian authorities discovered films coded "Necros Pedo" among those being distributed internationally by a child porn network based in Russia.

> "Last week Italian police seized 3,000 of Kuznetsov's videos on their way to client's in Italy; sparking an international hunt for paedophiles who have bought

his products. The Italian investigators said the material includes footage of children dying during abuse. Prosecutors in Naples are considering charging those who have bought the videos with complicity in murder. They say some may have specifically requested films of killings. . . The most appalling category was code-named 'Necros Pedo' in which children were raped and tortured until they died. . .The Naples newspaper Il Matino published a transcript of an alleged email exchange between a prospective client and the Russian vendors. *'Promise me you're not ripping me off,'* says the Italian. *'Relax. I can assume you this one really dies,'* the Russian responds. *'The last time I paid I didn't get what I wanted.'*, *'What do you want?'*, *'To see them die'.* "

— 'British link to snuff videos', The Observer, October 1 2000

The concept of a snuff film appears to have first been introduced into the public mind through the 1960 film *Peeping Tom*. In it the protagonist is the son of a behavioural psychologist who used him in experiments during early childhood to study the response of the central nervous system to fear. Because of this in adulthood, the protagonist has developed a sadistic fascination with fear and starts to capture it on the faces of women he murders on film.

The term 'snuff movie' was then coined a decade later by Ed Sanders in his 1971 book *The Family*, detailing his investigation into the violent escapades of Charles Manson and his followers during the late 1960s. Manson's cult had often recorded their group activities with super 8 cameras and screened these bizarro flicks at makeshift outdoor cinema events, held in private at the Spahn movie ranch. These films had mostly been of group sex and nonsense performance art, but some had included the torture and murder of animals. According to one individual Sanders interviewed who attended one of these screenings, they'd seen a short five minute super 8 reel of a young women being beheaded on a beach, referring to it as a "snuff movie."[2]

Sanders had posed as an art dealer looking to acquire Manson family films during the trial and learnt that, *"7-hours of assorted erotic films including Manson porn collected during the pre-trial investigations. But the price was $250,000."*[3] A friend of Gary Hinman, one of the Manson family victims, claimed to one reporter they'd been in possession of films of *"Malibu and San Franciso ax murders"*. One snuff movie was rumoured to have been sold to a famous New York artist, who Sanders does not name, though needlessly references Andy Warhol in the paragraph prior to mentioning this.[4]

In the mid 1970s law enforcement in New York started to receive tips from, *"very reliable underworld sources there are eight snuff films being circulated. Viewers at private screenings, he said, pay up to $200 to witness the filmed killings. . .He indicated the films begin with an actress and several actors engaging in a variety of sex acts. Soon, however, a knife appears, and the actress is stabbed to death and dismembered."*[5] Alan Dershowitz, a renowned civil liberties advocate for New York's Eastern Establishment, wouldn't help put these rumours to rest, when in 1977 he felt the need to defend the legality of privately screened snuff film events, provided the victims featured in them had been murdered overseas.[6]

In 1985 a prominent Manhattan art dealer named Andrew Crispo was accused of ordering the murder of a Norwegian fashion student named Eigil Vesti during a sadomasochist orgy held in a backroom of his art gallery, infamously known as the Death Mask Murder. Vesti's charred remains had been discovered in a smokehouse on the property of a United Nations official named John P. LeGeros. Vesti's naked body was found with a leather gimp mask slipped over his head punctured by a bullet hole. The UN Official's son turned out to be a personal assistant of Andrew Crispo named Bernard Legeros, who was charged with second-degree murder after a .22-caliber rifle deemed to be the murder weapon was discovered in Crispo's gallery.[7] The 22 year-old Legeros stated Crispo had gotten him hooked on cocaine and used him to procure victims for S&M encounters. He claimed Crispo had ordered him to execute Vesti during a cocaine-fuelled sadomasochist orgy. As Legeros' attorney explained to the uninitiated at the time, *"This case involved an S&M scenario. . .You have a master and a slave. . .The master was Andrew Crispo and he had a series of slaves,"* going on to point out, *"People seem to be losing sight of the fact that Vesti was wearing a bondage mask owned by Andrew Crispo, that he was wearing handcuffs owned by Andrew Crispo, and that he was whipped with whips owned by Andrew Crispo."*[8] As a reluctant witness at Legeros's trial, Crispo pleaded the fifth over and over until the judge dismissed him. A few year later in 1988 a man named Mark Leslie came forward and accused Crispo of having him tortured at gunpoint during another cocaine-fuelled sadomasochist orgy in the back room of Crispo's gallery in 1984. During courtroom testimony, *"The man said Crispo and the others, who included now-convicted Vesti killer Bernard LeGeros, 26, told him they had a 'need' to kill people and demanded that he give them a name of someone they could murder in a snuff movie."*[9] Bernard LeGeros agreed to testify against Crispo on defendants behalf, describing *"the man who has accused Crispo of the torture as 'crying' and 'frightened' on a September night in 1984, when it's charged he was handcuffed, whipped, and urinated on at the posh east side art gallery."*[10] The jury ultimately found Crispo innocent on account of the victim having consented to sadomasochistic sex.

An investigative journalist named Maury Terry, whose research intersected with the Andrew Crispo case during his own investigation into an alleged snuff film produced by Roy Radin involving one of the Son of Sam murders,[11] noted in his 1987 book *The Ultimate Evil*, *"Author Anthony-Haden Guest, who published a major story about Crispo in New York magazine, added another compelling lead when he told me Crispo had spoken about snuff films and a contact for them in Houston."*[12]

In 1994 Crispo's former assistant Bernard LeGeros alleged in a signed an affidavit, *"Mr. Crispo told me that Mr. Mammano was fencing stolen artwork, including sculptures, for him. Mr. Crispo also told me that Mr. Mammano sold cocaine to Mr. Crispo and that Mr. Mammano imported gay and straight 'snuff' movies into the United States from Mexico. Snuff movies are obscene movies in which a person is actually murdered on film. I heard that a man from Texas named John produced the snuff movies in Mexico and that John was subsequently arrested and convicted for committing a crime in Texas."*[13]

It would seem there had been demand for snuff films from at least one of New York's high society gallery owners by the early 1980s. And more tangible evidence of actual snuff film production had been found years earlier on the other side of the country.

In 1977 a Californian man named Fred Berre Douglas was arrested for soliciting a prostitute to help him torture, rape and murder two other women on film in the Yucca Valley desert. Douglas led two female undercover officers posing as aspiring models to a spot in the desert where, *"he kept saws, knives, chemicals, animal horns and ropes, which police later said were props for filming."*[14] Since no murder had been committed or snuff film found, the jury was deadlocked and Douglas escaped conviction. A few years later though he would lure a pair of teenaged girls into the desert for a porno shoot and murder them there with an associate named Richard Hernandez.[15] A female acquittance of the two men had testified,

"Douglas asked her if she would assist him in killing young women in the desert while making sex films that included bondage and sadism. Douglas apparently believed having a woman present would make it easier for the victims to trust him. Phillips testified that Douglas told her that his plan was to bury the bodies to eliminate any evidence and that they could make a lot of money selling the films to 'people in Las Vegas.' Phillips refused to participate in the scheme, but did not go to the police because of her drug habit. Her contact with Douglas ended when she was convicted of burglary and sentenced to jail."[16] The men claimed they hadn't filmed the murders and only the girls bodies had been found, so who knows.

A journalist named Robert Anson reporting on a growing trend of violent pornography in 1977 detailed a super 8 film called 'First Communion' he'd personally viewed in a $1 peepshow machine at an adult book store in New York.

> "The first reel shows five eight-year-old girls receiving their first communion, perfect innocence. Suddenly, a motorcycle gang breaks into the church. Right then, you know what is going to happen, but you can't stop from dropping in the second quarter. And here there is a surprise. For, instead of immediately commencing to rape the girls, the gang pauses to beat up the priest with chains. Then they crucify him to the cross above the altar. Finally, by reel four, the sex begins. You can actually see the little girls bleeding. All of them are screaming. Except the movie is silent, and you can't hear their cries."
> — 'The Last Porno Show', Robert Anson, New Times Magazine, June 24 1977

While it seems unlikely to have been real, Anson interviewed a vice detective investigating at that time, what were suspected to be the very real snuff film murders of young Mexican children smuggled into the USA by child pornographers in

LA.

"You don't have to suppose very long in Martin's business. Once you imagine the worst, it invariably happens, and, sure enough, it has already happened. Green plastic garbage bags keep turning up in and around Los Angeles, 18 of them so far in the last 18 months. Inside the bags are the dismembered, mutilated bodies of young boys, Mexicans mostly, some of the kids who Martin says are being smuggled across the border, sometimes in specially constructed compartments concealed in the floorboards and fenders of cars, to infuse fresh, exotic blood in the kiddie porn industry."
— The Last Porno Show', Robert Anson, New Times Magazine, June 24 1977

This vice detective then relayed quite a remarkable rumour. A snuff film, one being screened at private parties in Hollywood, featuring a victim of the notorious serial killer named Dean Corll.

"There was one film reportedly making the circuit, supposedly it had been a big hit at an L.A party a few weeks before, showing a boy actually being murdered. He had been one of Dean Corll's kids down in Texas, the story went. That had happened to a lot of Dean Corll's kids. By the time they finished digging them up, the Houston police had come up with 27 of them. Police strongly suspected that a number of young porn stars were among Corll's victims."
— The Last Porno Show', Robert Anson, New Times Magazine, June 24 1977

And so this unfortunate book begins in 1973, with the discovery of a mass grave of murdered boys in Houston, Texas.

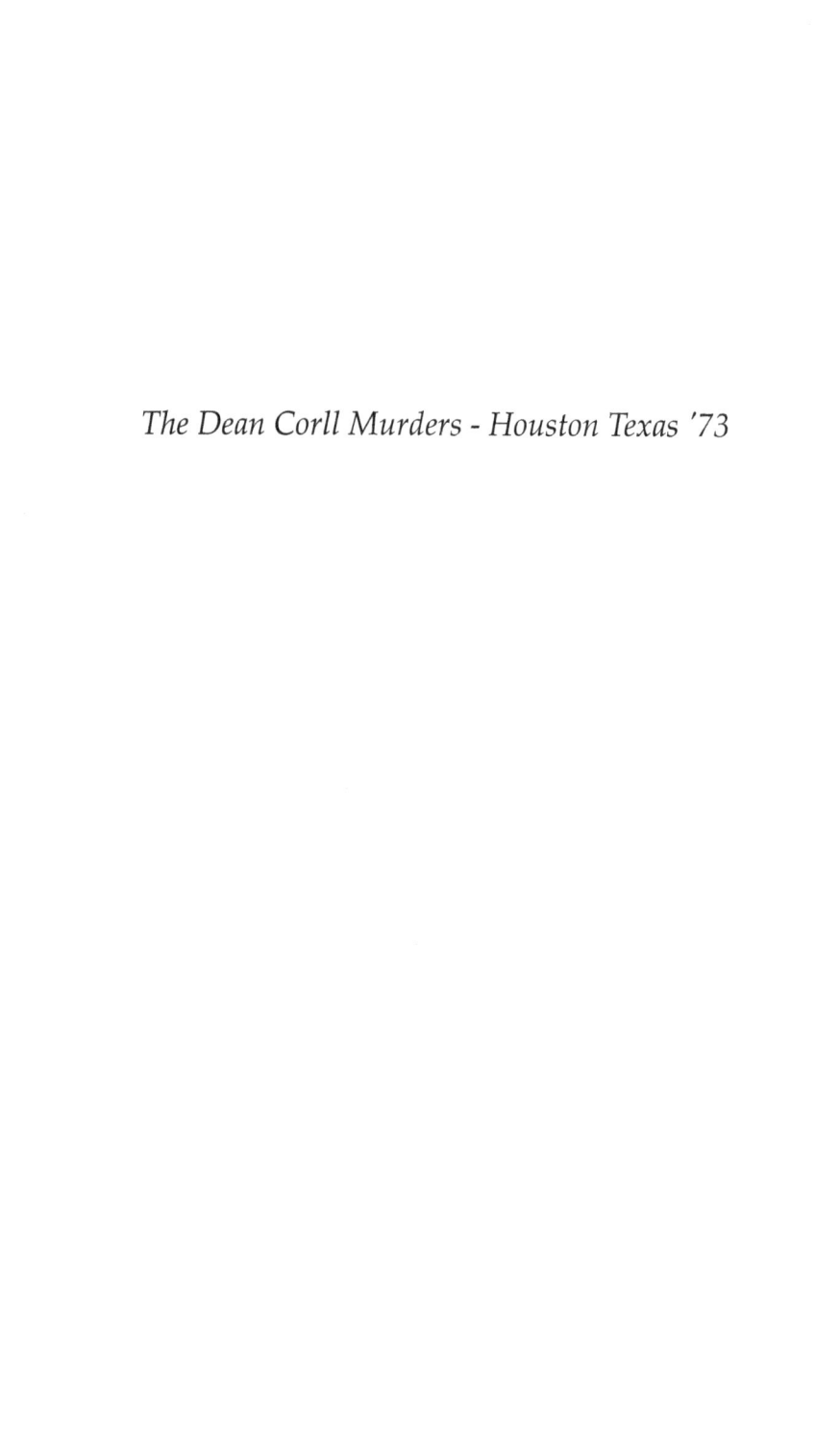

The Dean Corll Murders - Houston Texas '73

The Dean Corll Murders

On the morning of August 8 1973, 17 year-old Elmer Wayne Henley called Pasadena PD in Houston, Texas to report he had shot and killed a man in his home. When police arrived at the address they discovered the bullet ridden body of 33 year-old Dean Corll, lying naked in the hallway of his Pasadena bungalow. Henley had been waiting for police out front of the property with two other teenagers, 20 year-old Timothy Cordell Kerley and 15 year-old Rhonda Louise Williams.

According to the three's statements, which more or less aligned, Henley had invited his two friends over to Dean Corll's house for a paint sniffing party. They had all passed out and at some point Corll tied the three of them up and started to rape Kerley. Henley, who was friends with Corll, convinced Corll to untie him so he could do the same to Rhonda. When Henley was free he managed to get a hold of gun he used to shoot Corll with. He then untied the other two and called the police.[17]

In a living area of the bungalow police had found sprawled across the floor a sheet roll of polyethylene plastic and a large plywood 'torture board' with holes in each corner fitted with rope and handcuffs. Various sex toys and torture devices were found, such as a double-ended dildo, glass rods, and a hunting knife.[18]

Upon being taken into custody and questioned, Wayne Henley told police he knew of several missing teenagers Corll had killed and buried in a nearby boat shed. Henley directed police to 4500 Silverbell where Corll had rented a storage shed since 1970. Inside they discovered two ten pound bags of garden lime, a rake and shovel, plastic bags full of teenage sized boys clothing, an envelope containing pornographic literature, and disturbed soil beneath some carpeting.[19] A subsequent excavation of the site turned up the bodies of seventeen boys aged between thirteen and nineteen who had been reported missing over the past three years.[20]

While initially vague in the explanation he gave as to his relationship with Dean Corll, and how he came to know about the mass grave, Wayne Henley eventually confessed to having helped torture, kill and bury at least six of Corll's victims. He told police of another two locations where bodies had been buried. Four more were recovered from a wooded area near Lake Sam Rayburn where Corll's family owned a cabin, while further seven were found buried along a beachline on the Bolivar Peninsula. A total of twenty-eight known victims reported missing between September 1970 and August 1973. All of them males aged between thirteen and twenty years. Autopsies performed on the bodies indicated all had been raped and tortured before being killed, with the cause of death in most instances given as strangulation or a single .22 gunshot to the head.

During his confession Wayne Henley implicated an eighteen year-old friend of his named David Owen Brooks as a third accomplice, and the person who'd introduced him to Dean Corll two year prior. David Brooks was interviewed by police and confessed to procuring victims for Dean Corll and involvement in some of the murders. From both confessions detectives concluded the pair of teenagers had lived on and off with Dean Corll for the past three years, who paid them to procure victims, and over time the pair had progressively come to participate in the torture, murder, and disposal of victims themselves.[21]

Thus, we get the following case profile. A murder crew consisting of one adult and two teenaged procurers; engaged in the rape, torture, and murder of males under twenty buried together in a mass grave. This, is more or less where the official account of the case ends in popularised true crime. Dean Corll was nicknamed "The Candyman Killer" and the motive behind his murders was attributed to his 'modus operandi' as a 'serial *killer*'. Which is to say motive was looked for in the pathology of a single killer.

The first sign there had been more than one man's psychological profile behind these killings is found in the confession statements given by both Wayne Henley and David Brooks on August 9. The day after Dean Corll was killed. Both teenagers independently stated Dean Corll told them he was part of an organisation based in Dallas which bought and sold boys, and other members of this organisation were also murdering them.

Wayne Henley's signed confession on August 9 stated he was introduced to Dean Corll by David Brooks after he expressed an interest in making some money:

". . .and he took me to Dean Corll. Dean told me that he belonged to an organisation out of Dallas that bought and sold boys, ran whores and dope and stuff like that. Dean told me that he would pay me $200 at least for every boy that I could bring and maybe more if they were real good looking boys. . .I have come within an inch of killing him(Corll) but I just never got up enough nerve to do it until yesterday, because Dean had told me that his organisation would get me if I ever did anything to him."

— Elmer Wayne Henley signed confession given to

Pasadena PD, August 9 1973, 11:55am. David Brooks signed confession statement made the same day stated:

"During one of our conversations Dean mentioned that there was a group of people in Dallas which had similar activities to his. He mentioned a man by the name of Art who he said had also killed some boys in Dallas. One day while I was at his house I picked up a piece of paper with the name Art on it and all of a phone number but the last number and the area code was 214. Dean also mentioned Art has a wife. Lately Dean has been wanting to go to Dallas and I believe was supose[sic] to go at the end of this month."

— David Owen Brooks signed confession given to Harris County PD, August 9th 1973, 1:20pm.

Both confessions were made on August 9, with Henley's confession timestamped at 11.55 am and Brooks' at 1.20 pm. They were being held and questioned at separate police stations in Houston by two different teams of detectives. Henley had been held in the custody of Pasadena police since the morning of August 8. While Brooks had turned himself into Harris County PD on the morning of August 9 after having heard news of Corll's death.

It's unlikely the pair had an opportunity to communicate, making their statements mutually corroborating evidence Dean Corll claimed to belong to an organisation based in Dallas involved in trafficking and murdering boys.

Further more, Rhonda Williams, the female teenager who was tied up at Dean Corll's house when Henley shot him, stated something similar to investigators:

"Wayne has told Rhonda that he had been to Dallas several times with Dean and that a warehouse was in Dallas where she could make $1500 a week doing something illegal but Wayne reportedly had never told her what it was."

> — Houston PD Supplementary Offense Report No. D-68904, Progress Report - August 16 1973.

A total of three statements from two culprits and one witness suggested Dean Corll may have worked for an organisation based in Dallas which bought, sold, and killed boys.

- Signed confession of Elmer Wayne Henley, as given on the 9th of August 1973.
- Signed confession of David Owen Brooks, as given on the 9th of August 1973.
- Statement by Rhonda Williams, as recorded by police on the 16th of August 1973.

On August 11 Pasadena detectives noted in their report their intention to check with local postal authorities the number of a private post office box registered to Dean Corll in Houston, which David Brooks stated Corll had used to receive pornographic materials.[22] David Brooks would also later state, *"that Corll had been super secretive about his mail, picking it up at a post-office box, reading it then destroying it."*[23]

On August 13 detectives called Dallas PD to inform them of a possible connection between their murders and some in Dallas.[24] The very next day, on August 14, Dallas PD received a tip from an anonymous informant on a man running a mail-order boy prostitution service out of his Dallas apartment.[25] Acting on this information, police in Dallas arrested a 45 year-old man named John David Norman, found at the address in the company of five teenaged boys. From the apartment police seized photographic equipment, child pornography, and enough publishing stationary, files, and literature to fill an entire van, all pertaining to an organisation called *The Odyssey Foundation*.[26] Among the files seized were thousands of index cards with the names and addresses of, *"clients around the country, some of them prominent people and some federal employees in Washington."*[27] Mail correspondance taken from the apartment had been forwarded through a post office box registered in San Diego to *The Norman Foundation* and *Epic International*.[28] The foundation had been setup to ostensibly operate as a non-profit mentorship program which paired adult 'sponsors' with boy 'fellows' for inter-state educational trips. The 'sponsors' would provide lodging for 'fellows' and pay for their travel expenses. As Robin Lloyd explained in his book *For Money or Love: Boy Prostitution in America:*

> "Sponsors, selected from a master list of 50,000 prospects, were invited to join the Foundation for an enrolment fee of fifteen dollars. For an additional three dollars, they were sent a booklet called 'Fellows 1973,' which was a catalog of photos and mini biographies of hundreds of available boys. Foundation literature explained in decorous terms that Odyssey would arrange for sponsors to meet any of these young men should they so desire: *'At a surprisingly modest cost ($20 to $40 a day plus air fare), a sponsor may expedite a fellow's planned program and gain the opportunity to share the adventure.'*"
> — 'For Money or Love: Boy Prostitution in America', Robin Lloyd, 1976, page 80

Classified ads for Norman's callboy service were placed in both gay magazines and underground boylover newsletters circulated through the post. His operation spanned from coast to coast across the United States using mostly young runaways who were sent interstate, making them reliant on the men who would provide them with room and board. The service was popular among child pornographers, who sought an influx of fresh talent to use in their photographs and films, *"Sponsors would contact the Dallas headquarters of the foundation, which would then send a fellow to the sponsor's home. The sponsor would notify the organization how long he wanted the fellow to stay and then pay the boy's fare to his next assignment."*[29]

Among the files seized from Norman's apartment were photos and descriptions of available boys, of which four had the word "kill" written on them.[30] Apparently these were found in the apartment by a 21 year-old staying with Norman named Charles Brisendine, which led to the raid.

"Brisendine, then twenty-one, had replied to one of the published ads and was invited, by a sponsor to Dallas. When he arrived, he spent the night at Norman's apartment. They had sex together. Norman explained his operation to Brisendine, still maintaining the facade of a 'help' operation. But Brisendine wasn't so easily taken in. It was obvious to him that Norman was setting up a procurement service and many of the young men who would serve as 'fellows' were going to be lured to Dallas under false pretences. When Brisendine started to go through Odyssey's literature, he found that several of the 'Fellows' were missing and information pertaining to them had been stamped 'Kill'. This shook up Brisendine. At that time the horrors of the Houston murders were making headlines around the world and Brisendine recounted that Norman had been on the phone continually to Houston and seemed irritated whenever the subject of the Houston murders came up. Brisendine became convinced that Odyssey, somehow, was connected with the Houston murders."

— 'For Money or Love: Boy Prostitution in America', Robin Lloyd, 1976, page 81

To clarify the timeline:
- On August 8 Houston police discovered a mass grave of boys murdered by Dean Corll and two teenaged accomplices, Wayne Henley and David Brooks.
- On August 9 both Henley and Brooks gave indepen-

dent statements Dean Corll had claimed to belong to an organisation based in Dallas that bought, sold, and murdered boys.
- On August 11 Houston police discovered a private post office box they suspected Dean Corll used to 'secretively' receive pornography through the mail.
- On August 13 Houston police contacted Dallas PD regarding a possible connection between their murders and ones in Dallas. On this day the FBI also sent a memo to Dallas PD detailing information Charles Brisendine had provided others.
- On August 14 Dallas PD then bust an interstate boy trafficking network facilitated by a man named John David Norman using the postal service — The Odyssey Network. In his apartment were found photographs of boys used in the network who were missing, stamped with the word "kill" on them.

The possible link between the Houston murders and the *Odyssey Network* in Dallas were alluded to in the press but never substantiated. All that was publicly known was the tip received on the *Odyssey Network* had come from an informant spooked by the murders in Houston. And in the apartment of the man in Dallas four "kill" photographs had been found. As it was expressed in the New York Times, *"Assistant Police Chief Donald Steele reported that four pictures of young boys found in the apartment had the word "Kill" written on them. However, the police said they were told the word referred to their removal from the procurement ring's literature because they were uncooperative and did not mean they had been ordered killed."*[31]

The timing and discovery of 'kill' photographs in Dallas may raise an eyebrow, but what happened to the *Odyssey Network* client cards raises both. These would be handed over to Henry Kissinger's State Department and subsequently destroyed. This fact was confirmed by the State Department itself, both in an official statement given to the Chicago Tribune in 1977,[32] and then in an official letter of response to a request made by a US congressional inquiry into child exploitation held that same year.

"Lt. Harold Hancock of the Dallas police arrested Norman in March, 1973, on charges of contributing to juvenile violation of state drug laws. Hancock told The Tribune he confiscated from Norman more than 30,000 index cards listing clients around the country, some of them prominent people and some federal employees in Washington. *'I felt that some federal agency should get the cards and I contacted the State Department through the FBI. I think it was,'* Hancock said. *'All the cards were sent to Washington to the State Department, and that's the last I heard of it'*. The State Department confirmed to The Tribune that it had received the cards. Matthew Nimetz, a counselor for the State Department, said officials there determined *'the cards were not relevant to any fraud case concerning a passport'* and therefore destroyed them. Nimetz was unable to explain why the State Department looked at the cards only from the standpoint of possible passport irregularities or why it had not turned them over to the FBI or postal inspectors."

— 'Chicago is center of national child pornography ring', Chicago Tribune, May 16 1977.

According to the State Department's letter to Congress, just days after news of the *Odyssey Network* broke in Dallas one of its field agents in Los Angeles reported the case to Washington. On August 23 a State Department agent was sent to assist Dallas PD with their investigation. Apparently, this had been regarding the fraudulent use of a passport. Dallas PD mentioned to the agent that two of the names found on index cards had matched those of State Department employees, and this information was relayed to Washington sometime before September 5 1973. The State Department confirmed two of its employees had similar names to the ones found on client index cards. One of these had been assigned to the US embassy in Mexico City, though no further investigation was made into this. In December 1974 Dallas PD had then handed over to the State Department the entire trove of client index cards seized from John Norman. These were placed into State Department storage, where they remained 'without review' until they were eventually destroyed in September 1975.[33]

Around a year later in late 1976 the FBI requested to review the *Odyssey Network* items in State Department storage as part of an investigation into information it received government employees had been clients of the *Odyssey Network*. In response to an internal information request, one of the Dallas PD Lieutenants who'd arrested Norman in August 1973 advised, *"that NORMAN, at the time of his arrest, had in his possession an extensive card file and numerous pieces of correspondence from individuals located throughout the United States. Lieutenant [Redacted] stated the[sic] he recalls some of the pieces of correspondence were from individuals located in the Washington, D. C. area and who were possibly employees of the Federal Government"*.[34] The Lieutenant went onto mention all the evidence seized was handed over to the State Department in 1974, who then advised the FBI it had unfortunately all been destroyed except for a few items.[35]

A few weeks into the Dean Corll murder investigation, detectives in Houston received a letter, postmarked August 24 1973, from a Californian man named Steven Dale Ahern. They checked with the LAPD CI division, who told them Ahern *"was a member of the NAZI PARTY and writes letters and some of the information he comes up with is good."*[36] Ahern claimed to be a former male prostitute and model in pornographic films. Back in 1971 he responded to an advertisement in a magazine and received a paid offer to travel to Houston for a pornography shoot. There he'd been photographed by a man named Roy Ames, who Ahern said operated a large pornographic empire that exploited young boys. Ahern wrote some of the boy victims in Houston had been photographed by Ames, and that he had identified one of these victims in a child porn magazine published by Ames being circulated in California. Ahern then noted the reason for his letter. He wrote Ames had known Dean Corll and used him to exploit young boys.[37]

The detectives contacted Steven Ahern by phone for further information and he told them he met Dean Corll through Roy Ames in Houston, and was invited to a sadomasochist orgy at an apartment Dean Corll rented back in 1971. Ahern said Roy Ames was one of the largest producers of child pornography, responsible for around one third of the photographs and films produced in the United States, and provided detectives with a list of magazines published by Ames in Houston which were being distributed in California.[38]

The LAPD vice division was contacted sometime in late August 1973 to help Houston PD attain copies of these publication to see if any of Dean Corll's victims could be identified in them. In a copy of a magazine called *Hot Rods #3* detectives identified a boy who they felt looked similar to a 15 year-old victim of Dean Corll named William Lawrence. The photo was shown to the victim's father who said it was not his son, though in this part of their report detectives note that despite this, in their opinion there was a good possibility it was. They managed to trace these magazines to an address in Houston belonging to a record label called *Clarity Music*, owned by a music producer named Roy Ames.[39]

About a week after the LAPD vice division were contacted to help with this, they arrested a Hollywood-based child pornographer named Guy Strait on September 1 1973, for using underaged boys in his films, some of whom were from Texas. It was reported, *"Police said they were checking with Texas authorities in Dallas and Houston to find out whether there is any connection with an alleged ring in Texas which supplied hundreds of teen-age boys as prostitues for older men across the country."*[40]

Guy Strait was the operator of a mail-order child porn business called *Dom Studios,* and had launched a joint venture with another child pornographer named William 'Bill' Byars Jr., who owned a company called *Lyric Productions*. Together the pair operated, at that time in the early 1970s, California's largest child porn venture through a company called *DOM-Lyric Productions*.[41]

Guy Strait's arrest in September eventually led to those of his business partner and thirteen others later in October 1973, in bust-up described by vice detectives as, *"one of the nation's biggest 'chicken movie' operations."*[42] Among those arrested was a close associate of Williams Byars Jr. named William Johnson, a photographer from Houston.[43] It was reported:

> "The films sold for $50 each and the magazines for $5 and $10. Many of the alleged hardcore films were produced by Lyric Film Productions, reportedly owned by Byars. A Houston, Tex., photographer, William Johnson worked for Byars and also was named in the indictment. Grodin was quick to say there had been no link discovered between the alleged Los Angeles crimes and the mass homosexual murders in Houston, uncovered Aug. 8. He said Johnson and Byars may have transported some of their actors from the Houston area to California for the films."
>
> — 'Star's son faces sex charge', Independent, Press Telegram, Long Beach, California, October 27 1973

William Byars Jr., also from Houston, was heir to the Humble Oil fortune in Texas where his father, William Byars Snr., was a well established oilman with the kinds of friends in high places one would expect. One of these was J. Edgar Hoover, who Byars Jr. knew through his father. According to a book called *Official and Confidential* by Anthony Summers, Byars Jr. had supplied Hoover with boys used in his pornography shoots during visits Hoover would make to Byar's residence on Mulholland Drive.[44]

In April 1974, a few months after they were arrested, both Byars Jr. and William Johnston skipped bail and fled to Europe.[45] Guy Strait fled California as well, but was later picked up in Phoenix, Arizona in 1976 after he was arrested for having sex with a minor there.[46]

From prison, Strait told a reporter in 1977 he'd known John Norman,[47] and later that year during a congressional inquiry into child pornography, he testified to having known a child pornographer in Houston named Roy Ames.[48] When this mysterious Roy Ames would later be arrested, *"He told officers that, while Guy Strait had worked with him, Strait was small-time by Ames's standards, and that his own material was distributed worldwide."*[49]

To clarify the timeline of developments in the Dean Corll investigations thus far:
- In late August 1973 detectives in Houston received a letter from an informant in California claiming a Houston-based child pornographer named Roy Ames had used Dean Corll to abuse boys for pornography.
- Houston PD then contacted vice detectives in LA and obtained copies of child porn publications ciruclating there, in which they believed they may have identified one of Dean Corll's victims.
- At the same time, vice detectives in LA arrested a

child pornographer named Guy Strait who was in business with a wealthy oil heir originally from Houston named William Byars Jr. The pair operated through a company called DOMLyric.
- Guy Strait stated he knew John Norman who operated the *Odyssey Network* in Dallas, and had been in business with a child pornographer in Houston named Roy Ames.

So who was Roy Ames and how was he connected to the Dean Corll murders?

The answer to this may have been buried with two of the victims in Dean Corll's boat shed. The bodies of two brothers, Jerry Waldrop(13) and Donald Waldrop(15), were found buried in an area of the boat shed marked gravesite #5. They were the first victims to be identified on account of their identification cards having been buried with their bodies. In addition to this, found on top of the body of Donald Waldrop was a partially filled out police report.[50] Which is to say, Dean Corll for whatever reason, buried two of his victims with their identification cards and a police report.

The officer who recovered the police report separated it from the rest of the items found in the mass grave and placed it inside a lockbox back at the police station.[51] It remains unclear, at least to me, what happened to this report, as it isn't mentioned again in the case files available through FOIA.

> "Evidence Tagged: The partial Houston Police offense Report found above body #9 and below body #3 will be placed in the lab lock box in ID by Det. James, who recovered it and kept it in his possession, to be processed to try to determine if any writing was on it."
> — Houston PD Offense Report No. D-68904, Progress Report August 9 1973

On August 9 when the bodies of the Waldrop brothers were recovered, their father Everett Waldrop called Houston PD to inquire if any of the bodies reported in the news belonged to his two sons. After learning they were identified as victims, the father gave detectives the names of two men he said his boys were hanging around at the time of their disappearance. These were Bill Walls and Roy Ames.[52] The father had provided the same information in a missing persons report filed back in February 1971, in which he stated he though his sons were with a 'Roy Aimes' who *"gathers kids & takes movies"*.

"Parents came to 3381 & stated that subj. & his brother, Jerry Lynn Waldrop Wm/13 were dropped off at the above loc. & have not been seen since. Parents think that the subj.s are at Roy Aimes, 522 3679, add. unkwn when one of the boys was supposed to have placed a call from. XX this phone for reportee, & it XX's to Bill Roberts, 1311 Montrose, so they will go check it out. Reportee thinks that Aimes is a homosexual & gathers kids & takes movies."

— Houston PD Missing Persons Report for Donald Waldrop, No. 27736, February 9 1971

So Roy Ames was first mentioned in a missing persons report filed in 1971 when two of Dean Corll's victims disappeared. Dean Corll then buried identification cards with the bodies of these two specific victims, and only these two. When these two bodies were recovered Roy Ames was mentioned by the father once more. Then a couple weeks after detectives received a letter from an informant in California claiming Roy Ames had used Dean Corll to abuse boys in pornography.

On December 22 1973, Houston PD received information from another informant in California, a parolee in custody there named Richard Van Payne. He claimed, *"that he had been in the WAREHOUSE in Houston and had seen photographs of the dead boys in the mass murder."*[53]

It is unclear what warehouse the informant was referring to. However, sometime in December 1973 U.S postal inspectors raided a warehouse in Houston owned by Roy Ames and seized from it four tons of child pornography[54]. Also seized was letter correspondence between Ames and a man named Roger D. Smith regarding the sale of hardcore child pornography; films depicting children in sexual bondage. In one of these letters, Smith had written that a particular film would've been better if the producers had, *"tossed in a stiff 14-year old."*[55]

A little over a year later in February 1975 another warehouse belonging to Roy Ames was raided and two more tons of child pornography was seized.[56] This time, Houston PD identified 11 of Dean Corll's victims in the pornographic materials.[57] *"Juvenile officers say 11 boys who were victims in the Houston mass murders case are pictured in sex materials seized in what police called a homosexual ring."*[58]

"Juvenile Lt. H.A Contreras said Detective John St. John and a partner met with officers Wednesday about the case of photographer Roy Clifton Ames, convicted in 1975 for using the mails to distribute obscene material. Ames was sentenced to a Springfield Mo., federal prison after photographs of 11 Houston area victims of the mass murders were seized following the arrests and murder convictions of Elmer Wayne Henley Jr. and David Owen Brooks. *'We knew that they were shipping kids – boy prostitutes – back and forth to the West Coast in the Ames deal,'. . . 'Ames and some of his people were engaged in this. They would send California kids here and Houston kids to California.'* "

— 'Houston-Los Angeles Link Discussed In Mass Killings', The Napa Valley Register, 23 Sept 1976

As part of his confession in August 1973 David Brooks stated that, *"the first few that Dean killed were supposed to have been sent off somewhere in California."*[59] The grand jury which indicted Brooks lambasted Houston PD and the district attorney for neglecting to investigate obvious leads. In their report they stated that, *"the Houston police abandoned the investigation about Sept. 1, leaving unexplored 'the possible' involvement of others and related criminal activities."*[60]

"Sept. 1" 1973 was the day Guy Strait was arrested in California. This had launched an investigation into *DOMLyric-Productions*, his joint venture with business partner William Byars Jr, also linked to Roy Ames back in Houston, who had called the LA pair small-time operators.

> "Quite recently, a man with the unlikely name of Guy Strait was sentenced to a lengthy prison term in Rockford, Illinois for using children for pornography. Mr. Strait was considered to be a big producer. His partner, Bill Byars is the heir to the Humble Oil fortune and fled the country a couple years ago to Italy. These partners produced vast amounts of pornographic films and magazines. But when Houston police arrested Roy Ames, Ames described them as small-time operators. Houston police officers tried to make a deal with Ames offering him a light sentence in exchange for information about other producers. In spite of the fact that Ames was facing a ten-year sentence, he laughed at the police and told them his operation would run just as well while he was in jail as it would if he were out. He is now serving a lengthy sentence in a federal prison."
>
> — Statement by Robin M. Lloyd, Hearings Before Subcommittee on the Judiciary On Sexual Exploitation of Children, 1977

Very little can be found on Ames. He received a 10 year sentence after his warehouse was raided in 1975. By 1981 he had been released, as he was arrested in Boston for attempting to sell 25 master copies of some kind of pornography to undercover customs officers, for $20,000.[61] He went back to prison for a number of years. After that his legal difficulties seem to have mostly involved lawsuits brought against him by blue musicians exploited by his record label.

To summerise the facts so readers may draw their own conclusion:
- The bodies of 17 murdered teenagers were found in Dean Corll's boat shed.
- Two of these Corll buried with identification cards.
- Roy Ames was named in the missing persons report of these two victims.
- An informant from California stated Roy Ames used Dean Corll to abuse boys.
- 11 of Dean Corll's victims were identified in pornography seized from Roy Ames' warehouse.
- Letter correspondance seized from this warehouse addressed to Roy Ames' expressed the desire to see a *'14 year-old stiff'* in a film.
- Roy Ames shuttled boys to *DOM-Lyric Productions* in California.
- Dean Corll's accomplice David Brooks stated, *"the first few that Dean killed were supposed to have been sent off somewhere in California"*.
- *DOM-Lyric Productions* in California was busted on September 1. A grand jury stated, *"the Houston police abandoned the investigation about Sept. 1, leaving unexplored 'the possible' involvement of others and related criminal activities."*
- The vice detective who busted *DOM-Lyric Productions* later relayed rumours of a snuff film featuring one of Corll's victims.

In addition to this an inter-state boy trafficking operation was busted in Dallas. Both of Dean Corll's accomplices said he claimed to work for an organisation based in Dallas that bought and sold boys. Inside John Norman's Dallas apartment were four photographs of missing boys with the word 'kill' stamped on them. And for some reason the State Department took possession of the evidence taken from his apartment and destroyed it.

Perhaps this is all a coincidence. Perhaps it's a coincidence John Norman continued to operate somewhat unimpeded throughout the 1970s and 80s. Perhaps it's a coincidence, that during this time two boys who testified against him in separate cases were both viciously murdered. Perhaps it's a coincidence a suspect in those murders who worked for John Norman, even lived with him, also worked for the only other known mass murderer of teenaged boys in the 1970s. Another 'serial killer', who like Dean Corll had two teenagers help them bury their victims in a mass grave. Who just before their execution would claim John Norman was involved in making snuff films.

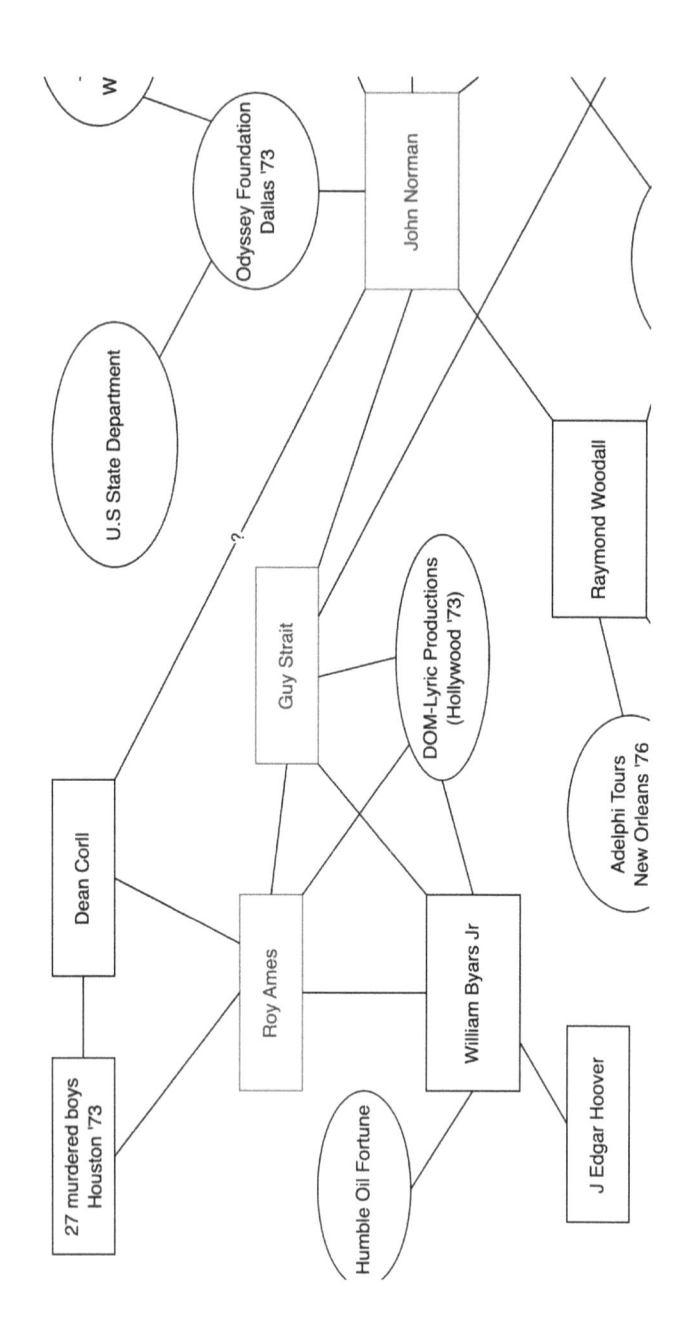

- Odyssey Foundation Dallas '73
- John Norman
- U.S State Department
- Raymond Woodall
- Guy Strait
- DOM-Lyric Productions (Hollywood '73)
- Adelphi Tours New Orleans '76
- Dean Corll
- Roy Ames
- William Byars Jr
- 27 murdered boys Houston '73
- Humble Oil Fortune
- J Edgar Hoover

The John Gacy Murders - Chicago Illinois 1972-78

Phillip Paske & The Delta Project

After Norman's Dallas arrest in August '73, an anonymous benefactor from California posted his $35,000 bail, which was forfeited a month later when Norman fled to Illinois in September 1973. He moved into an apartment in Homewood on the outskirts of Chicago using the alias "Steven Gurwell". The apartment belonged to a client of his named Charles Rehling who'd used a service Norman provided through an organisation called *Epic International*, which paired men with boys for overseas trips.

In late October 1973 Homewood PD were tipped off to a man at the apartment using underaged boys for sex and pornography. A local boy named Kenneth Hellstrom told police he'd gone there with a man who'd offered him beers and the man had performed oral sex on him.

Norman was out of town when police came knocking, but they got permission from Rehling to conduct a search and discovered the same *Odyssey Foundation* materials police had found in Dallas, including client lists and pictures of boys with descriptions.[62]

Rehling cooperated with police and told them he'd leased his apartment to a man from Dallas named 'Steven Gurwell' who operated a callboy service. Steven Gurwell's true identity was soon learnt from Dallas PD. Police surveilled the apartment and arrested Norman upon his return in November 1973.

Norman was sent to Cook County jail and his bail was set at a prohibitive $325,000. Which is where one might think his operation ceased, but one would be wrong.

From inside Cook County jail Norman was inexplicably granted access to the publishing, printing, and mailing facilities required to produce and distribute literature for his *Odyssey Network* under its new name *The Delta Project*. Nothing but a fresh coat of paint given to the same boy trafficking scheme he'd deployed through the mail for years. As it was reported by the Chicago Tribune in a retrospective article from 1977, *"The Cook County state's attorney's office and Chicago police have said that Norman's Delta Project was born in Cook County Jail last spring, while he was awaiting trial. They said that, unknown to jail officials, Norman used jail printing facilities to send out three 'newsletters' about the project to homosexual clients throughout the country and to those who answered his advertisements in pornographic publications."*[63]

Assisting Norman with *The Delta Project* was a young inmate named Phillip Paske. A tall slimly built twenty-something transvestite with long blond hair, serving time for accessory to murder he'd plead down to theft.

In June 1975 the charges against Norman from his Dallas arrest in 1973 were dismissed.[64] The reason for this may be inferred from the fact that two months after this the evidence seized from his Dallas apartment was destroyed by the State Department.[65]

As a result Norman's bail was reduced by $284,000 down to an affordable $36,000, which allowed his anonymous benefactor from California to post it once more, and Norman was set free in Chicago sometime in the early months of 1976.

"The State Department confirmed that it had received the cards[Norman's clients]. Matthew Nimetz, a counselor for the State Department, said officials determined 'the cards were not relevant to any fraud case concerning a passport' and therefore destroyed them. Shortly after Norman published his first newsletter from Cook County Jail last year, someone in California, whom police have not been able to identify, provided the $36,000 cash needed for his bail."

— 'Dallas man porno kingpin', Austin American Statesman, May 26 1977

Norman's young accomplice Phillip Paske was paroled in January 1976 and started helping Norman run *The Delta Project*,[66] and for a time even became its custodian while Norman was in prison.

Norman was summoned back to Cook County court in December 1976 to face charges relating to his Homewood, Illinois arrest. He was convicted and sentenced to 4 years with 23 months credited as already served.[67]

A month later a boy named Kenneth Hellstrom who testified against him in that case was viciously stabbed to death on his way home from work. Given the circumstances, and with Norman in prison, Phillip Paske naturally became the prime suspect.[68]

Then in May 1977 a judge inexplicably ordered Norman's early release and he moved with Phillip Paske into a basement apartment on W. Wrightwood Av in Chicago,[69] just a short twenty-minute drive from where soon, the bodies of twenty-nine teenaged boys would be exhumed from the crawlspace of John Wayne Gacy.

Norman and Paske set the apartment up as a photography studio with blacked out windows and started recruiting local area Chicago boys for pornography and assumedly prostitution. The apartment was raided in June 1978 after a boy named Michael Salcido reported Norman to Chicago PD for sexual assault. Inside the apartment police seized thousands of index cards listing details of Norman's extensive network of clientele, now 'sponsoring' boys through an organisation called *The Creative Corps*.[70] Norman was sent back to prison and Phillip Paske, found living with Norman at the address, was released without charge.

A few months later in February 1979, Michael Salcido was found with his throat slit in a car.[71] Salcido was due to testify against Norman at his upcoming trial, which made him the second boy to be murdered in the lead up to or after providing courtroom testimony against him. For a time Paske had been a prime suspect for both murders, but eventually others would be convicted for both murders. In one case, much more convincingly than the other.

> "Chicago and Homewood police are investigating a possible link between three youths whose bodies were found stabed[sic] to death Sunday and a Homewood youth whose fatal stabbing two years ago was never solved. One of the youths found slain Sunday was to have testified in the forthcoming trial of John D. Norman, who police have said is the leader of a nationwide child pornography ring. In the earlier killing, Kenneth Hellstrom, 17, of 18511 Lexington Av., Homewood had started home on Jan. 20 1977, from his job at a gas station several blocks away when he was attacked and stabbed six times in the back. He made his way home and collapsed. He died several hours later. . .In the Sunday stabbings, three youths were found dead in a car parked in an alley at 1460 W. Pensacola Av. about 3 a.m. Each of the youths had been slashed many times and their throats cut in what police described as an 'almost ritualistic' stabbings. . .Although Norman was in prison the night Hellstrom was killed, police want to question his alleged accomplice in the child prostitution ring,

> Phillip R. Paske, who was once tried for murder but later pleaded guilty to theft after plea-bargaining with prosecutors."
>
> — 'Police seek '77 killing link to slain youths', Chicago Tribune, February 28 1979

The Salcido murder was attributed to local drug dealers, though any inquisitively paranoid readers should perhaps look into the boys connection to the Maryville Academy, a rather questionable Catholic institution.

The murder case of Kenneth Hellstrom had been cold for decades, when in 2005 his sister picked out a John Wayne Gacy biography from her local library. In it she discovered someone had penciled in notes remarking on her brother's connection to John Norman, and that this, had some relation to John Wayne Gacy. It turned out Gacy had been interviewed in the 1990s about John Norman's possible connection to Kenneth Hellstrom's murder.

Two years after Hellstrom's sister made this discovery, and before the cold case was about to transferred to Cook County PD, Homewood police performed a traffic stop on a man who turned out to be an old classmate of Hellstrom's named Fred Rogers. Apparently Rogers had been a suspect all along but police never questioned him because he left Chicago. Thirty years later Rogers returned to the area after his father's death, he was pulled over, confessed to the murder and the case was closed. Detectives said Hellstrom had made sexual advancements towards Rogers while the pair shared a joint, and in response Rogers had stabbed Hellstrom in a fit of rage.

> "Some years before his murder, Kenny was the state's key witness in a criminal proceeding against a local man convicted of running a nationwide homosexual prostitution ring. Some family members suspect Kenny's murder was retaliation for his testimony. When Rees checked out John Wayne Gacy's biography from a northwest Indiana library, she noticed

penciled marks on a page that talked about Kenny and that man. The notes were a potential tip, the family thought, but it went nowhere. . .In the early 1990s, Homewood police investigators interviewed Gacy about the retaliation connection. That's not one of the angles investigators are looking at now, Janich said. Before he was killed, Kenny asked his mother if he could switch bedrooms with his sister. '*He asked me if he could go upstairs because he was afraid,*' Carol Hellstrom said, adding that Kenny thought somebody was looking for him. '*We let him go upstairs, and he went and put paneling up over the windows. But he would not tell me what he was scared about.*' "

— 'Mother still hopes son's killer will be caught',
Southtown Star, December 11 2005

After John Norman went back to prison in June 1978, Phillip Paske lost his job as a children's supervisor at a public swimming pool,[72] and as records show, went on to work at John Wayne Gacy's construction company, *Painting Decorating Maintenance*(PDM). Receipts for three payslips made out to Phillip Paske from PDM, dated 12/9/1978, 19/9/1978, and 25/9/9178, were found in the archives of the companies financial records from that period.[73] These receipts corroborated claims made by Gacy just prior to his execution in the early 1990s. Gacy, who should of course only ever be believed if the evidence supports what he claimed, said he had known Phillip Paske, who worked for him and frequented his house in the months just prior to the discovery there of the largest mass grave of murdered boys since the excavation of Dean Corll's boat shed in 1973.

What led to this discovery had been the disappearance of a 15 year-old Maine West High school student named Robert Piest on December 11 1978.

* * *

Robert Piest disappeared from a pharmacy where he worked part-time. Gacy was an acquittance of the pharmacy owner and his company PDM had recently completed a remodelling job there. Robert was seen out front of the pharmacy by his mother, who'd arrived to pick him up at the end of his evening shift. His mother said Robert had gone inside then never returned. The pharmacy's owner, Phil Torf, told Robert's mother her son had gone to speak with someone about a job. When Robert didn't return home later that night his mother reported him missing, and his case found its way onto the desk of a police captain named Joseph Kozenzcak, whose son just so happened to be a classmate of Robert's at Maine West High school.[74]

The pharmacy owner was interviewed the following day and he gave police the name 'John Wayne Gacy' as the man Robert had gone to see about a job. Robert's co-worker, a girl named Kim Byers, told police Robert had told her, *"the contractor guy wants to speak with me about a job,"* just before he'd left the pharmacy.[75]

Police pulled Gacy's criminal record and discovered he'd sexually assaulted a boy around Robert's age in 1968. A search warrant was obtained for Gacy's home at 8213 West Summerdale Avenue in Norwood Park, which was executed by a team of detectives led by Cpt. Kozenczak on December 13.[76] Items seized from Gacy's home included pederasty pornography and literature, chemist 'date rape' drugs, a hypodermic syringe, a wooden board fitted with two wrist-sized loops of rope, a pair of handcuffs, two driver's licences, and a Maine West High School graduation ring inscribed with the initials 'J.A.S'.[77]

The ring belonged to a teenager named John Szyc, who graduated from Maine West High School in 1975 and was reported missing in January 1977. It was learnt Szyc had worked for Gacy's construction company shortly before his disappearance and a few months after his car had been found in the possession of another teenager who worked for Gacy named Michael Rossi.[78] Rossi had lived with Gacy on and off at his Norwood Park house, which also served as a home office for his business, along with another employee named David Cram(20).[79] All three were placed under police surveillance after police searched the house on December 13.

On December 16 police interviewed David Cram. Cram told detectives Gacy claimed to be part of a crime syndicate,[80] and said he'd found drivers licenses belonging to dead people in Gacy's garage.[81] He also mentioned that after detectives had conducted their search of the house on December 13 Gacy went down into the crawlspace beneath the house with a flashlight.[82]

The following day Michael Rossi was interviewed on December 17. When asked about having been found in possession of John Szyc's car, Rossi told detectives Gacy had given it to him.[83] Rossi then repeated the same thing David Cram had told detectives about finding the drivers licences of dead people in Gacy's garage.[84]

On December 17 a third missing youth was also added to the list of prospective victims. Cpt. Kozenczak reported speaking with Gacy's ex-wife, Carole Hoff, who provided him the name of another teenager who worked for Gacy named John Butkovich, who was reported missing in 1975.[85]

So by December 17 Gacy had become the prime suspect in the disappearances of three missing youths: Robert Piest, John Szyc, and John Butkovich. Two of these had attended the same high school as the son of the lead detective, Cpt. Kozenczak. Maine West High School.

On December 21 Cpt. Kozenczak obtained a second search warrant for Gacy's home based on the following two pieces of evidence.

The first was Cpt. Kozenczak's claim that a photo processing receipt, which had been in Robert Piest's jacket pocket when he went missing, was found inside Gacy's kitchen bin during the December 13 search. As Cpt. Kozenczak recounted in his book *The Chicago Killer*:

> " 'Wait one minute,' I suddenly said, and, jumping up, bolted down the hall to the polygraph room. There, in a clear plastic bag, shining like a piece of gold, was the bright red receipt I had plucked out of John Gacy's garbage bag. . . . This was the first and only piece of evidence we had showing that the Piest's boy had even been in the house on Summerdale. I felt as if I had just dropped a noose around the burly contractor's neck."
> — 'Joseph R. Kozenczak, Des Plaines detective chief on the Gacy serial-slayer case, dead at 75', Chicago Sun Times, June 25 2016

However, according to both the case files and a statement made by an evidence technician named Karl Humberg, who was present during the search and in charge of the inventory of items taken from Gacy's home, the receipt had never been logged into evidence. Other detectives who were present during the search later stated the receipt hadn't actually been found on Gacy's property at all, but on the curb out front of it.[86]

The second piece of evidence was a claim made by a detective named Robert Schultz. Schultz was on the surveillance team assigned to monitor Gacy's movements. Schultz claimed Gacy let him inside his Norwood Park home on December 19 to use the bathroom, during which time the detective smelt an odour he recognised as decomposing dead bodies.[87]

Based off this and the photo receipt, a second search warrant was secured and executed on December 21. When detectives arrived at Gacy's home the crawlspace was found flooded on account of a water pump having been disconnected. After it was turned back on and the crawlspace drained, the first human remains were unearthed, in what over the coming weeks and months would lead to the discovery of twenty-nine bodies buried on Gacy's property.

Gacy was arrested at a gas station that same day and when he arrived at the police station he reportedly said, *"Who else do we have in the police station. There are others involved."* During his interrogation he named both David Cram and Michael Rossi as accomplices who had buried the bodies.[88] He claimed to have multiple personalities and confessed somewhat in third-person to the murders of Robert Piest, John Butkovich, and John Syzc. He said David Cram and Michael Rossi were involved and dug graves in the crawlspace, which the pair would later admit to during Gacy's trial but deny knowing what purpose the trenches they'd dug down there were for.[89]

According to testimonies provided by Cram and Rossi, Gacy claimed to work for a crime syndicate involved in 'setting people up'.

"Rossi and Cram testified Gacy, despondent over a 10-day police surveillance in the disappearance of a Des Plaines youth, told them he had admitted to police he was involved in the 'syndicate' slayings of more than 30 youths. Cram said in 1976 he found several wallets in Gacy's garage — so called 'souvenirs' of Gacy's victims — and asked Gacy if he could use the identification cards to drink in cars. 'He told me I didn't want those,' Cram testified. 'He said they were from some kind of deceased people. It had something to do with setting people up for the crime syndicate'."

— 'Gacy ordered youths to dig graves', Daily Republican Register, February 13 1980

The suggestion Gacy had associates involved in his crimes was attested to by a man named Jeff Rignall, who was chloroformed and raped by Gacy at the Norwood Park home in early 1978. Rignall stated at least one other person was present when the assault occurred.[90] It was reported in 1979 police were looking at three other suspects as possible accomplices, including the teenager Michael Rossi.[91]

One of the victims was a 19 year-old named John Mowery who moved into an apartment with Michael Rossi just days prior to his disappearance.[92] Two of Mowery's friends went to the apartment and spoke with Rossi about Mowery's whereabouts at the time.[93] According to them, Rossi said Mowery was away for a few days, but then strangely asked if they would take his dog. Even more strange, Mowery's friends claimed Rossi also mentioned a place where dead bodies were buried during that same conversation.

> "Becker and Stephenson said they recently spoke with two women and a man who knew Mowery. According to their accounts, a man[Rossi] who knew Gacy moved into Mowery's Chicago apartment three days before Mowery went missing. The day after Mowery disappeared, the two women went to his apartment looking for him. While there, they say, the roommate told them he knew of a location in the Chicago area where dead bodies were stored. *"He told us that he knew of a location where there were a bunch of dead bodies that nobody knew about, not even the police, which I remember very clearly because he said this with such a terrible smirk on his face,"* one of the women told WGN."
>
> — 'Witnesses shed new light on John Wayne Gacy murder, suggest he had accomplice' MSNBC, February 17 2012

In 1980 Gacy was convicted as the 'serial killer' of thirty-three victims and sentenced to death. He spent the next decade on death row postponing the date of his execution through the process of appeals.

The prosecuting attorney who secured his conviction, Terry Sullivan, got a book deal and published an authoritative accounting of the case called *The Killer Clown*, which was entered into the annals of 'true crime' in 1983.

Apart from a tiny hiccup published in the *Chicago Tribune* in 1987, this account would remain relatively undisturbed until the early 1990s. The Tribune passingly noted that the leader of the *Chicago Ripper Crew*, suspected of killing 17 women in 1981 and 1982, had at one time worked for John Wayne Gacy, *"Gecht twice had done construction work for John Wayne Gacy, the convicted murderer of 33 young men and boys. A friend quoted Gecht as saying, 'The only mistake Gacy made was burying bodies under his home'."*[94]

In 1992, with the date of his execution looming after having exhausted his appeals all the way up to the supreme court, Gacy went public with new information regarding accomplices in a last-effort attempt to have his case reexamined and prolong his life.

During a series of TV interviews with multiple outlets Gacy claimed police looked into four of his accomplices in 1979. This had in fact been reported at the time, though the number of accomplices was three.

> "In the meantime we've also learnt three former Gacy associates are still under investigation for their involvement in or knowledge of the assaults and murders. One of them, Mike Rossi, will be ordered to hand over handwriting samples in connection with a forged title transfer. Rossi sources say has already hired former state attorney Ed Hanrahan to represent him."
>
> — 'Missed Gacy Leads', WLS Channel 7 Eyewitness News,

February 13 1979

Gacy named the pair of teenagers who lived with him, David Cram and Michael Rossi, but now he named a third, Phillip Paske, and by extension a fourth, John David Norman. Gacy said was introduced to Phillip Paske through David Cram, describing Paske as a dangerous child pimp who procured boys for sex and movies.[95] Gacy said David Cram, Michael Rossi, and Phillip Paske all had keys to his house and frequently used it during periods he'd been out of town.[96] Found in the archives of Gacy's company records were travel documents and financial statements which did appear to show Gacy was out of Chicago during times when some of his victims disappeared.[97]

In 1994 just a month before his execution it was reported a $1.99-a-minute reverse charge telephone number was playing a recording of Gacy proclaiming his innocence.

"Callers can hear Gacy proclaim his innocence in his high, intense voice full of outrage. In the messages, Gacy suggest the murders were committed by his contracting employees, who had keys to his house. *'There were 12 keys out to the house,'* he says. Gacy says the recorded message was taped without his knowledge during phone conversation with an attorney."

— 'On death row, time is running out for Gacy', The Philadelphia Inquirer, April 17 1994

A collectables store owner named Andrew Matesi played what appears to be a segment of this recording in a video uploaded to youtube in 2012. In the recording Gacy states, *"Well aside from the twelves keys, we already know that Rossi, Cram, Paski, and Norman were involved in the case. And you know something, what's funny, these sons of bitches know it too."*[98]

It appears authorities were indeed aware of Phillip Paske's connection to the Gacy case back in 1979 and 1980.[99] A lawyer named Steven W. Becker who compiled a report on the court

files at the time found:
> "John Wayne Gacy was arrested on December 21, 1978, just six months after Norman's latest arrest. Gacy's trial was conducted during the term of Cook County State's Attorney Bernard Carey. Moreover, Phillip Paske was listed as a witness on the State's discovery disclosures, as well as a possible witness for the defense"
> — HUMAN TRAFFICKING, HOMICIDE AND CURRENT PREVENTION EFFORTS IN THE UNITED STATES OF AMERICA, Steven W. Becker, October 2022.

If John Norman's connection to the case was based on Gacy's claim alone it would hardly be worth mentioning. But the evidence demonstrates some basis of truth to his claim which makes it worth discussing. Especially given Gacy's murders are almost identical to those of Dean Corll in Houston five years earlier. These similarities are as follows:

- Dean Corll used a handcuff trick to incapacitate his victims and tie them to a wooden torture board. John Gacy used a handcuff trick to incapacitate his victims and tie them to a wooden torture board.
- Dean Corll had a total of twenty-eight victims, all male youths between the ages of thirteen and twenty. John Gacy had a total of thirty-three victims, all male youths between the ages of fourteen and twenty-one.
- Dean Corll buried seventeen of these victims in a mass grave beneath his boatshed. John Gacy buried twenty-nine of these victims in a mass grave beneath his home.
- Dean Corll lived with two teenaged accomplices who said Corll claimed to work for a crime organisation. John Gacy lived with two teenaged (suspected) accomplices who said Gacy claimed to work for a crime organisation.
- The investigation into the Dean Corll murders led to

a suspected link to John Norman's boy trafficking network. The investigation into the John Gacy murders led to a confirmed link to John Norman's boy trafficking network.

There is a further connection. As explored in the prior chapter, there is evidence to reasonably believe Dean Corll had been involved with a Houston child pornographer named Roy Ames in the production of snuff films. A skeptic could say this isn't proven, but they cannot say it is unreasonable to conclude.

When John Gacy named Phillip Paski and John Norman as accomplices in his 1992 media interviews, it hadn't been entirely clear in what capacity he meant. Gacy was evasive and even stated he was unsure if he had even met John Norman. The only thing he did say was that Phillip Paske and John Norman had been making snuff films. The following is an excerpt of a statement Gacy made during an interview with Robert Roessler, *"Here we've got Phillip Paske, who had a newsletter going out of Cook County jail. Here he is involved with a guy named John Norman. And John Norman was running boys for hire. They were making snuff films with young boys. To me, they were pimping them off, selling them."*[100] This does seem to suggest Gacy never met Norman personally, and only learnt his name reading about his connection to Phillip Paske in the paper. Though it also seems where ever John Norman goes teenaged boys die, and I'd be willing to bet David Cram and Michael Rossi did know John Norman since they were friends with Paske. Of course, this likely possibility was never investigated.

According to court documents obtained by Tracy Allman, a documentary producer who spent nine years investigating the Gacy case for a Peacock documentary called *John Wayne Gacy: Devil In Disguise,* a household inventory list filed by Gacy's lawyers which was signed and received by the Cook

County courthouse prior to his trial, mentions an 8mm movie camera, editing deck, and other film production equipment.[101] It also mentions the following item in a drawer of 'one executive desk', *"drawer F. confidential files, list of payoff, city inspector, political men, personal income tax files, files on five bank accounts, check books, credit cards files, insurance files personal, private list of known homo, politicians, sports figures, count and city employees."*[102] It's important to note this is the inventory of household items *Gacy's lawyers* filed. None the less, one of the better known aspects of John Wayne Gacy is how active he'd been in local politics. Gacy had been appointed a democratic precinct captain of the Norwood Park township in 1975 by the democratic party commissioner there, Robert Martwick, who also served as Cook County's school superintendent.[103] Gacy was also secretary and treasurer of the township's Lighting Commission, where he served alongside the commission's legal counsel Sam Amirante, who would go on to represent Gacy at his trial and file the aforementioned household inventory list with the interesting items listed in *drawer f*.[104]

Gacy had further aspirations of holding elected office and often hired a photographer named Marty Zielinski to photograph him alongside politicians at local events. Soon after his arrest a photo appeared in the *Chicago Tribune* of Gacy shaking hands with Mayor Michael Bilandic.[105] A year later another one appeared, taken in May 1978 just seven months before his arrest. An infamous photo of Gacy shaking hands with Firs Lady Rosalynn Carter. The photo even showed Gacy with a Secret Service special clearance button pinned to his lapel.[106]

After his arrest Marty Zielinski, who tailed Gacy at these political events, told the *Chicago Trbiune* Gacy once asked him to film illegal pornography and *"that there was a good buck to be made"*.[107] If this was true, to whom would Gacy be selling his pornography? Well, *illegal pornography* is precisely what John Norman and Phillip Paske were producing in a basement apartment 20 minutes from his house up until July 1978, just before Paske went onto to work for Gacy himself.

When looking at a timeline of Gacy's victim disappearances, there is a correlation between an uptick in these during periods when John Norman is free in Chicago. The official list of victims attributed to Gacy is thirty-three, of which twenty-eight have been identified, some perhaps incorrectly though we'll leave that matter aside. These twenty-eight all disappeared within a seven year period spanning January 1972 to December 1978.

January 1972 - January 1976 (John Norman not in Chicago or in Jail/Prison)	Timothy McCoy, 18, January 3, 1972 **John Butkovitch**, 17, July 21, 1975 Darrell Sampson, 18, April 6, 1976 Randall Reffett, 15, May 14, 1976 Sam Stapleton, 14, May 14, 1976
February 1976 - December 1976 (John Norman free in Chicago with Phillip Paske)[108] May 1976 (Michael Rossi starts living with Gacy) July 1976 (David Cram starts living with Gacy)	Michael Bonnin, 17, June 3, 1976 William Carroll, 16, June 13, 1976 James Byron Haakenson, 16, August 1976 Rick Johnston, 17, August 6, 1976 Kenneth Parker, 16, October 25, 1976 Michael Marino, 14, October 25, 1976 William George Bundy, 19, 26 October 1976 Francis Wayne Alexander, 21, 1 December 1976 Gregory Godzik, 17, December 12, 1976

January 1977 - May 1977 (John Norman in Prison)	**John Szyc**, 19, January 20, 1977 Jon Prestidge, 20, March 15, 1977
June 1977 - June 1978 (John Norman free in Chicago)	Matthew Bowman, 19, July 5, 1977 Robert Gilroy, 18, September 15, 1977 John Mowery, 19, September 25, 1977 Russell Nelson, 21, October 17, 1977 Robert Winch, 16, November 10, 1977 Tommy Boling, 20, November 18, 1977 David Talsma, 19, December 9, 1977 William Kindred, 19, February 16, 1978 Timothy O'Rourke, 20, June 1978
July 1978 - December 1978 (John Norman in Prison)	Frank Landingin, 19, November 4, 1978 James Mazzara, 21, November 24, 1978 **Robert Piest**, 15, December 11, 1978

Only seven victims disappeared during the five years John Norman was either in prison or jail or not in Chicago. Twenty disappeared within the two years Norman was free in Chicago with Phillip Paske. That's more than twice the amount of disappearances in less than half the amount of time.[109] (this is a rather extensive footnote for those interested)

During this period Norman was involved with a group of Chicago men who published a 'boylover' newsletter called *Hermes*. This underground publication was printed in Chicago and used coded classified ads to propagate Norman's *Delta Project/Odyssey Network* and advertise mail-order hardcore child pornography. It catered to a readership of predatory pedophiles who between themselves did away with the pretence of 'boylove' to self-identify using the pronoun 'chickenhawk'. A hawk that hunts little chickens, or in their case boys. Many were men who liked to dominate children who sought pornography or prostitution services of this type. The sort of thing which could not be advertised openly and circulated in private mailing lists advertised in *Hermes*.

Aside from carrying advertisements for Norman's trafficking network, *Hermes* also published advertisements for clandestine groups providing support and instructions on how to infiltrate community groups, such as the boy scouts, big brother programs, or church affiliated youth groups, including guides on how to groom children.[110]

Hermes was printed and edited by men associated with John Norman in Chicago, and was allegedly financed by a philanthropist in the neighbouring state of Michigan named Francis Duffield Shelden. A scion of the old money families of Grosse Pointe, Detroit, who owned a private island in Lake Michigan called North Fox Island. The island was used as part of a child pornography and prostitution network of international scope. Its exposure in 1976 led to the cascading exposure of other interlinked operations setup under an incorporated umbrella across the United States, including the publication of *Hermes* in Chicago. It also bled into yet another child murder investigation. This time another 'serial killer' in Michigan, dubbed "The Oakland County Child Killer".

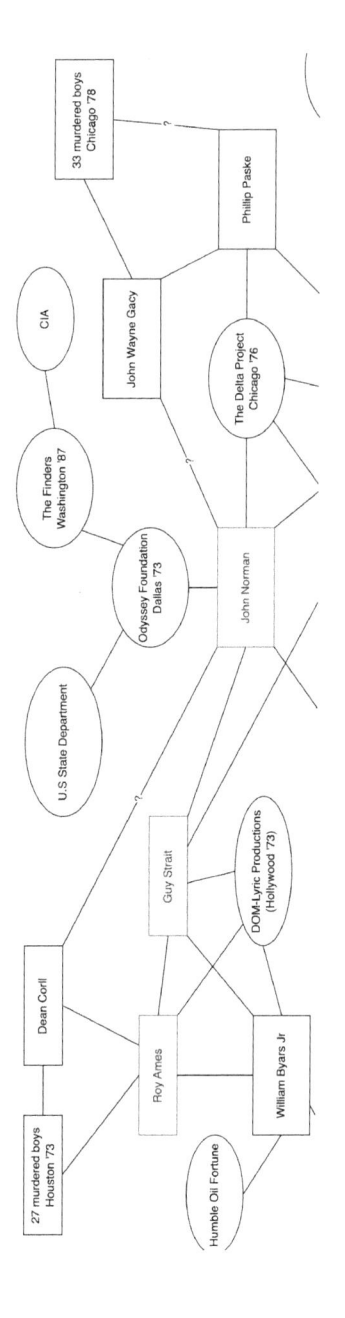

```
                                    33 murdered boys
                                    Chicago '78
                                          |
                                          |
                                    John Wayne Gacy ——— Phillip Paske
                          CIA            /                    |
                           |            /                     |
                    The Finders '87    /              The Delta Project
                    Washington          \                Chicago '76
                           \             \             /
                    Odyssey Foundation    \           /
                    Dallas '73             \         /
                          |                 John Norman
                          |                /    |
                    U.S State Department  /     |
                                         /      |
                                        /       |
                                    Guy Strait
                                       /  \
                                      /    DOM-Lyric Productions
                                     /     (Hollywood '73)
              Dean Corll ——— Roy Ames ——— William Byars Jr
                  |              |              |
          27 murdered boys    Humble Oil Fortune
          Houston '73
```

55

North Fox Island - Michigan '76

Hermes & The Delta Project

In May 1977 a Chicago man named David Berta was arrested after producing child pornography using two 14 year-old foster children and a 19 year-old go-go dancer named John Bell.[111] Police described Bell as 'disturbed'. He'd been one of several hundred kids sent to an orphanage in Texas by the Illinois Department of Children and Family Services in the 1960s which was shutdown after rampant abuse of the wards in its care. Bell was reportedly, *"chained to a bed when he killed a dog and forced to wear the dog's tail around his neck for two weeks."*[112]

This experience appears to have made Bell an excellent candidate for John Norman's *Odyssey Network*, as he ended up on the boy prostitution circuit working with child pornographers in New York and Chicago by age 15, before graduating to become an exploiter as part of a 'Delta dorm' arrangement with David Berta.

The pair were arrested after attempting to sell 8mm filmstocks of Bell abusing foster children pimped to Berta by their foster parent, a third man arrested named David Welch.[113]

David Berta was found to be an editor of the *Hermes* newsletter, which led to the arrest of two others named Patrick Townson and Elden Gale Wake as principal figures behind the publication. Investigators linked all three men to John Norman and his trafficking operation, *The Delta Project*.[114]

> "The investigation also has disclosed that a clandestine newsletter is being published in Chicago which serves as a conduit for perverts throughout America in engaging children in pornographic modeling and prostitution and in making contact with one another. Both operations, the police said, were controlled by separate groups of men working together in an interlocking web of vice. The ring trafficking in young boys goes under the name Delta Project. According to police in Chicago, Los Angeles, and Dallas, it is masterminded by 49-year-old John D. Norman, a convicted sodomist serving a four-year sentence in the Illinois state prison at Pontiac. His closest associate is Philip R. Paske, 25, a convicted murderer and thief who police said is now on probation and is carrying on the project in Norman's absence. The clandestine newsletter is known as Hermes. Police said the principal figures in its publication are Elden Gale [Rusty] Wake, 40, an employe of Trinity College in Lake Forest; Patrick Townson, a Chicago man who operates a citizens band radio information show for homosexuals and is connected with the Gay News and Events newspaper, and David Berta, who along with Townson was involved in Norman's operation."
>
> -- 'Chicago is center of national child pornography ring', Chicago Tribune, May 16 1977

A collection of 8mm child pornography films were seized from the home of a dentist associated with the *Hermes* men named Arthur Langford. Of sixty-nine 8mm filmreels taken from the dentist's home, one was labelled "John Bell – Michigan trip."[115] It turned out Langford and John Bell were directors of a children's summer camp in Michigan,[116] as had been the man identified as *Hermes* printer, Elden Gale Wake.[117]

In February 1977, two months prior to the arrests of the *Hermes* men in May, it was reported by a Michigan newspaper that a financial backer of the *Hermes* newsletter was a wealthy philanthropist there named Francis Duffield Shelden.[118] A fugitive who'd fled the state in late 1976 after it was discovered a summer camp called *Brother Paul's Childrens Mission* incorporated on a private island he owned had been setup as a front in an international child porn operation.

"State police believe they have uncovered evidence that links Leelanau County's North Fox Island to an international network that uses children to produce homosexual pornography. Photographs allegedly taken on North Fox Island have been reproduced in hard-core pornographic magazines, according to state police. And, state police say the island's owner, Francis D. Shelden, has been named by informants as a staff writer of Better Life, an international publication which advertises itself as a monthly paper with articles, photos, poems. etc. relating to the subject of boylove. Associates of the Ann Arbor millionaire also have told state police that Sheldon[sic] is alleged to have financial interest in Hermes, another explicit homosexual magazine with worldwide distribution."
— 'Police say photos link area island, porn ring', Traverse City Record-Eagle, February 16, 1977

July 1976 — In the quant little city of Port Huron, Michigan just North East of Detroit, a high school gym teacher named Gerald Richards with a concerning combination of other vocations, such as masseuse, magician, hypnotist, and republican candidate for local government; was arrested after the mother of a boy told police Richards had molested her son on a camping trip.

On July 12 Richards had taken four of his students, ages 8-14, to a private airstrip to meet with a man who flew them in his plane to his private island, called North Fox Island, located 17 miles off the coast of Michigan's Leelanau peninsula. There, the four boys and two men spent two nights lodged at the bungalow facilities of *Brother Paul's Childrens Mission*. Upon their return one of the boys told his mother Richards and the other man had performed sex acts on him and photographed him naked.[119]

> "[redacted] said MR. RICHARDS picked him up in his car around noon on Monday (7-12-76). He also picked up 3 other boys, [redacted] (all students at St. Joseph School Port Huron), then took them to the St. Clair airport where they were picked up by a MR. FRANK SHELDON in his 2 engine airplane. MR. SHELDON took the group to his Island (North Fox Island). where they spend that night, all day Tues. (7-13-76) and then returned home on Wed. (7-14-76). [redacted] said that he slept in the same bed with MR. SHELDON and wasn't allowed to sleep in other empty beds. During both nights, SHELDON would rub his back and play with his Penis. He then took [redacted] hand and placed it on his (MR. SHELDON'S) penis. He then took [redacted] hand and placed it on his (MR. SHELDON'S) penis. This would last for about 15 minutes. [redacted] said that SHELDON also tried to have anal intercourse with him, however he refused to cooperate. In interviewing [redacted] and others later listed in complaint 23-1728-76 related report, it is understood that SHELDON ownes[sic] one of 4 or 5 cottages on NORTH FOX ISLAND. When he lands his plane, there is a jeep available for his use. He takes the boys hiking &

etc. while on the island."
— Michigan State PD, Incident Report 70-355-76, D/Sgt. Joel Gorzen, 12-17-76

Beginning on July 15 a week long investigation into these allegations took place. It was learnt Richards had a 'naturopathy clinic' located in a commercial basement dwelling where he molested boys during 'massage therapy' sessions. One of these was a 12 year-old neighbour of his he used as an assistent in his 'magic shows'.

Richards drove around in an orange pinto with "Jerry the Magician" marked on the side, and was pulled over in his distinguishable vehicle on July 23. Inside the glove compartment detectives discovered two envelopes. One contained naked photo's of boys, the other was a letter Richards had written to a "Frank Shelden", warning them to *"watch his files & mail & to check his files & get all stuff to North Fox Island."*[120]

Richards confessed to molesting boys and in exchange for partial immunity gave detectives the names of two other men he said were principal figures in a nationwide child porn operation, of which he claimed to be merely on the periphery of. These were Francis Duffield Shelden and Dyer Grossman.[121]

Francis Duffield Shelden belonged to an old money establishment family in Michigan. His great-grandfather on his father's side had been Michigan governor and senator Russel A. Alger, the United States Secretary of War from 1897-99. And on his mother's side were the Duffields, an industrial dynasty of money old enough to have forgotten from where it came.[122]

As such, Francis Shelden was endowed with a trust which allowed him to pursue a leisurely life of 'philanthropy', which in his case took a particular interest in youth charity. So far as appearances went, Shelden had a number of commercial property developments and worked part-time as a geology Professor at Wayne State University. He served on the board of a private arts academy and boarding school called the *Cranbrook institute*, as well as *Boys Republic*, a boarding school for delinquent youths funded by the General Motors' charity, *United Foundation*.[123] He also volunteered his time to Big Brother programs.[124]

According to Gerald Richards, he'd met Shelden through an advertisement he placed for his 'magic show' in a pedophile newsletter called *Better Life Monthly*, abbreviated to BLM, or *Boy Lovers Monthly* for the initiated. Richards told investigators Shelden was a 'prolific writer' for the publication, that it was *"one of several magazines that dwells on boy-boy-man sex, SHELDEN writes articles for this magazine & personally knows editor/publisher. SHELDEN said[told Richards] the address is a box that re-mails correspondence. He believes it is printed & published in different cities in America. A second such magazine is 'HERMES' from California that is published by F&F Distributors."*[125]

Richards 'magic show' was really a coded message used to swap his 12 year-old 'magic assistant' for other boys groomed by pedophiles in the Michigan area. Later during testimony given to a congressional inquiry into child pornography, Richards would refer to the boy in question as a 'fellow', the term used for boys exchanged between 'sponsors' of John Norman's *Odyssey Network*, which he referred to in another part of his testimony as a 'Cadet racket'.[126]

Richards and Shelden started corresponding by mail, then started meeting in person at hotel rooms and Shelden's Ann Arbour estate, where together they would use boys they knew for sex and pornography.[127] As their relationship progressed Shelden mentioned a private island he owned called North Fox Island, and his desire to start a summer camp there for boys, which he wanted Richards to become the director of.

To this end Shelden put Richards in touch with an organisation called the *The Church of New Revelation* located in New Jersey, and a reverend there by the name Dyer Grossman. This wasn't a real a church and Dyer Grossman wasn't a real reverend. He was a science teacher from a wealthy family on Long Island who worked at an exclusive boarding school for boys in New York.[128]

Grossman travelled to Michigan to meet with Richards and draft an incorporating charter for *Brother Paul's Childrens Mission*. The charter allowed the camp to derive a non-profit status as a subsidiary of Grossman's tax exempt church in New Jersey, which had of course only existed on paper.

A news article from 1970, entitled 'New Organisation To Present Magic Shows With Meaning', shows Richards had setup an organisation prior to this called *Brother Paul's Educational Entertainment Missions*, described as *"a non-profit society dedicated to furthering safety instruction and religious education through the media of magic and allied thespian arts and crafts."*[129]

In August 1976 Gerald Richards handed over a letter he'd received from Grossman, postmarked July 19 1976. In it Grossman detailed plans to set up a series of foster homes in Michigan, citing the profitability in receiving monthly payments from the government for taking in "runaways" and "problem kids". The letter also mentioned a 12 year-old boy Grossman said he'd procured through a Big Brother program who he described as 'innocent' but that, *"some camping trips may change that."*[130]

The letter had a return address for an organisation based in New Jersey called *The Ocean Living Institute*. This was seasteading foundation incorporated by a man of the curious name Adam Starchild, who'd also served as the incorporating agent for *Brother Paul's Childrens Mission* on North Fox Island.[131]

Adam Starchild was actually a man named Malcolm Willis

McConahy, or at least he had been; an offshore tax attorney who appeared to have faked his own death in 1975.[132] Starchild, as we shall call him for clarity's sake, had been a scout master in Minneapolis kicked out of the organisation in 1965 after he expressed a desire to engage in sex with boys there. He'd then been apprehended in Wisconsin on his way to New York with four boys in his car, and was charged for possession of child pornography.[133] As it was reported, *"An investigation of incorporation papers in three states confirms that a central figure in all the organisations cited by Richards goes by the name of Adam Starchild, an alias according to new Jersey authorities. Starchild is listed as the president of the Church of the New Revelation and was the primary incorporator of Brother Paul's."*[134]

According to its mission statement, *Brother Paul's Childrens Mission* provided temporary lodging and mentorship programs on North Fox Island for juvenile delinquents sent there by court order.[135] Through *The Church of New Revelation* it was linked to another program in Illinois called *The Educational Foundation for Youth*. The program solicited donations from 'sponsors' by mail, who in return received pornography produced using boys in the program. Sponsors could then pay to visit the boys, which the pornography was really an advertisement for, in a brothel type arrangement. The mailing list for this service was advertised in underground pedophile newsletters such as *The Broad Street Journal*, *Better Life Monthly* and the aforementioned *Hermes*. The same ones used by John Norman.

In September 1976 Gerald Richards was sentenced to a 2-20 year variable length prison term.[136] This appears to have inspired within him the motivation to further cooperate with the ongoing investigation into his wealthy accomplices.

From prison Richards sketched out a large network diagram of a child pornography operation. One which spanned from state to state, coast to coast, right across the United States, and even the Atlantic Ocean.[137]

Network diagram drawn by Gerald Richards, September 1976

Richards admitted to processing child porn sent to him from another organisation linked to *The Church of New Revelation*. He first mentioned this to Michigan detectives in September '76:

> "Informant GERALD RICHARDS w/m dob [redacted] (Arrested & Now in jail for sex crime involving 10 yr old boy)advised officers that he has learned of an organization catering to PEDOPHILIA inclined sex deviates. He first heard of this operation thru magazines that portray this type of activity. (Better Life & Herme's). RICHARDS believes a man can go to a place called FATHER BUD'S BOYS FARM at MONTEAGLE, TENNESSEE & with proper credentials, pay for a vacation-type visit there & be furnished with a young boy to be sexually abused."
>
> — Michigan PD Supplementary Report 23-1728-76, September 27 1976, D/Sgt. Joel Gorzen

Filmstocks would be mailed to Richards from a rural farm in Monteagle, Tennessee called *Father Bud's Boys Farm*. Richards would develop these and mail copies onto a forwarding service located in North Carolina called MAIL-O-MATIC,[138] and named a distribution company in California at the end of this pipeline called F&S Distributors operated by Guy Strait.[139] Richards had identified F&S as the Californian distributor for *Hermes*,[140] a publication Guy Strait himself admitted involvement with,[141] and a detective who arrested Strait had told press that, *"Hermes. a clandestine newsletter for the 'boy love' market that is published in Chicago, is well known in Los Angeles."*[142]

> "Strait said he knows John Norman, who ran a national male prostitution ring employing young boys and helping put together 'a neater package' to attract customers. He also said he wrote an article for Her-

mes magazine, a Chicago-based journal publishing philosophy and sex stories of boy love."
— 'His only regret: I got caught', Chicago Tribune, May 17, 1977

Father Bud's Boys Farm in Tennessee was a foster home located on a rural farm owned by an ordained episcopal priest named Rev. Cladius Vermilye. Juvenile delinquents were sent there by the youth corrections and welfare agencies in Tennessee,[143] where they were supplied with drugs and alcohol to make them pliant and perform in orgies. These would be filmed and photographed and sent out to a mailing list of 'sponsors' who could, if they wished, further pay to arrange visits to the farm.[144]

The farm was raided on November 10 1976 and authorities in Tennessee linked the foster program's incorporation to *The Church of New Revelation* in New Jersey.[145] Francis Shelden's name had also been found on a list of 'sponsors' seized.[146] The attorney general's office there stated there was no church, *"it's just a referral agency which distributes the pornography around the country."*[147]

What led to the raid, in conjunction with the information provided by Gerald Richards in Michigan, had been the discovery of yet another interlinked operation two months prior in September 1976, this time in New Orleans.

September 1976 — Film reels of child pornography discovered by technicians in a broken down commercial film processing machine in Dallas were traced to a man in New Orleans named Harry O'Cramer. He was an assistent-scoutmaster of a troop there called Troop 137, and boys from the troop and their scoutmasters were subsequently identified engaging in sex acts on the discovered film. This led to the arrest of three other scout leaders: Richard Halvorsen, Raymond

Woodall, and Robert Lang.[148]

The home of head scoutmaster Richard Halvorsen was raided on September 10. Found living with him were two foster children, both boys aged 9 and 11, as well as an 18 year-old named Lloyd Schwegmann, taken into custody alongside Halvorsen for possession of the date rape drug Tuinal. Along with child pornography, police seized hundreds of index cards with information on boys in other states, accompanied by computer generated forms detailing their sexual preferences and personality types.[149] Halvorsen had filing cabinets full of documents and letter correspondance with men in other states involved in what appeared to be an organised child pornography production and prostitution network, utilising mailing lists and advertisements placed in underground magazines.[150]

Among the mail correspondence was a letter sent to Halvorsen by Cladius Vermilye, personally inviting him to visit *Father Bud's Boys Farm* in Tennessee.[151] This had served, in conjunction with the information provided by Gerald Richards in Michigan, as the basis for the search warrant of this farm a few months later in November.

Other documents seized from Halvorsen's home revealed he and another scout leader named Raymond Woodall were in the process of applying for federal and state funding to establish a number of group foster homes for boys in New Orleans.[152]

Inside an address book belonging to Raymond Woodall, police found John Norman's name and contact details,[153] and a few months later in November 1976 the New Orleans PD juvenile division would relay this information to authorities in Chicago to alert them of 'chicken men' operating in their area.

"Attached you fill find a copy of a listing of all porno

magazine suppliers involved in our case. Also, you will find a listing of all chicken men in your area who corresponded with the arrested subjects in our case... We recently received literature from THE DELTA PROJECT and another group known as The HERMES Gay Magazine. It is apparent from the literature that they 'chicken men' are attempting to set up a large scale operation in your area"
— FBI FOI/PA# 1352511-001, File No. 166-2548-1A5, Date received November 1 1976

Weeks after this memo was received, John Norman was hauled back into Cook County court and handed a four year prison sentence, from which he'd then strangely been granted an early release from months after.

Another memo, this one sent by the FBI in February 1977, perhaps provides the reason why Norman was hauled back to prison for such a brief stint. It confirmed *The Delta Project* connection to Troop 137 in New Orleans, and noted that Norman's conviction in December 1976 ended an on-going investigation into *The Delta Project*, which had continued to operate under Phillip Paske.

"That investigation concerned the Delta Project, headed by PASKE and NORMAN, a male prostitution ring involving young males, with operations in New Orleans, California, and Chicago. Newsletters were sent out regarding the boys available and other Delta Project services...The Cook County States Attorney's Office has conducted an extensive investigation into the Delta Project, however, that investigation has been closed following conviction of NORMAN and the closing of the Delta Project."
— FBI FOI/PA# 1352511-001, Memo sent February 11 1977

Further investigation in the Troop 137 case revealed Richard Halvorsen and Raymond Woodall previously worked at a private children's school in Florida called *Adelphi Academies*, owned by a wealthy individual named Peter Bradford.[154] The pair moved to New Orleans in the early 1970s and were approved as juvenile probationary officers. They used these positions to access, and in some instances reactivate, case files on juvenile offenders to leverage against their families in scholarship offers for their boys to attend the *Adelphi Academy* in Florida. At least six boys from New Orleans had been trafficked to Florida in this way, where they were used for sex and pornography. The academy's owner Peter Bradford was charged, but in New Orleans rather than Florida.[155] Which allowed him to pay for his crimes in money instead of time, by simply forfeiting his bond and returning home where he faced no charges.[156]

Halvorsen and Woodall chartered Troop 137 in 1974, alongwith a mysterious figure named Robert Lang. Around forty boys from low income families were recruited into the troop, from which around ten aged between 8 and 12,[157] were groomed and supplied as boy prostitutes to a network of wealthy clients located across the United States.[158] Among those charged as clients were: a millionaire from California named Robert B. Mallers, a Boston real estate mogul named Hugh Mellor, and a Boston financier named Richard C. Jacobs, who was a minority-owner of the New England Patriots NFL team.[159] All up over twenty men were charged as accomplices or clients of the Troop 137 boy prostitution network. Many of the wealthier among them, such as Peter Bradford and Richard Jacobs, simply absconded on their bonds and never saw the inside of a prison cell.[160]

In a bizarre turn of events the district attorney responsible for prosecuting their cases, Harry Connick, was implicated in the case during court testimony provided by one of his own witnesses.

An associate of Raymond Woodall's named Lewis Sialle, who'd been given an immunity deal to testify, claimed under oath DA Harry Connick had been the lover of a boy pornographer named John Reed Campbell, a fugitive wanted in connection to the Troop 137 case. Sialle had alleged, *"I knew that Harry Connick was involved with John Campbell as his lover, and there was a cover-up."*[161] Connick at first refused to dignify the allegation with a response, but was then promptly forced to admit he knew John Campbell, but only as a political supporter during his campaign for office.[162]

John Campbell was a prime suspect in the case from the very beginning. Some of the victims told police they were introduced to the Troop 137 leaders at Campbell's residence after posing as models in a series of "Huck Finn and Tom Sawyer" portraits Campbell had painted of them.

> "Richard Halvorsen and Robert E. Lang, had moved suitcases containing pornographic materials into their friend John Campbell's residence for safekeeping... Using the statements of the boys and other information, officers obtained search warrants for the residences of Halvorsen and Campbell...In the pre-dawn hours, juvenile division detectives served the search warrants. They arrested Halvorsen, scout leader Raymond Thomas Woodall and another man at Halvorsen's home. At Campbell's residence, police seized the suitcases, some of the artist's work and other pornographic material. But Campbell was not arrested."
>
> — 'Chronology of John Reed Campbell Affair', The Times-Picayune, November 2 1979

The John Campbell connection to the case was a revelation, learnt three years after the fact by reporters at a New Orleans newspaper who published a series of articles on it beginning in November 1979, which had touched on Campbell's connection to Harry Connick.

> "Campbell met with Connick and Wessel Sept. 10 1976, a few hours after New Orleans police served the search warrant at the artist's West Laverne Street residence and art studio, seizing pornographic materials. Police said Campbell was a suspect by the time of his meetings with Connick and Wessel. They were building a case against him. And Campbell, a self-described friend and political supporter of Connick, has said in interviews that he went to see the district attorney to find out what the police had on him. The circumstances under which Campbell left New Orleans, and his encounter with the law in connection with the 'Boy Scout Cases,' have been at least partially pieced together by the Times-Picayune reporters."
> — 'Chronology of John Reed Campbell Affair', The Times-Picayune, November 2 1979

It turned out three days after meeting with Connick, Campbell fled New Orleans and wasn't charged in the case for another ten months. In response to this report Harry Connick subpoenaed the newspaper in question, *The Times-Picayune*, for all materials related to the source of their information.[163]

When Campbell was eventually brought back to New Orleans to face prosecution, Connick dropped some of the charges against him before reassigning the case to another prosecutor after Campbell told a judge he'd known Connick, *"for several years, as a personal friend, a legal adviser, and as an active campaign supporter when Connick ran for office."*[164] The remaining charges were then dismissed by the prosecutor Connick reassigned the case to.[165]

John Campbell had gone from prime suspect, to wanted fugitive, to a free man. A remarkable achievement well summarised in the evolution of newspaper headlines at the time.

"Man Claims Connick Fugitive's Gay Lover" - March 5 1980

"DA Connick Denies Lover Accusations" - March 6 1980
"Reporters' data subpoenaed" - April 6 1980
"Connick May Try Scout Sex Case" - September 20 1980
"Prosecutors Drop Case Against Scout Sex Suspect; Case Stale" - July 23 1982

According to an inside scoop published by NAMBLA, an otherwise unreliable partisan source, though given the circumstances an exception has been made, someone close to Campbell recalled, *"Campbell told me much more but I definitely remember him saying that he and Connick were lovers, that he had action pictures to prove this, that Connick had a good ass and he used to fuck the shit out of him."*[166]

The initial source on the John Campbell connection to Connick appears to have been Raymond Woodall, who Connick had sentenced to a hefty 75-year prison term.[167] In November 1979 writing from prison, Woodall had penned a letter, which just so happened to fall into the hands of journalists at the *Times-Picayune,* disclosing yet another revelation in the Troop 137 case.

It turned out in 1976 detectives had also investigated a side operation setup by Woodall and the mysterious Robert Lang, which allegedly supplied out of state politicians with male prostitutes through a tour guide service called *Adelphi Tours.*[168]

> "Sources told The Times-Picayune the tour guide service, which police said was called Adelphi Tours, catered mostly to out-of-town homosexuals. The tourists allegedly included influential men whose sexual preferences ran to young men and boys. Customers of the service allegedly included at least two U.S congressmen, a U.S senator, other politicians from around the country and a Protestant clergyman from Texas. The congressmen and senator were not from Louisiana, sources said. The service, which one

of the operators said was also named simply 'Tour Guide Service (TGS),' was owned and operated by Ray Thomas Woodall and Robert E. Lang, according to Woodall. Both men were arrested in 1976 and charged in the Scout cases."

— 'Scouts Case Figures Ran Gay Tours', The Times-Picayune, New Orleans, November 25 1979

Woodall said only legal age prostitutes were used by the escort service, but according to his associate Lewis Sialle, who was familiar with the operation, *"The service started out using adults, but they began ripping off the customers. That's when Woodall said we could use the kids. They'll get $50, a good meal and all that jazz. The customers will enjoy themselves and everyone is happy."*[169] According to Sialle boys from Troop 137 were used, and *"several of the boys had been originally introduced to those men by local artist John Reed Campbell, who has been a fugitive and wanted by police in the cases since September of 1976. Sialle said some of the boys had first been 'turned out' and had their first sexual experience with men after posing as models for Campbell."*[170]

New Orleans detectives who investigated *Adelphi Tours* said they were prevented by the U.S postal authorities from accessing the P.O box used to facilitate it, *"Police who worked the case said they were 'stonewalled' after postal authorities refused to allow them to open the mail...'We knew about it' said one detective. 'But we never had the evidence on who was involved...as customers or the kids'. 'We heard there was a list kept of clients, but we could never get our hand on it'."*[171]

Harry Connick's office had been aware of the operation too, but claimed they hadn't pursued the matter as those involved were already prosecuted on the boy scout charges.[172] Which had been at best, misleading. While Raymond Woodall had received a 75-year sentence, the other man mentioned, the mysterious Robert Lang, somehow managed to have his entirely suspended.

"Ray Thomas Woodall, a former scoutmaster who is serving a 75-year prison sentence for his role in the scandal, told the newspaper that several politicians used the tour service when they visited the city. Woodall said he and Robert E. Lang, a committee member of the Scout troop, formed the service in 1973 or 1974. Lang pleaded guilty to a conspiracy charge in the sex case in 1976 and received a suspended sentence."

— "Legislators linked to 'callboy' service", The Roswell Daily Record, November 27 1979

The New Orleans detectives who investigated Robert Lang later said in interviews with a documentary maker covering the case, they believed Lang had been an intelligence asset on account of evidence they discovered indicating he served in all four branches of the United States Military.[173]

Aside from John Campbell, Robert Lang was the only key figure involved in the Troop 137 case to avoid a prison. Richard Halvorsen, Raymond Woodall, and Harry O'Crame all received lengthy prison terms. As for some reason the State Department of Corrections put in a good word with the judge on Lang's behalf.

"The report recommended Lang for probation in view of his minimal involvement, which the report stated was largely unsubstantiated. The report recommended Lang be excluded from programs involving juveniles. A probation officer considered Lang of high morale character and unlikely to have committed the crime charged against him. The charge stemmed from formation of Boy Scout Troop 137 in eastern New Orleans. Lang was accused of having knowledge that the troop would be used as a cover for sexual activity between scoutmasters and scouts. <u>Lang said he is</u>

<u>now a businessman in Saudi Arabia</u>."
— 'Sentence Is Suspended In Boy Scout Sex Case', The Times-Picayune, December 22 1977

To clarify the interlinked chain of investigations sparked by the one into North Fox Island in Michigan.

- In July 1976 Gerald Richards was arrested and police in Michigan learnt a summer camp called *Brother Paul's Childrens Mission* located on a private island owned by Francis Shelden had been setup as a front in a child pornography network.
- *Brother Paul's Childrens Mission* was then linked to a parent organisation in New Jersey called *The Church of New Revelation* and two men there, Adam Starchild and Dyer Grossman.
- In August and September 1976 Gerald Richards provided detectives in Michigan with information on a nationwide child porn network, and told them of a Boys Farm in Tennessee.
- In September 1976 a child porn and prostitution ring operated by leaders of Troop 137 in New Orleans also turned up evidence of a Boys Farm in Tennessee. Their operation was linked to John Norman and his *Delta Project* in Chicago and a publication there called *Hermes*.
- In November 1976 *Father Bud's Boys Farm* in Tennessee was raided and linked to *The Church of New Revelation* in New Jersey. That same month John Norman was sent back to prison, ending an investigation into *The Delta Project*.
- In May 1977 men involved with the *Hermes* publication in Chicago were arrested.

Despite the North Fox Island investigation having been the first among these interlinked operations uncovered in July 1976, it wasn't reported on until December 1976. The four month delay of news breaking about the case appears to be due to a district attorney named Peter Deegan, who postponed the authorisation of arrest warrants for both Francis Shelden and Dyer Grossman during that period.

Francis Shelden frequently used an airstrip in Charlevoix, Michigan to privately transport boys to and from North Fox Island. Shelden was on good terms with a district attorney there named Don Berlage, a former FBI agent who visited North Fox Island with his two teenage sons on at least one occasion.[174] Shelden used another airstrip in St. Clair County, where Gerald Richards lived in Port Huron, to shuttle the four boys to North Fox Island on July 12. And as a result the charges against him originated from victim complaints in that County, handled by the district attorney there named Peter Deegan.

On July 30 '76, a week after Gerald Richards' arrest, a detective Lambourn noted in their report, *"that as soon as a warrant is obtained for SHELDON, they will check Isl. and if he is there, pros. at Leelanau County will auth. a search warrant for Fox Island."* A few days after this on August 2 the report noted, *"Deegan wants to wait on warrant for SHELDON until invest is completed."*[175]

On August 30 a detective Gorzen noted, *"Officer will contact St. Clair Pros. & attempt to obtain warrant for GROSSMAN in near future. Contact will be made with Federal agency having Jurisdiction (or MSP Operations to send letter to State Agency) Ref. GROSSMAN apparently abusing IRS laws, and converting monies intended for Child welfare to own use in sexually abusing boys. This could entail activity in California, Washington & Oregon."*[176]

On September 7 detective Gorzen noted, *"Referred info & pros report to Pros. DEEGAN. He wants to delay issuing warrant for SHELDON & GROSSMAN until his office has time to spend on case. (Presently involved in several major trials)"*.[177]

On September 27 detective Gorzen noted, *"SHELDEN'S ATTORNEY: Attny L. Bennett Young of Birmingham, Mich. tx 642-5555 called officer requesting info as to investigation. He represents the SHELDEN family & none of family has seen FRANCIS SHELDEN since search warrant was served at his home on 7-28-76. An acquittance found the search warrant return & initiated investigation thru attorney to determine what info the police have regarding SHELDEN & alleged criminal sexual acts stated on search warrant. MR. YOUNG was given limited info & assured that if/when a warrant is issued, he would be notified. If possible he would produce SHELDEN to answer charges."*[178] It was also noted on this date, *"The St. Clair Prosecutor was contacted with request for warrant for GROSSMAN for Sex crime last summer. He has not authorised as yet due to work load. If/when warrant is issued, the information will be relayed to same authority the above info will be referred to."*[179]

On September 30 a detective Sgt. Wolak noted, *"DISPOSITION OF ARREST: On 9/13/76 GERALD STEWART RICHARDS pled guilty to Criminal Sexual Conduct in 1st Degree. RICHARDS sentenced to 2/20 years in Southern Michigan Prison in Jackson by Judge Ernest Oppliger. STATUS: CLOSED by arrest."*[180]

On October 8 detective D/S Gorzen noted, *"RE-OPEN COMPLAINT: Complaint was closed in error. Attempts will be made to obtain warrants for DYER GROSSMAN & FRANCIS SHELDEN. . .Prosecutor to be contacted ref warrant requests for GROSSMAN & SHELDEN."*[181]

Almost two month later an arrest warrant for Francis Shelden was finally authorised on November 24. Followed by a fleeing felon warrant request, as Peter Deegan had noted that, *"Defendant fled before he could be arrested and arraigned."*[182]

Arrest warrants for Francis Shelden and Dyer Grossman were then issued in early December 1976, days after which news of the investigation was broke by Marilyn Wright in the *Traverse City Record-Eagle*. Wright had covered developments in the case for months and published her findings in a series of articles, the first of which appeared on December 11.

One day prior to this, an 18 year-old named Joe Moore from Charlevoix was found dead on December 10. It was learnt the teenager had known Francis Shelden for over a decade since age 9, and often accompanied the wealthy pedophile on trips. His cause of death was reported as a suicide. The youth had placed a rifle in his mouth and shot himself in the head.[183]

At the time there was another on-going investigation in Michigan into a series of child murders known as the Oakland County Child Killings, which took place over the years 1976 and 1977. That investigation ended in 1978 one day after a key suspect was found dead of a reported suicide. The suspect was found lying in bed with one arm tucked beneath a pillow, and with a blood alcohol content in excess of .40, had aimed a rifle to their forehead and pulled the trigger.

The suspect in question had also known Francis Shelden, whose name would later be mentioned in that same investigation in relation to the production of 8mm child pornography films, including a snuff film allegedly featuring one of the victims.

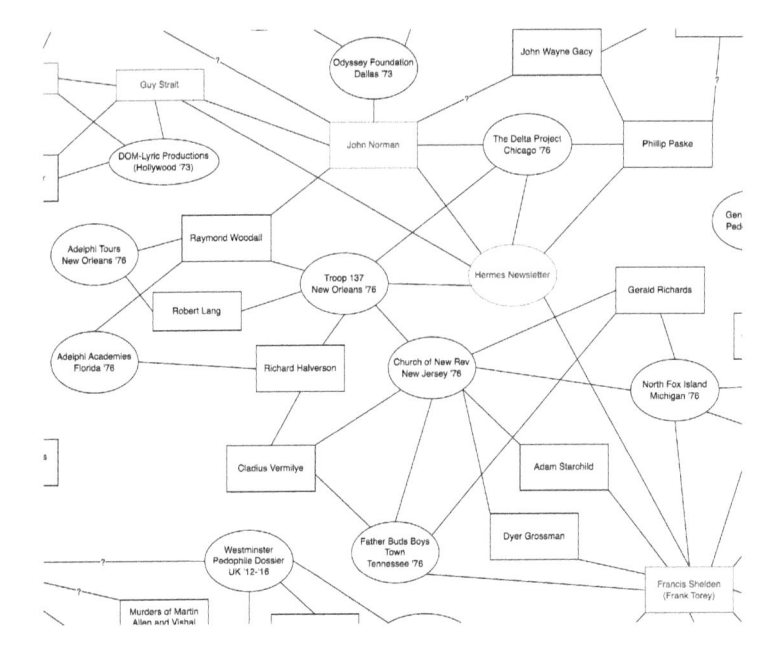

- Odyssey Foundation Dallas '73
- John Wayne Gacy
- Guy Strait
- John Norman
- The Delta Project Chicago '76
- Phillip Paske
- DOM-Lyric Productions (Hollywood '73)
- Raymond Woodall
- Adelphi Tours New Orleans '76
- Troop 137 New Orleans '76
- Hermes Newsletter
- Gerald Richards
- Robert Lang
- Adelphi Academies Florida '78
- Richard Halverson
- Church of New Rev New Jersey '78
- North Fox Island Michigan '76
- Cladius Vermilye
- Adam Starchild
- Westminster Pedophile Dossier UK '12-16
- Father Buds Boys Town Tennessee '76
- Dyer Grossman
- Francis Shelden (Frank Torey)
- Murders of Martin Allen and Vishal

*Oakland County Child Murders - MIchigan
1976-77(Cold Case:2004-2009)*

North Fox Island Connection

The Oakland County Child Killer was the moniker given to whoever murdered four children in Oakland County Michigan between February 1976 and March 1977. The victims were two boys and two girls, all aged between ten and twelve, whose bodies were found in the following sequence:
- 12 year-old Mark Stebbins went missing February 15 1976. His body was found dumped in the corner of a parking lot four days later. He had been bound with rope, sexually abused with a foreign object, and his cause of death was determined to be suffocation.
- 12 year-old Jill Robinson went missing December 22 1976. Her body was discovered in a highway ditch four days later. She had been shot in the face with a shotgun and showed no signs of sexual assault.
- 10 year-old Kristine Mihelich went missing January 2 1977. Her body was found roadside nineteen days later. She showed no signs of sexual assault and her cause of death was determined to be suffocation.
- 11 year-old Timothy King went missing March 16 1977. His body was discovered in a ditch six days later. He had been sexually abused with a foreign object, and his cause of death was determined to be suffocation.

Two of these murders were unlike the other two, and one was unlike the other three. The assumption all four fit a pattern attributable to the same behavioural profile of a single killer, which they would be, 'The Oakland County Child Killer', doesn't stand to reason or even pattern recognition. The two which are alike, and upon which this chapter narrows its focus, are the murders of the two boys, Mark Stebbins and Timothy King.

The investigation into these two murders is convoluted and further obfuscated by limited public disclosure of original case files, which are heavily redacted and riddled with what appear to be anecdotal red herrings. So to put the case simply for clarity's sake before we enter into it. The murder of Mark Stebbins can reasonably be attributed in some way to a pedophile named Christopher Busch, who was the son of a General Motors executive seemingly involved with a pedophile ring made up of executives at the company.

The murder of Timothy King can reasonably be attributed to members of a child pornography ring located in the Cass Corridor region of Detroit, likely financed by Francis Shelden.

A member of the Cass Corridor ring named Richard Lawson, a somewhat reliable police informant who dealt in half-truths, provided nondescript identifications of three men he claimed were linked to the murder. Suspect #1 was likely one of Shelden's pedophile associates, either a man named Josiah Tazelaar or another named Kent Schultz. Suspect #2 was a child pornographer in Cass Corridor named Robert Moore. Suspect #3 was a Ford motors employee named Ted Lamborgine.

In September 1976 Gerald Richards had given detectives working the North Fox Island case the name 'Josiah Tazelaar' as a pedophile associated with Francis Shelden's child porn operation. He also identified a boy named Mark Shuck who would accompany Tazelaar on trips to North Fox Island.[184]

Although his name never appears or has been redacted from the limited release of case files related to the North Fox Island investigation, Josiah Tazelaar, a 42-year-old elementary school teacher, had in fact been arrested on January 21 1977 by the lead investigator in that case, detective Joel Gorzen, on charges relating to the sexual assault of four boys during a camping trip in 1975, for which Tazelaar would be sentenced to 1-15 years prison.[185]

Tazelaar had given detectives in the North Fox Island investigation the name of another man named Titus "Duffy" Jones, who he said procured boys for a child pornography ring financed by Francis Shelden.[186] However, the address Tazelaar provided had in fact been his own previous address of 88 Stevens in an area of Detroit called Highland Park, where he had employed Titus Jones as a landscaper. Titus Jones actually lived in an apartment with another man Tazelaar had known, a Ford motors employee named Ted Lamborgine, who would later become a prime suspect in the murder of Timothy King.[187]

About a year after Tazelaar gave his name to detectives, Titus Jones was found stabbed to death in a basement, most likely by someone he knew.[188]

Detectives had taken a victim's statement from one of Tazelaar's victims named Mark Schuck, who said he'd met Tazelaar through Gerald Richards. Schuck stated boys were frequently brought to Tazelaar's property in Highland Park, which had been used as a child pornography studio and a venue to host 'pedophile parties'.[189]

Prior to moving to Highland Park Tazelaar lived with his brother just a few blocks away from where OCCK victim Timothy King had lived with his family in the neighbourhood of Birmingham.[190]

During his police interview, Tazelaar had mentioned a boy

named Ralph who was the 'boylover' of another pedophile living in Highland Park named Kent Gilbert Schultz, the caretaker of a Methodist Church just around the corner from where Tazelaar lived at 88 Stevens.[191]

Kent Schultz was then arrested in October 1977, by which time he'd become a prime suspect in the OCCK murder investigation based on a tip police received earlier that year from a child trafficker named Richard Lawson,[192]

> "A social worker, charged with sexually assaulting a 12-year-old boy, may face similar charges involving as many as six other youths, authorities say. Police say they also plan to question Kent Schultz, 32, again in connection with the sex slayings of four Oakland County children last winter. . .Lt. Robert robertson, a member of the Oakland County task force investigating the killings, said Schultz was questioned earlier this year but released after his work records gave him an alibi. Schultz was arrested Thursday after the 12-year-old boy told police Schultz had sexual relations with him about a dozen times since June 1."
>
> — 'Other Charges Possible', The Times Herald, 29 October 1977

Richard Lawson was an informant involved with a pedophile ring which used youth programs sponsored by the *Cass-Methodist Church* in downtown Detroit to procure boys. One of the men involved had been a U.S customs agent stationed at the Ambassador Bridge on the Detroit/Ontario border during the late 1970s.[193]

The leaders of the *Cass-Methodist Church* were Felix Lorenz and Rev. Lewis Redmond, who had in some instances personally introduced boys to these pedophiles.[194] Redmond was a well known Methodist Priest who lived and worked in this poverty stricken region near downtown Detroit dubbed the Cass Corridor. He'd owned a number of dilapidated properties in the area and turned one into a foster home for juvenile delinquents that was shutdown in 1972 over the questionable allocation of its funding.[195] His son Robert Redmond, who had been an organiser for the *Cass-Methodist Church* youth programs, had been shot and killed in 1976.[196] According to a source who lived with the Redmond family at the time, the murder had something to do with a dispute which had arisen after Robert Redmond confronted two others over the rape of a kid.[197]

The *Cass-Methodist* youth programs were affiliated with a student program at Wayne State university, where Franchis Shelden had worked part-time as a geology professor.[198] A student at the university named George McMahon, who helped organise these programs, was suspected of supplying boys in them to a child pornographer named Robert Moore, who had a film studio setup in the basement of a bike shop he owned in Cass Corridor.[199] Bob Moore would later become a prime suspect for the murder of Timothy King.

The aforementioned Kent Schultz had also been an alum Wayne State University, and during a retrospective investigation into his involvement in the OCCK case, a detective would note he was, *"connected to Josiah Tazelaar, Francis Sheldon, & ex-Michigan Senator Jack Faxon at that time. Faxon was in public office at the time of the killings and was friends with Schultz, along with the others."*[200]

It was also noted that when the OCCK taskforce arrested Schultz in October 1977, *"they were certain they had arrested the Oakland Count Child Killer,"* but that Schultz had been cleared as a suspect based on the results of a polygraph test.[201]

Schultz was later convicted in 1984 for the sexual assault of four children, one of which had been an 11-year-old girl.[202] Which actually made him the only suspect ever looked at with a record of assaulting both boys and girls.

A polygraph test was used to clear another prime suspect who also briefly attended Wayne State University. A pedophile named Christopher Busch who was arrested in 1977 alongwith a man named Gregory Greene for sexually assaulting a boy they procured through a church sponsored big brother program.

Gregory Greene was a convicted pedophile who was charged with attempted murder in California in 1974 after he raped and choked a boy unconscious. He'd been sent to a state mental hospital but was released after 12 months and then moved to Detroit.[203]

Greene was arrested on January 25 1977 after multiple complaints were received by police in Flint, Michigan that he had been sexually assaulting boys he coached on a baseball team.[204] During his interview Greene confessed to raping a boy named Kenneth Bowman with another pedophile named Christopher Busch. Greene stated Busch would take boys on trips to his family's cabin in the woods surrounding Michigan's Ess Lake, and that on one of these trips a boy had been murdered, whom he identified as the first OCCK victim Mark Stebbins.[205]

The victim of these two men, Kenneth Bowman, stated he was picked up by Greene and Busch from his home sometime in May 1976 and they'd driven him to a deserted area where he'd been raped by both men and at one point choked unconscious by Gregory Greene. He said Chris Busch wanted to take him into the woods, but he had refused to go because, *"GREG had told him that CHRIS BUSCH had killed one kid out in the woods up by CHRIS's house a couple of years ago."*[206] Bowman also stated Greene had once asked him, *"to go to a local playland store and help him kidnap and kill a young boy. If he did Greg would cut off the boys penis and put it in a box and give it to him."*[207]

While Gregory Green was a low-life degenerate, Christopher Busch turned out to be the son of an Executive Financial Director at General Motors named Harold Lee Busch.[208] His father had worked in Europe during his high school years where Chris attended an exclusive Swiss boarding school called *Institut Le Rosey*. Upon returning to the United States Chris then briefly attended Wayne State University for a year in the early 1970s, before becoming the owner of restaurant his father bought him, called *The Scotsman*.[209]

Busch was arrested at his restaurant on January 28, and when police searched his home they found a suitcase full of 8mm child pornography films. These were described as being, *"8-10, 8mm type homemade movies involving children having sex in a tent in a wooded area. . .this suitcase also contained commercially produced child porn magazines, photos and movies."*[210]

Busch confessed to the incident involving Kenneth Bowman but denied having anything to do with the murder of Mark Stebbins. He submitted to a polygraph examination and based off the results, just like Kent Schultz, was cleared as a suspect.[211] However, while in custody Busch had bizarrely admitted to a fantasy he shared with Gregory Greene to, *"kidnap a young boy, tie him up, and sexually abuse him."* When detectives asked what the pair planned to do with the boy after this, according to their report Busch had remained silent.[212]

Busch was charged with the sexual assault of Kenneth Bowman and his bail was set at $75,000. The judge assigned to his case reduced this to $1000 within a matter of days, which his father paid, and Busch was released from police custody on January 31.[213]

A few weeks later it was reported on February 18, *"Four Flint men have been charged with engaging more than 30 boys in oral sex and sodomy, and photographing the acts. . .The prosecutor refused to reveal the identifies of the men. The prosecutor said an eightweek probe failed to turn up indications of an organized ring. But Leonard said some of the men knew each other and traded or referred the boys to other men."*[214]

On February 28 Busch was arrested once more on separate charges. This time for sexually assaulting a boy he'd taken to his family's cabin.[215] The victim was named Vincent Gunnels and had attended same school as Busch's other victim Kenneth Bowmen.

Vincent Gunnels stated to police Busch had shown him 8mm films on a projector at the cabin which featured boys bound with rope being anally raped, and that Busch had tried this with him but hadn't persisted after Gunnels fought him off.[216]

A couple days after this it was reported on March 1:

"Busch's arrest resulted from a Oakland County investigation into the kidnap-slaying of six county youngsters in the past 13 months. Busch has been cleared in all six of the slayings. He is to be arraigned before District Judge Gerald E, McNally in the Oakland County case. He was released on $1,000 cash bond in Genesee County on the sex charges there. Busch is one of three men arrested by Flint police last month on other multiple charges of criminal sexual conduct involving young boys there. Busch and the other two men, both of Flint, allegedly used gifts, threats and physical force to persuade 12- to 14-year-old boys to engage in sexual facts[sic] and lewd photography sessions."

— 'New sex charges filed in Oakland', Detroit Free Press March 1 1977

Then a few weeks later Busch was named alongside Francis Shelden in a newspaper report on the production of 8mm child pornography films in the Michigan area. The article, published March 12 1977, reported:

> "State police seized 18 rolls of film from a Marine City man who was named in the corporation papers of Brother Paul's Childrens Mission, an alleged homosexual pornography ring involving young boys in Port Huron and on North Fox Island off Grand Traverse Bay. Photographs allegedly taken on the island have been reproduced in hardcore pornographic magazines, police said earlier. Two principals of Brother Paul's, Francis D. Shelden and Dyer Grossman, are still being sought by state and federal authorities on criminal sexual conduct charges. Flint police also confiscated eight rolls of film from Christopher Busch, 25, of Birmingham, one of three men arrested and charged with criminal sexual conduct involving 10 to 14-yer-old boys. Police there say as many as 50 youths could be involved."
> — 'Legislator to sponsor outlawing child porn', Traverse City Record, March 12 1977

A detective named Corey Williams, who would later head up a cold case investigation into the OCCK murders, would state of his findings, *"I know Busch's name was on a ledger filled with Francis Shelden's child porn customers and I have no doubt Busch and Shelden knew each other."*[217] The link between the two had indeed been under investigation in February 1977, when it was reported:

> "Genessee County Prosecutor Robert F. Leonard said yesterday the defendants may have passed boys from one to another, and the scheme may have had 'nationwide' ties. He said his office is investigating the possibility the defendants may have been linked to Grosse Pointe multimillionaire Francis D. Shelden, missing since allegations that his youth camp on a

Lake Michigan Island near Traverse City was a homosexual haven became public last year. Busch is free on $1,000 cash bond, while Bennett and Green are in Genesee County Jail in lieu of $15,000 and $75,000 bonds, respectively."

— "Oakland County link probed in sexual exploiting of boys." The Detroit News, February 22 1977

This prosecutor, Robert F. Leonard, had then penned a letter in March 1977 on behalf of the National District Attorney's Association to the Assistent U.S Attorney General expressing his concerns of a nation-wide highly organised child exploitation network. Leonard had written:

"It seems there may very well be a national conspiracy made up of an inter-relating network of foster homes, churches, nature camps and other similar programs ostensibly set up to handle wayward, incorrigible, homeless youngsters. . . These adult perverts appear to be aware of the network and travel between states attending these camps and sexually abusing these children for money usually paid to the camp officials. Many of these people involved in this type of activity are very wealthy individuals and some are respectable community leaders in their home towns."[218]

— Letter from Robert F. Leonard Prosecuting Attorney, Genesee County, to Benjamin Civiletti, Assistant U.S. Attorney General, March 4, 1977.

In April Robert F. Leonard had then organised a meeting for information sharing between local law enforcement agencies in Michigan on ties between various pedophile rings concurrently under investigation in the region. The meeting was scheduled for April 11 with a list of agenda items including :"Identification of Individuals", "National Conspiracy and its effect on Michigan", and "Civic organisations vulnerable to infiltration."[219]

In May Leonard then testified before a House of Representatives Sub-Committee of the Judiciary hearing on child sexual exploitation, and emphasised during his opening statement, *"The tentacles of this illegal activity form an underground network reaching from New York to California and Michigan to Louisiana. Prosecutors in cities across the country have uncovered and compiled information pointing to a high degree of exchange and communication among those who prey on our children. Seemingly isolated cases of such deviancy reveal a frightening set of sophisticated intercommunications upon closer scrutiny."*[220] Later that year Leonard became the target of a federal investigation which led to his conviction in March 1979 for embezzlement of federal funds, the loss of his legal license, and a five year prison sentence.[221]

After the disappearance of the final OCCK victim Timothy King in March 1977, the task force investigating the OCCK murders had shifted their focus away from the promising leads into the aforementioned pedophiles rings operating in Michigan, and towards the psychological profile of an elusive serial killer.

Academics were consulted as part of 'Operation Burial Ritual' to determine similarities between the murders of Mark Stebbins and Timothy King, two boys raped then strangled, and two girls not raped then strangled, one of whom had been shot in the face.

One anthropology PhD determined, *"After studying the pictures of the drop sites, Dr Peebles indicated that it would appear they exemplified the Judeo-Christian traditional burial ritual."* Further consultation with academics from Wayne Sate University identified more similarities between the four victims. They noticed that, *"One boy (Timothy King) and one girl (Jill Robinson) had red jackets"* and that, *"One boy (Mark Stebbins) and one girl (Kristine Mihelich) had blue jackets"*; That, *"All had shoulder length hair"* and that, *"All had fair complexion"*; So that, *"This might lead one to the conclusion that the killer does select a specific target or victim."*[222]

Two days after the discovery of Timothy King's body on March 22 an article appeared, headlined 'Weird Pattern Links Deaths of 4 Children':

> "The children, in the apparently related cases, all disappeared or were found dead on days when it snowed, and although the killer murdered his first victim last February, he did not strike again until cold weather returned more than 10 months. . .A psychological profile of the killer developed by police departments working on the murders said the killer is fanatically clean, bright, but sexually abnormal."
> — 'Weird Pattern Links Deaths of 4 Children', Detroit Free Press, March 24 1977.

The investigation gained quick notoriety in the media through an assumption there was a 'serial killer' driven by a 'modus operandi' defined by their 'psychological profile'.

For all kinds of pathological reasons people insert themselves in things that receive publicity. This is especially true for murder cases. The task force started receiving hundreds, if not thousands of tips and possible leads from people seeking to become personally involved in the public story telling of the mystery unfolding each morning in their newspapers during breakfast. Soon, the case was reduced to the granular details of a police sketch of the killer and the make and color of their car.

Behind the scenes however there seems to have only been two prime suspects. Kent Gilbert Schultz and Christopher Busch. Both convicted pedophiles tied to Francis Shelden, who were both cleared as suspects based on the results of polygraph tests.

After his arrest in October 1977 Schultz had been questioned and polygraphed in December.[223] On December 12 the OCCK task force chief had put in a request to INTERPOL concerning reports of child snuff pornography in the media, *"Enclosed are pictures of the youngsters who have been killed in this area. We would like to request they be distributed throughout your network with information on the aforementioned 'snuff out' pornography theory. Further, we would like to alert your field agents to be cognizant of these films and any child participants and victims of same."*[224]

Nothing would come of this though, and in 1978 the 'serial killings' apparently stopped and rumours for why started to circulate in the press. Supposedly the killer's family had them committed to a mental hospital. Then in November 1978 the investigation was then closed, unsolved, one day after Christopher Busch was found dead of a reported suicide.

On the morning of November 20 1978, Chris Busch's brother Charles Busch received a phone call from their parent's housekeeper. The parents were away and Christopher Busch had been staying there and the housekeeper locked out of the home. Charles arrived at the house and waited for a patrolman named Richard McNamee to arrive before entering. McNamee would later be charged for sexually assaulting a minor in 1982.[225]

Charles Busch and Officer McNamee entered the house together and discovered the body of Chris Busch inside the room he kept there, lying in bed with one arm tucked beneath a pillow, next to a .22 rifle with a gunshot wound in his forehead.[226]

When crime scene investigators arrived they discovered the following items in this room: ropes cut to the length required for binding limbs on the floor, a box of shotgun shells on a dresser, and pinned to the wall a handdrawn portrait of a little boy in a parka coat screaming. This portrait appeared to resemble Mark Stebbins, the OCCK victims

Gregory Greene claimed Busch had killed.[227]

The convenience of this was remarkable. Ropes for the ligature marks discovered on both boys. A handdrawn portrait of one. Shotgun shells for the girl who'd been shot in the face with a shotgun. And the body of a prime suspect who couldn't be questioned. The very next day the OCCK task force was dissolved,[228] and just like that the case went cold.

Then—some twenty-five years later—a Michigan detective named Cory Williams investigating an unrelated cold case murder from 1989, stumbled upon information which would reignite the link between the North Fox Island investigation and the OCCK murders.

In 2004 Det. Williams received a tip on a prisoner in California who had confessed to being an accomplice to murder back in 1989. The inmate, Richard Mudica, was a teenager at the time running around with a then 32 year-old man named Richard Lawson. Mudica claimed Lawson shot the owner of a taxi company named Exavor Giller in the driveway of his home with a shotgun he'd disposed of in nearby lake. Mudica was able to lead detectives to the lake in question and divers recovered the murder weapon, all but confirming the validity of his claims.[229]

At the time, Richard Lawson was recently paroled in California after having served time for his involvement in a human smuggling ring which operated across the San Diego-Mexico border.[230] He was arrested and extradited to Michigan to face trial. With the evidence stacked against him, and facing the prospect of a life sentence, Lawson told Det. Williams he had information on the OCCK murders to exchange for a deal.

It turned out Lawson had been an informant for the Detroit Sexual Crimes Unit back in the 1970s and provided a number of tips on pedophile rings that operated within Michigan.

Det. Williams checked with Lawson's police handler from that period, Isiah "Ike" McKinnon, who confirmed Lawson was part of a pedophile network operating in multiple states, and that Lawson had been a reliable source of information.[231]

During a series of interviews conducted in 2005, Lawson provided drips of information which described three individuals involved in the murder of Timothy King, who he claimed was murdered in a snuff film financed by Francis Shelden.[232]

Based off information Lawson provided, the identifies of these three suspects were determined to be : 1# Josiah Tazelaar, #2 Robert Moore, and #3 Ted Lamborgine.

Suspect #2, Robert Moore, was a child pornographer who used the basement of his bike store as a studio to produce 8mm films, allegedly commissioned by Francis Shelden according Lawson.[233]

Suspect #3, Ted Lamborgine, was a Ford Motors employee and a roommate of Titus 'Duffy' Jones, who Josiah Tazelaar had said supplied boys to Francis Shelden back in 1977. Lawson said Lamborgine supplied boys to Robert Moore, and had shown him a photograph taken by Moore of a naked boy who Lawson believed to have been Timothy King.[234]

Suspect #1, most likely either Josiah Tazelaar(possibly Kent Schultz), was never directly named by Lawson, who had withheld the identity of #1 as part of his bargaining position.[235]

It turned out this wasn't the first time Lawson had leveraged this information in exchange for clemency. Back in 1988 Lawson was picked up on four counts of sexual assault of a minor. Oddly enough, Lawson had known the father of Timothy King, who'd been a lawyer named Barry King, and contacted him claiming to have information on his son's murder. Detectives along with a representative of Barry

King's law firm met with Lawson in 1988 and he had supplied them with the same information, only in more detail.[236]

Back then Lawson said Shelden was the major backer of a "chickenhawk" organisation which shipped child pornography to Amsterdam. He said Suspect #1 was part of that operation and told him during a poker game while high on cocaine they'd seen a child porn film with Timothy King in it.[237]

> "Lawson was frequenting poker games near the Wonderbread plant in Detroit in the mid to late 70's. Lawson was also frequenting this same poker game where they would share pedophile stories about kids. Faye confirmed this along with the 1988 report when Lawson called Timothy King's father at home and told him that he knows who killed his son. Lawson was pretty sure he knew, again, but couldn't prove it. In this report, Lawson told Detective Studt from Birmingham PD that he met the person he described in the report as #1 at a poker game. Lawson described these subjects as #1, 2 & 3 and told detectives that he believed these to be the people responsible for the killing of Timothy King and possibly the others. Lawson also told detectives in the 1988 report that #1 was high on cocaine one night at a poker game and told Lawson that he had seen a child porn movie with Timothy King in it."
>
> — Casenotes of Det. Corey Williams, 11-27-06 entry

Lawson claimed to be part of Shelden's operation and said he'd travelled to Amsterdam in 1979 to meet with a child porn distributor there named Kim Tam Ang. Ang had told him Francis Shelden and Suspect #1 were involved in the abduction and murder of the Timothy King.[238]

> "Approximately a year and a half ago, John Ouelett (FBI) forwarded a request to the FBI & Dutch police

in Amsterdam to pursue a possible connection between a large distributor of child pornography in Amsterdam, according to Lawson, named Kim, Francis Sheldon and the possibility of a connection with the Oakland County Child Killings. Lawson had told authorities in 1988, when he was facing life in prison for child molestation, that he had travelled to Amsterdam in 1979 and had a conversation with this Kim. Lawson said that Kim named Francis Sheldon and #1 by name as having involvement in the abduction/ murder of Timothy King. Lawson had mentioned in the 1988 report that Francis Duffield Sheldon, pedophile from the southwest Michigan area, was the person who was financing the child porn photos and films in the Detroit area and shipping them to Amsterdam for distribution to the eye of the chickenhawk organization."
— Casenotes of Det. Corey Williams, 2-7-07 entry

Det. Williams was able to confirm that Lawson had in fact travelled to Amsterdam in 1979, and Dutch authorities were able to confirm that both a 'Kim Tam Ang' and 'Francis Shelden' were named together in a 1993 investigation into child pornography.[239]

"Today, the FBI in Washington D.C., forwarded a response they received from the Dutch police in Brussels in regards to our request. In this response, the Dutch authorities, state that they compared all the photographs of our OCCK victims to photos and films they confiscated during a large child porn sting in Amsterdam in 1993, with negative results. However, they state that Kim was identified in the 1993 investigation as Kim Tam Ang, born 4-16-1933, a British national from Selangor, Malacca, living in Amsterdam. Ang was well known to Dutch police for

child pornography and sexual abuse of minor boys in 1997. The Dutch police, also provided that Francis Duffield Shelden, w/m", born 9-5-28, from Wayne County, Michigan, U.S.A. died 7-9-96, was also named in their investigation. Ang & Sheldon were both mentioned in an investigation by the Danish police in 1993 concerning child pornography and sexual offenses against minors. This confirms Lawson's story."
— Casenotes of Det. Corey Williams, 2-7-07 entry

Cross referencing the information Lawson had provided in 1988, with what he then partially regurgitated once more in 2005, Det. Williams tentatively identified Suspect #1 as Josiah Tazelaar.[240] Another possibility had been Kent Gilbert Schultz.[241] The reasoning for this was as follows.

- Lawson stated Suspect #1 supplied boys to Robert Moore used in child porn films financed by Francis Shelden. Josiah Tazelaar had known Gerald Richards and Francis Shelden and been questioned about North Fox Island in 1977.
- Lawson stated Suspect #1 was still alive in 2005. Josiah Tazelaar was still alive in 2005.[242]
- Lawson stated Suspect #1 had lived in Highland Park. Josiah Tazelaar had lived at 88 Stevens in Highland Park. And prior to that he had lived with his brother in the same neighbourhood as Timothy King.[243]
- Lawson stated a child porn distributor in Amsterdam told him Suspect #1 and Francis Shelden were involved in the Timothy King murder. Josiah Tazelaar had family in the Netherlands.

Aall the charges Lawson faced in 1988 had been dismissed, seemingly in exchange for this information, yet the information itself had never been followed up on.[244]

By the time Det. Williams stumbled across this in 2005, both Robert Moore and Francis Shelden were dead, which just left Ted Lamborgine and Josiah Tazelaar as suspects for the murder of Timothy King.

Josiah Tazelaar was interviewed about his pedophile activities in the 1970s. He was evasive and caught in multiple lies, but was smart enough not to implicate himself in any past crimes. When it became clear he was being questioned over the OCCK murders, Tazelaar lawyered up and refused to take a polygraph.[245] He would later agree to submit to one, but only in exchange for immunity from any past non-violent crimes. Tazelaar was granted immunity, but when it came time to hold up his end of the deal, the polygraph got called off due to 'a heart condition' and Tazelaar never ended up taking the test.[246]

When Ted Lamborgine was questioned he corroborated much of what Lawson had claimed. He admitted to involvement with other pedophiles in the Cass Corridor during the 1970s, and admitted to sexually assaulting boys and taking them to Robert Moore's bike shop to be filmed. Though he denied having anything to do with the child murders.[247]

Lamborgine submitted to a polygraph, which in the assessors opinion he failed, and that led to him becoming the new prime suspect in the OCCK cold case. He was charged for the past sexual assaults he admitted to, and these were leveraged against him for either a confession or further information on the murders. However, Lamborgine maintained he knew nothing about them and received a life sentence for his past crimes.[248]

Around this time Richard Lawson stopped cooperating with the investigation also, and in 2007 received a life sentence for his 1989 murder charge. But just as this aspect of the cold case had dwindled, another into Christopher Busch resurfaced.

* * *

In July 2006 a polygrapher named Patrick Coffey, who just so happened to be a childhood friend and neighbour of Timothy King, met another polygrapher named Larry Wassar at a trade convention in Las Vegas. The two got to talking shop when Coffey learnt Wassar had worked in the Oakland County area during the 1970s, and the OCCK case came up. Wassar then casually mentioned he polygraphed the guy who'd killed Timothy King back in 1977.[249]

Patrick Coffey relayed this information to the King family, who forwarded it onto the FBI and Det. Williams, whose focus to that point had been firmly on the Francis Shelden child porn ring connections in the case.

It was learnt Larry Wassar was hired by Christopher Busch's attorney, Jane Burgess, back in 1977 to perform a preparatory polygraph prior to the one used to clear Busch as a suspect.

There was a whole legalistic fiasco over whether the information Wasser 'may or may not have had' was privileged since he'd administrated the polygraph acting on behalf of Busch's lawyer. When he was pushed for further information by cold case investigators he more or less insinuated Busch had admitted to some level of culpability in the OCCK murders.

Det. Williams then went back over the OCCK case files from 1977 and discovered a polygrapher named Ralph Cabot had administered the tests given to both Gregory Greene and Christopher Busch in 1977. Records of these tests were shown to another polygrapher, who determined the results should not have been indicative of Busch being truthful. [250]Thus, Busch shouldn't have been cleared as a suspect based off those results.

In 2008 the FBI interviewed Christopher's brother Charles Busch, and requested a DNA sample to match against DNA evidence taken from the bodies of OCCK victims. Charles agreed, but only on the condition that should a match be returned on his family's DNA profile, it be withheld that the DNA sample came from him, and that his nephews in Michigan be placed in the FBI witness protection program.[251] Charles also mentioned that near the end of his father's life, Harold Lee Busch shredded all of the family's documents, including birth certificates, marriage licenses, passports, and family photos. Which Charles had found rather strange.[252]

Harold Lee Busch started his career at General Motors as a low-level accountant within the Fisher Body Division of the company. A division founded by the Fisher family, another from Detroit's high society well acquainted with Francis Shelden's.[253] A member from this family named Everett E. Fisher Jr. also had a tip called on them in during the OCCK investigation back in the 1977.[254]

According to Barry King, when Richard Lawson met with a representative of his law firm in 1988 regarding his son's murder, *"Lawson advised Binkley that his associate Bobby Moore, used to take young boys to visit with H. Lee Busch, the father of Christopher Busch."*[255] Lawson also mentioned in his 2005 interviews with Det. Williams he and Robert Moore, *"took a young boy to a Chrysler executives home on the east side (possibly Warren) back in the mid to late 70's and the executive paid Moore to have sex with the boy."*[256]

In January 1977 the owner of stamp and coin collectables store in Michigan named Fred Minch supposedly had a rather interesting conversation with a regular customer of his, a Chrysler executive at General Motors named Harwood Rydholm. The GM executive allegedly said that, *"The killer is the son of a high-level GM executive but the police aren't doing anything because GM is protecting the father."*[257] This story was told by the daughter of Fred Minch, who contacted the sister of

Timothy King, a woman named Catherine Broad who has been keeping a blog(www.catherinebroad.blog) on the renewed investigation into her brother's murder.

Since starting her website in 2013, Broad has been contacted by people who grew up in Michigan and have given accounts of a pedophile ring made up of General Motors executives active in the 1970s.

In one account, a person claiming to be the child of a personal assistant to GM executives *"and other affluent men like Dick Chrysler of Cars and Concepts"* alleged they were been passed around to various "babysitters" whose job it was to prepare children for appearances in child porn films. The filming took place at the home of a General Motors accountant with a large storage shed at the back of the property where these films were kept in Scooby Doo VHS cases.[258]

In another account someone claimed the daughter of a GM employee had been 'made available' to her father's superiors in the upper management of the company. A private investigator was engaged in the matter and the apparent theory was, *"that offering up a child was a kind of ticket into the upper ranks of management."*[259]

Det. Corey Williams and a journalist named Marney Keenan, who wrote a book on the OCCK case called *The Snow Killings*, interviewed others who gave similar accounts, *"The women claimed to have been sexually abused as children as part of an organized ring of pedophiles operating within GM's executive management during the mid-seventies and into the eighties."*[260]

"Yet another woman, who claimed she was abducted in 1970 by a pedophile ring operating out of Auburn Hils (the site of GM's now shuttered massive truck and coach manufacturing facility) spoke of being held with other kids for several days in private homes. 'We were treated like toys, rather than human beings,' she said. Her account was specific and detailed. Both boys and girls were ritually drugged and raped. No penetration for the girls, no ejaculation inside boys, with emphasis on scrupulous bathing and cleansing afterwards. She said large sums of money - upwards of $100,000 - were involved. When she went to the police, she said, she was humiliated. *'I was not taken seriously,'* she said, *'because I'm a psych patient'*. "

— The Snow Killings: Inside the Oakland County Child Killer Investigation, Marney Rich Keenan, page 172

"With her attorney and therapist present, she spoke at length about her abuse at the hands of her father, beginning at age four and lasting well into her teenage years. What began as incest escalated into forced sex acts with several of her father' associates. She said she was sold as entertainment at pedophile orgies; she described helping create child porn movies. She gave the names of many of the well-known suspects in the OCCK and North Fox Island cases, and she described their respective roles in the ring."

— Ibid, page 173

An FBI report filed in 1992 gave an even more disturbing account. It stated the victim's father, an accountant for a company located in Ann Arbour, the name of which had been redacted, was part of a child abuse ring led by a 'prominent and powerful person' from the Ann Arbor community. The victim claimed they were made to watch their father and other members of this group murder two other children sometime around 1975-'76. It stated the father impregnated the victim's sister and they were forced to watch the abortion procedure.[261]

General Motors was a DuPont family controlled company from 1920 until they divested their controlling stake in the mid 1960s.[262] For almost that entire period a single man name

Alfred P. Sloan had managed the company on their behalf from 1923 until his death in 1966. It would be fair to assume that the corporate culture instilled within GM during this forty year period was largely attributable to Alfred Sloan and the DuPonts, which persisted into the 1970s amongst executives at the company who, like Harold Lee Busch, had spent their entire careers there.

I bring this up because the DuPont family were fascists. This term has lost most of its punch due to semantics, but allow me to emphase this with another term which has likewise lost its meaning - literally. The Du Ponts were literally fascists.

The DuPont chemical firm maintained cartel arrangements with the Nazi chemicals conglomerate I.G Farben throughout the 1920 and 30s. Alfred P. Sloan was personally involved in the patent transfer of Ethyl lead to I.G Farben during that period, a compound used to improve the engine efficiency of planes and automobiles. As late as 1938 Sloan had authorised the transfer of 500 tons of the stuff to the Luftwaffe.[263]

In addition to this, the largest tank manufacturer in Nazi Germany was a wholly-owned subsidiary of General Motor called Opel, which persisted its operations under the GM umbrella throughout WW2, where its factories had been mostly spared during allied bombing raids.[264]

Perhaps this could've been explained away with that old motif that doesn't explain anything—the profit-driven motivation of the capitalist system—if of course, the DuPont family also been primary backers of a fascist coup attempt in the United States.

In 1933 the DuPonts were involved in what has become euphemistically known as the Business Plot. A conspiracy to replace the US Presidency of Franklin Roosevelt with a fascist dictatorship.

In November 1934 a Major General named Smedley Butler

informed Congress he'd been approached by a director from the Guaranty Trust Company named Grayson Murphy, to lead a paramilitary group formed from US military veterans as the means for backing a plot to install Hugh S. Johnson, at that time the head of the National Recovery Administration, as dictator of the United States.

The plot was financed by the Guaranty Trust Company, a J.P Morgan financial firm backed by City of London financiers, with armaments for the prospective paramilitary units raised to be supplied by the DuPont family firearms subsidiary Remington Arms Co.[265] The plan was to relegate the Presidency to the purely ceremonial role played in 2023 by President Joe Biden. Who himself having been a Senator from Delaware, has the DuPont family to thank for his political career.

Biden's first senatorial campaign was fully funded and staffed by DuPont employees in the early 70s.[266] His victory party was held and celebrated in a DuPont ballroom, and soon after his family moved into an old DuPont family mansion. As Biden put it himself in the 1980s, he prostituted himself to these people.[267] And when a member of the DuPont family raped his 3 year-old daughter, Joe Biden's son Beau as district attorney decided not to prosecute the case.[268]

Joe Biden shared a questionable relationship with his own daughter, whose leaked diary, and the authenticity of this diary is confirmed by Ashley Biden herself, contained the following entry: *"Hyper-sexualized @ a young age. What is this due to? Was I molested. I think so – I can't remember specifics but I do remember trauma – I remember not liking the woolzacks house; I remember somewhat being sexualized with [a cousin]; I remember having sex with Friends @ a young age; showers w/my dad (probably not appropriate). Being turned on when I wasn't supposed to be."*[269]

Perhaps Biden had prostituted more than just himself to advance his career. The Bidens, like the DuPonts, are a very strange family.

As for who murdered Mark Stebbins or Timothy King? The aspects of the case covered in this chapter are much too convoluted to draw any firm conclusions. The one draw by investigators early into the renewed cold case investigation pretty much aligned with what Richard Lawson claimed.

> "The only connection so far between Lawson and Francis Shelden's pedophile ring is that Lawson talked about Shelden financing the film of Timothy King, produced by Bob Moore. Lawson told detectives this during the interview in 1988, after he contacted Timothy King's father from the Macomb County jail, stating that he knew who killed his son. John and I agreed that the motive behind the kidnappings and killings was probably the money the suspects were getting for filming and selling the Snuff films of these children."
>
> — Casenotes of Det. Corey Williams, 12-13-05 entry

If Francis Shelden had been funding snuff films as part of his operation, then perhaps it would explain why a local art dealer named John McKinney, also closely affiliated with the Cranbrook Institute, was murdered in his Birmingham gallery in September 1977.[270] By that time though Shelden had fled Michigan, and even the United States, to join up with another network of British pedophiles in Amsterdam, the eye of the chickenhawk. It only gets worse from here.

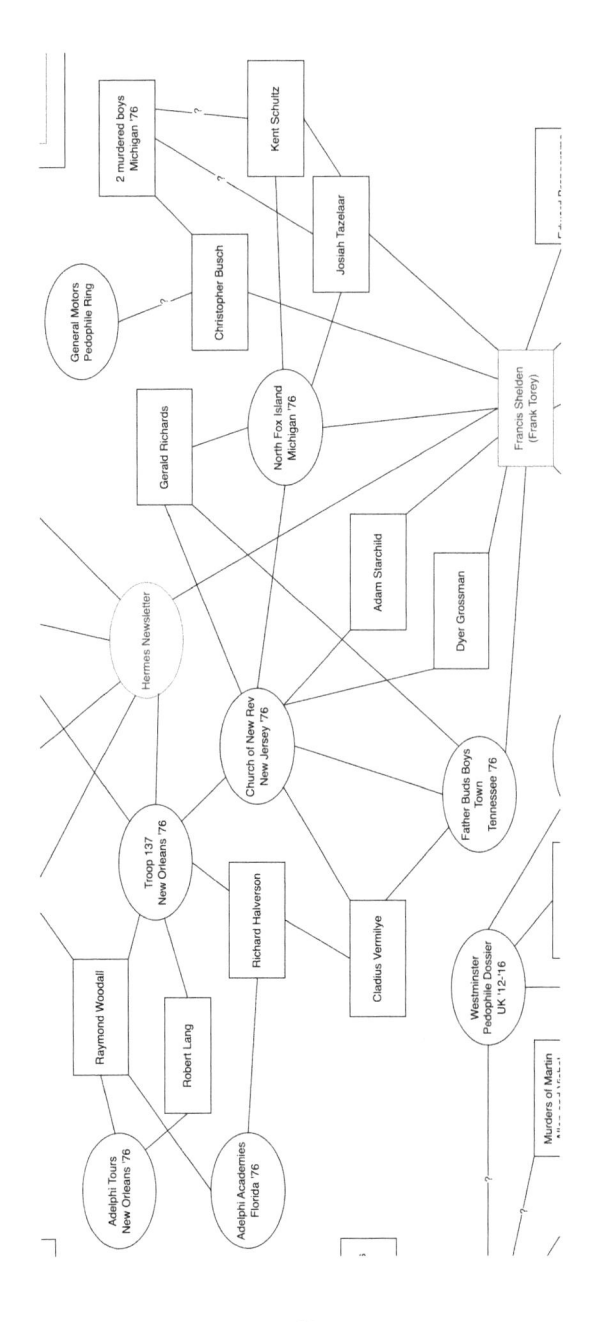

Spartacus International - UK, Amsterdam, Germany, Australia '79-95

Francis Shelden & John Stamford

Francis Shelden fled Michigan almost as soon as the investigation into North Fox Island had commenced in July 1976. The four month delay in the authorisation of his arrest warrant bought him enough time to get his affairs in order, transfer his estate into offshore holdings, and then himself to Amsterdam sometime in the latter months of 1976. And through his political connections there was fast tracked for Dutch citizenship protecting him from extradition.[271]

One of the front organisations Shelden had used for his operation was *The Educational Foundation for Youth in Illinois*. This foundation derived a tax exception status as the non-profit subsidiary of an offshore profit making parent company called *The Trust Company of The West Indies Inc.*, which had ostensibly operated as an export business shipping surplus books overseas.[272] The incorporating agent for both of these was Adam Starchild, the same offshore tax attorney Shelden used to incorporate the summer camp on North Fox Island.

In September 1976 Shelden had given Adam Starchild his power of attorney and transferred all of his assets, including the deed to North Fox Island, into an offshore trust called *The Trust Company of the Virgin Islands, Ltd*. Two years after this in 1978 Shelden then appointed a Dutch Senator named Edward

Brongersma as the primary trustee of his off-shored estate using an Amsterdam attorney.[273] Brongersma was a prominent advocate for the legalisation of pedophilia in the Netherlands as a senior member of the Dutch Senate's Judiciary Committee, and assumedly the political connection Shelden used to attain Dutch citizenship so quickly.

In Amsterdam Shelden started a new newsletter called *PAN(Paedo Alert News): A Magazine about Boy-love*, under the penname 'Frank *Torey*'.[274] *Pan* was of course the son of *Hermes* in the homeric verse of Greek myth, a hint to the publishing legacy Shelden now continued abroad. Just as *Hermes* was used in North America to facilitate John Norman's *Odyssey Network*, *PAN* was be used to platform its European equivalent called *Spartacus International*.

The first edition of *PAN* was first published in 1979 through a publishing house owned by fugitive child trafficker named John Stamford.[275] Stamford was a British foreign-national and defrocked Anglican priest who fled to Amsterdam in 1972 after he was charged with operating a child pornography service through the mail.

> "In Amsterdam John Stamford, who runs the Spartacus Club, said he was forced to flee Britain because the British 'are too pig-headed' and can't understand the quality of sexual relationships between men and boys'. He left Britain for Holland shortly after being convicted for sending obscene literature through the post in 1972. His club is part of Spartacus international, a British-registered company described as 'general publishers of trade and business directories, periodicals, newspapers and journals'. In fact, its publishing is confined to a host of homosexual literature including books for pederasts, and Paedo Alert News, described as 'a magazine about boy love'."
>
> — 'Scandal of Britons who buy young boys for £3 a night',

The Sunday Times, August 3 1986

From Amsterdam through the late 1970s, 80s, and early 90s, Stamford operated a child sex tourism business under the guise of an international homosexual travel guide, which also sponsored boy brothels around under the franchise *Club Spartacus*.

To skirt child sex trafficking laws Stamford had inverted the process, delivering pedophiles to children in countries such as the Phillipines and Thailand. His operation was exposed by the Fleet Street press in the mid 1980s, which led to a raid of his estate on the outskirts of Amsterdam and the discovery there of copious amounts of child pornography.[276] Stamford's operation, no doubt aided through his association with Francis Shelden, extended all the way to the United States in affiliation with NAMBLA.

"NAMBLA officials also don't deny that several of the group's members belong to Club Spartacus. The names of the Westchester members of Club Spartacus were discovered along with thousands of other men and women in the London computers of a British man, John Stamford, 55, who was identified by authorities as a Club Spartacus official, according to FBI and other federal law enforcement records. . .Club Spartacus, according to one investigative document, is a clandestine organization that operates through a box number in London. Vital information on each member — stored on a computer and guarded with secret codes — include their sexual preferences, the desired age of the children and preferred country of origin. Members receive personalized lists of children, mainly from outside Europe, and are invited to select a child and indicate the choice to a local middleman."

— 'NAMBLA: Investigation launched against pedophile group', The Daily Times, April 10 1995

When authorities cracked down on his operation in Amsterdam, Stamford hopscotched across to Germany and transferred control of *Spartacus International* over to a German publisher called *Bruno Gmunder Verlag*. He'd then fallen under investigation by German authorities and fled to the pedophile's last bastion, Belgium, where he would finally be charged with "incitement to the sexual exploitation of children" in 1993 and be brought to trial in 1995, facing a maximum sentence of 1 year.[277]

An article published in a German tabloid called *Gossenblatt Berliner BZ* in 1992 reported Scotland Yard hadsuspected Stamford of having trafficked in snuff films, *"He fled to Berlin after the police confiscated 16 boxes of child pornography and 25,000 customer addresses from his villa near Amsterdam. Scotland Yard, the famous London police, has a terrible suspicion: Stamford filmed 20 boys dying after sex orgies in England. On these perverse films: after the children have been repeatedly raped by men, they have been strangled, suffocated, strangled. The videos were sold for around 1,500 marks per strip - to particularly good customers"* [German to English] [278]

A similar accusation was given by a former associate of Stamford's, read out at at his trial.[279]

"The ambiguity is likely to benefit John Stamford who is nevertheless a key figure in the dissemination of sex tourism. Marie-France Botte explains that the "Spartacus" guide and the "Paedo Alert News" ("PAN") magazine are visible in most hotels in Thailand that make children available to their customers. In one of these establishments, recommended by the "Spartacus" guide, an RTBF team was able to "obtain" a ten-year-old boy without any problems. You can even buy children for a few hundred dollars. Worse still: in a P.-V. written by a PJ officer who investigated the Stamford affair, we find the testimony of a Briton accusing Stamford of having made a video film where a Filipino child is tortured and put to death. His body would have been buried under a house under construction" [French to English]

— 'LAW APPEARS POWERFUL IN THE FACE OF SPARTACUS AND HIS SLAVE TRADERS, THE PUBLIC MINISTRY ONLY REQUIRES ONE YEAR AGAINST STAMFORD', Le Soir, February 16 1995

The trial came to an abrupt end in December 1995 when Stamford died of a heart attack during a hospital stay. Some months later Francis Shelden died as well, of unknown cause in September 1996.[280] A month earlier it was reported Belgian authorities had been looking into a possible connection between Stamford's network and the child trafficking activities of another one of those 'serial killers', Marc Dutroux. We'll place a pin in that connection for now and return to in a later chapter.

"The Belgian police, for the first time, have also pooled their information on 15 children who have disappeared over the past six years. Seven of those are known to have been killed. There seems to be no indication that Britain is involved in this apparent paedophilia web, although Belgian police have been alert to a possible British connection since the arrest last year of John Stamford. He was head of the Spartacus International Paedophile Group and died during his trial before a Belgian court last December."

— 'Belgian police link child sex victims to trade with East', The Times, August 21 1996

Over a twenty year period tendrils of Stamford's network can be found creeping in the background of various political 'scandals' and 'affairs', in countries as far away as Australia.

In 1979 a Brisbane woman reported a man to police for photographing her son naked. He was placed under surveillance and was soon caught doing the same to boys he'd taken on a trip into the bushlands. The man police arrested was a 61-year-old retired stenographer named Clarence Henry Osborne, a well placed civil servant who for years had transcribed government hansards and supreme court proceedings in the Australian state of Queensland.

At Osborne's home police, *"discovered thousands of pictures of naked children, hundreds of hours of tape-recorded conversations with boys and a meticulously organised filing cabinet filled with index cards bearing the details of his victims, from their names, ages and addresses, to their physical measurements. It was later estimated that Osborne had been involved with more than 2500 under-aged males over a 20-year period."*[281]

Osborne was taken into police custody and interviewed by detectives, who decided not to charge him and instead drove him home, where, later that night, Osborne promptly committed suicide using the exhaust pipe of his car.

The materials seized from Osborne's home were forgotten about in storage, until a year later a detective stumbled upon all twelve boxes of them, *"he noticed dozens of boxes on the shelves marked 'Osborne'. 'Within those boxes were all these index cards ... I recognised names ... it was quite obvious there were members of the judiciary, the legal fraternity, there were politicians, it was the top end ... there were no bloody truck drivers and bricklayers amongst them,' the retired officer, who requested anonymity, said."*[282]

A detective from the juvenile division who inspected Osborne's files commented there'd been enough evidence, *"to bring down the [then Queensland] government overnight."*[283]

Among Osborne's boxed possessions were magazines published by *Spartacus International* in which detectives identified some of the Brisbane boys Osborne had photographed, *"And the thing that was very disturbing about them was that the Brisbane kids [photographed by Osborne] were appearing in the German magazines ... then we'd find a copy of the same magazine in English ... and it was almost like a tourist guide for paedophiles."*[284] Osborne's letter correspondance indicated he had acted as a sort of concierge for members of the Spartacus network who visited Australia.

" *'They could come to Brisbane and meet these kids. And this was all arranged through bloody Clarry. We discovered that the motto of the paedophile group over there was – sex before eight [years old] before it's too late'. 'One of the German magazines was named Spartacus and it was the codename of an international underground paedophile network. It was run by a bloke called John Stamford out of Amsterdam. He originated from the UK and I think sort of got himself in a bit of strife there and went over to Amsterdam and he was running this network, and Clarry Osborne was part of that.'* "

— 'Paedophile Clarence Henry Howard-Osborne's files could have brought down government', Matthew Condon, The Courier-Mail, March 18 2016

According to the detectives who uncovered this, their investigation was obstructed after they attempted to setup up a sting operation using Osborne's Spartacus code to communicate with John Stamford in Amsterdam. One detective said they found a bullet in their desk drawer after pursuing the matter.

Following the media reports of this in 2016, a former Queensland Premier named Mike Ahern accused a senior police official of having covered up the Osborne investigation, and referred the case to a royal commission being held into historic institutional child abuse in Australia at the time. The commission rejected former Premier's request, so he put it bluntly to the press, should there be any doubt as to what would've been found.

"FORMER premier Mike Ahern believes further in-

vestigation is needed into an organised gang that operated in the '70s and '80s. The gang, he said, was led by Clarence Howard-Osborne, who worked at Parliament House as a part-time Hansard reporter while Mr Ahern was in Parliament. It delivered hundreds of schoolboys, some as young as eight, in black Humbers to predators around Brisbane during those decades. He said it was a blot on the state's history and wanted to know why the case was suddenly closed after Howard-Osborne killed himself. He is unhappy a royal commission into institutional child sex abuse rebuffed his submission to include the case in its inquiry. *'Pedophilia was part of the overall corruption of society at the time,'* he said."
— 'Mike Ahern demands fresh probe into gang that delivered kids to Brisbane pedos', Des Houghton, September 15 2017, The Courier-Mail.

A few years after Osborne's death John Stamford's *Spartacus Network* would then be concretely linked to another, much more high profile and consequential case in the UK. A *Club Spartacus* child brothel operating out of a suburban townhouse in London was found servicing a VIP clientele, including some parliamentary ministers. The discovery of this served as the genesis to what later become known as the Westminster Pedophile Dossier in 2012.

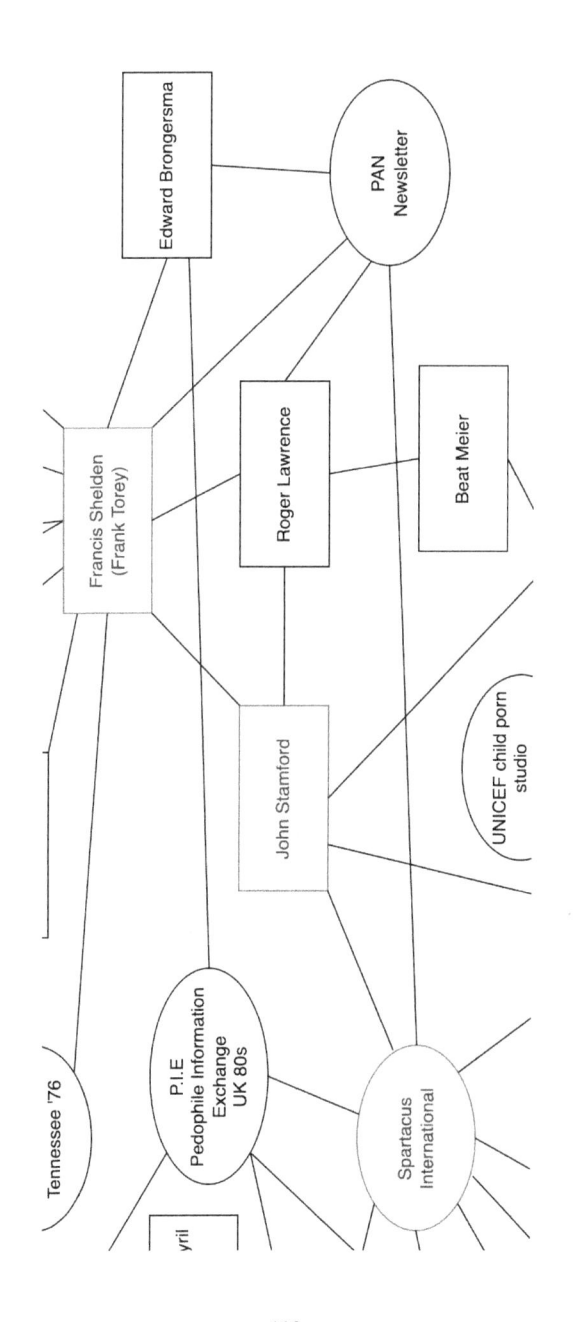

- Edward Brongersma
- PAN Newsletter
- Francis Shelden (Frank Torey)
- Roger Lawrence
- Beat Meier
- John Stamford
- UNICEF child porn studio
- Tennessee '76
- P.I.E Pedophile Information Exchange UK 80s
- Spartacus International
- yril

The Elm Guest House - UK 1982, 1990(Cold Case: 2012-2015)

Elm Guest House & Westminster Pedophile Dossier

UK, June 1982 — Metropolitan police raided a suburban terrace townhouse suspected of operating an illegal brothel on a residential street near central London. The owners, a German couple named Haroon & Carole Kasir, operated a suburban hotel at the address called the *Elm Guest House,* with a sign out front which read "Spartacus, Club - Welcome".[285]

After the premise was raided, it was reported visitors were provided with a price-listed menu of sex to indulge in with boys as young as ten. That twenty-three men were detained, found amongst bedroom suites festooned in whips, chains, and ropes; and among communal areas such as a lounge bar, spa and sauna facility, and a screening room for pornography.[286] That, according to police sources, three of the guests who visited the brothel were parliamentary ministers, while a fourth a member of the Queen's royal staff.[287] Strangely, it was even reported that in relation to this Scotland Yard had been, *"expected to reopen files on the murder of one boy and the disappearance of another in their investigation into a VIP homosexual vice network in London."*[288]

All reporting on the matter was subsequently denied in official statements provided by the authorities involved in the investigation, or those seemingly not involved with it.

"A Scotland Yard official said: *'It is just a routine investigation into a brothel, something that goes on all the time'*. But a source close to the investigation said: *'The top brass have ordered everything to be played down. Officially we aren't saying anything at this stage'*. *'Every attempt is being made to make sure the names of the VIPs who have been using this place don't leak out.'* "

— 'Cover-up Bid In Vice Scandal', News of The World, August 8 1982

"Claims that a police investigation into an alleged homosexual brothel had revealed a possible security risk were denied yesterday by Scotland Yard. The Metropolitan Police confirmed that four people had been charged after allegations that gay sex was for sale at a London suburban guesthouse. The Daily Express reported yesterday that at least 30 men prominent in public life—including three MPs—were believed to have been named after undercover inquiries and that security officials were called in. But the Yard said yesterday that the Special Branch—which is automatically called in whenever questions of security arise—was not taking part in inquiries."

— 'Gay Security Threat Denied', Sunday Times, August 8 1982

The mixed reporting appears to be the result of a pretty common phenomenon. Law enforcement officers at the operational level of an investigation leak information to the press, which is then subsequently denied in official statements given by their administrative superiors, who have to deal with the political ramifications.

Whoever the clients of the *Elm Guest House* may have been, the ones detained that night were all released without charge, and soon after all reporting on the matter ceased, possibly upon intervention by Attorney General Sir Michael Havers.[289]

The owners of the *Elm Guest House* were charged for keeping a disorderly house and possession of child pornography.[290] However, the latter charge was then dropped the following year after seven hours of video footage seized from the premise as evidence was ruled inadmissible.*"By agreement with the defence lawyers the prosecution has slashed eight hours of videos that were to be shown to the court, to just 45 minutes. The judge made an order forbidding the press to say anything which might identify the child in the case. Reporting restrictions were not lifted."*[291]

That same year, 1983, a Tory MP named Geoffrey Dickens handed the Secretary of the Home Office Leon Brittan a dossier on members of parliament and the Queen's royal staff alleged to have been part of a VIP pedophile ring, with ties to a group called the Pedophile Information Exchange(PIE).[292]

"Several public figures have been named in a Scotland Yard dossier on child sex offences, a member of British Prime Minister Margaret Thatcher's Conservative party said Wednesday. Geoffrey Dickens, a campaigner against child pornography, said in a radio interview that he has compiled a list of names and plans to disclose them in Parliament. The Office of the Director of Public Prosecutions confirmed it is studying a report on a police inquiry into a group called Pedophile Information Exchange. . .Interior Minister Leon Brittan has ordered a copy of the report by Friday, his officials said. Dickens said the Scotland Yard report, like his own dossier, contains the names of a number of top people in public life and show business."

— 'Public figures may be tied to child-sex group', Red Deer Advocate, August 25 1983

"British Home Secretary Leon Brittan is studying allegations of a homosexual vice ring in Buckingham

Palace, a government spokesman said Friday. The allegations came from MP Geoffrey Dickens, who compiled a massive dossier alleging that young males who joined the palace staff as footmen, cooks or servants are being dragged into a web of vice."
— 'Vice ring charged', Nanaimo Daily News, November 26 1983

Shortly after Dickens first handed the dossier over in August of '83, he started to receive death threats and his home was burglarised multiple times. His name and other personal details were then found in a notebook belonging to a fugitive named Arthur Hutchinson, wanted for a triple homicide. As a result a security detail had been placed on Dickens for a number of weeks until Hutchinson was apprehended.[293]

Little was made of this at the time, but thirty years later Dicken's dossier would serve, at least in part, as the basis for an investigation into historic allegations of child sexual abuse by a VIP pedophile ring linked to parliament and Prime Minister Margaret Thatcher's office at No. 10.

The circumstances surrounding the *Elm Guest House* resurfaced in 1990 during an inquest into the death of its former owner Carole Kasir, who died from an insulin overdose in July that year. A social worker named Mary Moss testified Kasir had approached her in 1989 with evidence boys from a foster home called *Grafton Close Children's Home* were supplied as prostitutes to VIP guests of the *Elm Guest House* back in the early 1980s. *"It was alleged the home, run by Richmond Council, supplied boys under the age of 14 to the gay guest house during the early 1980s said to be frequented often by top MPs and judges."*[294] According to Mary Moss, Kasir had been involved with a group of child pornographers linked to the foster home's management and was in fear for her life in the lead up to her death.[295]

The manager of the *Grafton Close Children's Home* at the time was a man named John Stingemore, who would later be charged in 2014 for sexual abuse of the children there.[296] Stingemore died before his trial could commence, but a priest named Anthony McSweeney who worked with Stingemore at the home was convicted over the same charges in 2015.[297]

During the 1990 inquest Mary Moss, alongside a more questionable figure named Christopher Fay, claimed Kasir was murdered over evidence she had kept on the *Elm Guest House's* VIP clientele. Fay testified Kasir had shown him a photograph, *"of a former Tory Cabinet minister in a sauna with naked boys,"* and that, *"a bishop, a high court judge, **social services director** and top businessman were also among those captured on video at the hotel."*[298]

The alleged cabinet minister in question turned out to be Leon Brittan, the Secretary of the Home Office who Geoffrey Dickens handed his VIP pedophile dossier to in 1983. *"Fay, now 69, claimed on oath that Brittan had been involved in abuse and that in March 1990 he had seen a photograph of the former Tory politician in a French maid's uniform, with a young boy."*[299] Another parliamentary minister named during the inquiry was Cyril Smith, who would be posthumously exposed as a serial violent sexual abuser of boys in 2013,[300] confirmed to have been a frequent visitor to the *Elm Guest House*.[301]

Following this inquiry, in 1992 a **social services director** named Peter Righton, *the* top UK government adviser on child protection services, was arrested after customs officials intercepted child pornography addressed to him from Amsterdam.[302] Righton had been a member of the *Pedophile Information Exchange* named in the VIP pedophile dossier from '83, and two years later in 1994 he was arrested once more during a Scotland Yard investigation into allegations of historic sexual abuse at children's homes.

"Former child care chief Peter Righton has been arrested as part of a nationwide abuse inquiry. Mr Righton, 68, a leading consultant on children's homes, has been questioned in connection with indecent assaults on children in the London area. . .This countrywide inquiry followed the closure of New Barns, a school for emotionally-disturbed children in Gloucestershire. Staff are now facing abuse charges. . .Mr.Righton held a senior post with the National Children's Bureau and was a respected figure in the child care field."

— 'Child care chief held in abuse inquiry', Evening Standard, London, November 9 1994

This VIP pedophile dossier Righton was mentioned in was dredged up again in October 2012 when a Labour MP named Tom Watson asked Prime Minister David Cameron before parliament to investigate evidence of, *"a powerful paedophile network linked to parliament and No 10"*.[303]

"In 2012 Tom Watson, the Labour MP who played a key role in exposing the phone-hacking scandal at the News of the World, stood up in parliament to ask the prime minister to ensure that a dossier of information used in 1992 to convict a notorious paedophile called Peter Righton was examined thoroughly. Watson said he believed the file, if it still existed, would provide some evidence of a 'powerful paedophile network linked to parliament and No 10'. "

— 'Edwardian house at hear of a long-simmering sex scandal', The Guardian, July 5 2014

This was then followed in November by more specific accusations levelled against Cyril Smith by an MP named Simon Danczuk, who held Smith's former parliamentary seat of Rochdale.

"Theresa May will this week be challenged to launch an investigation into allegations that an 'establish-

ment coverup' prevented claims that Sir Cyril Smith was a child abuser from being revealed for almost 50 years. Rochdale MP Simon Danczuk will ask the Home Secretary to order an inquiry into the handling of a police investigation into the activities of the former Liberal MP, who died two years ago, after a series of men came forward to claim they were abused by him in the town in the 1960s."
— 'Cyril Smith abuse claims covered up', The Independent, November 18 2012

Off the back of these statements, made publicly by reputable figures in the wake of what was recently acknowledged of Jimmy Savile, an investigation was launched by metropolitan police into historical allegations of child abuse at the hands of a VIP pedophile ring, allegedly made up of high ranking government officials who frequented the *Elm Guest House* in the early 1980s.

Documents and notes compiled on information Mary Moss had gathered from Carole Kasir shortly before her death in 1990, were then leaked online by Moss in January 2013 shortly before they were seized under warrant by police.[304] Soon after the two aforementioned heads of *Grafton Close Children's Home* were arrested, and Mary Moss in an *ITV* interview said the *Elm Guest House* had been used to make child pornography.

"Asked who visited there, Ms Moss, a former chair of the National Association of Young People in Care, said: *'MPs. All sorts of prominent[people]…It was a child porn racket. I don't think that necessarily anyone would be accused of just simply being perverts. This was a money-making business.'* She added: *'One of my cases that walked into the office was a young boy who had been abused there. And another case…was a boy who had been abused in another children's home and it all linked up. In a*

> *nutshell he [the abuse victim] was abused at Grafton Close children's home and procured for the Elm Guest House where they were filmed to make child porn, which was then distributed.'"*
> — 'Two arrested over claims that MPs took part in child sex ring', The Independent, February 7 2013

According to the information Mary Moss leaked online, Carole Kasir had said two men named Terry Dwyer and John Rowe persuaded her to renovate her townhouse into a spa and sauna facility for members of *Club Spartacus* in 1979. To this end she had been put in touch with a man named Peter Glencross, who was a close associate of John Stamford and acted as the commercial agent for *Spartacus International*.[305] The *Elm Guest House*, had of course displayed a sign out front which read *Club Spartacus*, and letter correspondence from *Spartacus International* addressed to the *Elm Guest House* dated from 1981 exists as well.[306]

> "Papers[Mary Moss's] seized by police name the man who helped turn a guest house into a paedophile brothel allegedly used by MPs and other VIPs. Exaro can reveal that the key figure who persuaded Carole Kasir, co-manager of the guest house, to create a haven for homosexual men to have sex with boys is Peter Glencross, who was part of an underground paedophile network called 'Spartacus'."
> — 'Files reveal who turned Elm Guest House into paedo brothel', exaro news, February 2 2013

Notes on records from a *Elm Guest House* sign-in book were included among the photos leaked online of files seized by police. Among those named, under alleged monikers, were MP Ronald Brown, MP Harvey Proctor, Royal staffer Anthony Blunt, a barrister named Colin Peters,[307] as well as Cyril Smith and Leon Brittan. Many of these figures, particularly those last two, became targets of an investigation launched by

Metropolitan police in February 2013 called Operation Fernbridge.

This investigation took an ominous turn in November 2014 when Scotland Yard announced they would be reopening the cold case files of two child murders(one missing presumed murdered) from 1979 and 1981 due to a possible connection to the *Elm Guest House* and its VIP guests.

This aspect of the investigation, called Operation Midland, was initially opened based on claims made by an anonymous accuser named 'Nick' who would later be discredited. As such, the claims made by this accuser have been omitted, along with those made by six other anonymous witnesses. This connection, as previously noted, had been reported way back in 1982, long before Operation Midland got underway:

> "Scotland Yard is expected to reopen files on the murder of one boy and the disappearance of another in their investigation into a VIP homosexual vice network in London. Members of Parliament and a member of the staff at Buckingham Palace have been mentioned as being clients of male prostitutes in the capital. And boys as young as the tragic children have been involved. One of the old dossiers detectives will examine again concerns eight-year-old Vishal Mehotra, who disappeared while returning to his home in Putney after watching last year's Royal Wedding procession."
>
> — 'Vice police reopen file on boys', Daily Express, August 10 1982

Thirty years later, a retired magistrate solicitor named Vishambar Mehrotra, whose son Vishal disappeared within a mile of the *Elm Guest House* in 1981, claimed he had been contacted shortly after his son's disappearance by a male prostitute who said his son may have been taken to the *Elm Guest House* and murdered by a group of "highly placed" pedophiles. The father said he relayed this information to authorities at the time but they'd refused to investigate, *"I was contacted by a young man who seemed to be in his 20s. He told me he believed Vishal may have been taken by paedophiles in the Elm Guest House near Barnes Common. He said there were very highly placed people there. He talked about judges and politicians who were abusing little boys."*[308]

Another boy named Martin Allen had also gone missing not far from the *Elm Guest House* two year earlier in 1979. The boy was the son of the chief chauffeur of Australian High Commissioner Sir Gordon Freeth, and his family lived in the caretakers cottage on the grounds of the Commissioner's residence.

It was reported at the time the father believed his son was abducted by a gang of pedophiles to make child pornography. And after Vishal's disappearance in 1981 it was reported police believed both boys were abducted by the same gang.[309]

Vishal's body was found in February 1982 confirming he'd been murdered, and a few months after this it was reported Scotland Yard planned to examine a possible connection between the two boys and the *Elm Guest House*.[310]

> "Vice squad officers probing London's homosexual scene have reopened their files on two schoolboys who went missing. Vishal Mehrotra, eight, was found murdered seven months after disappearing on the Royal Wedding day last year. Martin Allen, 15 son of the chauffeur to the Australian High Commissioner in London has never been found after being whisked away by an unknown man. Both cases have connections with South West London where police have raided a gay guest house. Vishal was last seen in Upper Richmond Road, Putney, just a mile and a half from the guest house. Martin, of Kensington, was

picked up as he approached Kings Cross station. Police believe many prominent people are linked with homosexual vice rings involving young boys."

— 'Lost Boys in Gay Probe', Daily Star, August 10 1982

In 2014 detectives rexamining the case learnt a gang of murderous pedophiles led by a man named Sidney Cooke were looked at as suspects for the murder of Vishal Mehrotra. Cooke and three others had been convicted of the abduction, rape, and murder of three boys during the 1980s and were suspected to have killed up to twenty more.

During an investigation into Sidney Cooke in the 1980s, called Operation Orchid, it had been learnt one of Cooke's accomplices named Lennie Smith had been a rent boy in the West End thought to have been linked to the Elm Guest House.[311] When detectives checked the original case files in 2014 to see if any further links between Cooke's gang and the *Elm Guest House* had been discovered, they found the files pertaining to that aspect of the investigation were missing.[312]

According to Martin Allen's older brother Kevin Allen, the pair had often washed government cars at the Commissioner's residence and other surrounding buildings under Australian embassy jurisdiction. Because of this, Kevin said when his brother dissappeared in 1979 Australian intelligence officers launched an internal investigation into stand-in drivers hired by vistors to the residence, which often hosted civic functions attended by those close to Margaret Thatcher's circle. Among these had been her private secretary Peter Morrison - an alleged pedophile, a deputy-director of MI6 Peter Hayman - a known pedophile, as well as her Home Secretary Leon Brittan.[313]

According to Kevin Allen, there had been a private chauffeur company used by the Australian High Commission to hire stand-in drivers on occasion. The company in question had a number of convicted pedophiles on its payroll, including at one time Sidney Cooke.[314] Another had supposedly been David Smith, the personal driver of Jimmy Savile, a convicted pedophile who died of a heroin overdose the day before his Saville-related trial was to take place.[315]

> " Kevin says it was standard practice for the high commission to supplement its regular drivers with stand-in and casual drivers from a particular chauffeur firm located just across the Thames. His research has revealed that this chauffeur firm had, at various times, employed Sidney Cooke, whose gang the "Dirty Dozen" would later be convicted and jailed for the torture and murder of three young boys in the 80s. Jimmy Savile's chauffeur, David Smith, who killed himself last year before standing trial on sex charges, is believed to have had links to the same car company in the late 70s. Cooke and his pedophile cohort are understood to have been some of the drivers who would pick up young care-home boys and rent boys in the expensive cars and deliver them to organised orgies in Barnes, Pimlico and Kensington."
> — 'A missing boy and the Australian high commission in London', The Australian, February 1 2015

The Operation Orchid files weren't the only ones to go missing. It was also learnt the dossier Geoffrey Dickens handed over to Leon Brittan in 1983 had since been either lost or destroyed by the Home Office. And because Leon Brittan had been the minister in charge of overseeing domestic intelligence agencies at that time, it was soon suspected past investigations into an alleged VIP pedophile ring had been covered-up by MI5.[316]

One instance of this allegedly involved Cyril Smith, who was allegedly arrested in the mid 1980s for possession of child pornography found in the trunk of his car by Northamptonshire police.[317] An investigation into the incident by a journalist named Donald Hale turned up evidence suggesting Smith had made a phone call from custody and was soon released without charge upon intervention by MI5.[318]

Another alleged incident involved Leon Brittan himself. A customs official named Maganlal Solanki told Operation Fernbridge detectives in 2014 he'd stopped Leon Brittan at the port of Dover in the late 1980s, travelling into the UK from Amsterdam with child pornography in his car.[319]

> " A senior Tory politician said to be part of a child sex ring was allegedly stopped by a customs officer with child pornography videos but got off scot-free, police have been told. The former MP was driving back to the UK via Dover when a customs officer pulled him over because he was 'acting suspiciously'. The border guard, who is now retired, has told detectives that when he searched the MP's car he found videotapes of children *clearly under the age of 12* taking part in sex acts. He passed the material on to his superiors, but the MP was never arrested or charged."
> — ' Tory MP allegedly found with child porn in 1980s faced no charges, police told', The Telegraph, July 4 2014

This incident was learnt after journalists discovered Solanki had confiscated 8mm films and videotapes from a man named Russell Tricker at the port of Dover in 1982. Tricker's name had drawn their attention because he operated a coach service called *Toff's Travel* across the English Channel in the 1980s used to smuggle boys into Amsterdam, and he was also a known associate of *Spartacus International* commercial agent Peter Glencross, who was tied to the *Elm Guest House*.[320]

The films confiscated from Tricker featured child abuse of an undisclosed nature, and one had been entitled 'LB'.[321] This had led the journalists to speculate(incorrectly) that "LB" stood for Leon Brittan, and that the tape in question featured a boy being abused in Brittan's presence. While Solanki refused to comment on the Russell Tricker incident, stating he was bound by the Official Secrets Act, he did mention another incident involving Leon Brittan later in the 1980s. Solanki was then interviewed by Operation Fernbridge detectives, whom he confirmed the incident with.[322]

Despite the totality of evidence accumulated over thirty years, the renewed investigation into the *Elm Guest House* and a VIP pedophile ring was dismantled and relegated to the status of a hoax through the insertion of a single witness into the entire investigation.

In November 2014, two years into the investigation, a witness dubbed "Nick" came forward with claims he had witnessed children murdered at the *Elm Guest House* by politicians. These claims were treated to a brief period of credibility during which time the witness "Nick" became the focal point of evidence in the investigation, especially in the press and especially by the BBC. "Nick" was then exposed as a pedophile named Carl Beech who'd provided false information. This had allowed for all the evidence in the investigation to be dismissed as a hoax, and for the media narrative to flip from "the accused" to the "the wrongly accused". Which it should be noted, thanks to Carl Beech, some politicians had been. After this the investigation was closed.

The claims made by Carl Beech have been omitted from the accounting of the case provided in this chapter. Which is to say, the account that you have read here is not at all based on things Carl Beech claimed.

Despite this, the authoritative accounting of these events as it currently stands in a Wikipedia entry in February 2023, entitled 'Elm Guest House hoax', cites an article by *The Telegraph* from September 2015 for the following claim, *"No evidence of abuse connected to the Elm Guest House was uncovered, and the operation was closed in March 2015."*[323] When you read the article in question you'll notice it omits everything prior to November 2014, and dedicates no more than a single sentence to this period.

> "Detectives launched Operation Fairbank as a scoping exercise to probe the claims of VIP child abuse and later Operation Fernbridge, looking at the former Elm Guest House in south west London, where it was rumoured children had been molested by high profile figures. **While the internet was alive with rumour and speculation, little firm progress was made in lifting the lid on the so-called parliamentary paedophile ring. But then in November 2014** the saga took a scarcely believable twist when a man in his 40s went into a police station claiming he had been abused for almost a decade by a powerful cabal of politicians, establishment and military figures."
> — 'Operation Midland: The story behind the Met's controversial VIP paedophile ring investigation', The Telegraph, 21 September 2015

The reason everything prior to November 2014 has been omitted is because it can't so easily be dismissed. Skeptics who would try, either make themselves appear ridiculous in reducing all historical evidence to a series of coincidences, or end up with a conspiracy theory of their own in contending it's an intergenerational hoax, fabricated over a thirty year period by people unknown to each other. It's much easier to frame it all on the claims of one man beginning in November 2014 and ignore the larger context.

Remember, we have only entered into the events of this chapter through those in North America in the 1970s. We arrived here through a direct, concrete link between Francis Shelden and *Spartacus International*, then *Spartacus International* to the *Elm Guest House*. And this link was through Amsterdam.

* * *

At the time of the inquest into Carole Kasir's death in July 1990, Scotland Yard had investigated the possibility Sidney Cooke and his gang of pedophiles had produced films of the deaths of boys during orgies held at a flat in east London, *"The inquiry is closely linked to the murder of Jason Swift, aged 14, in Hackney, east London, in 1985. He was sexually abused and strangled during a male orgy. Mr Hames said it had been rumoured that Jason's killing had been filmed but no copies of a video have been found."*[324]

This investigation was launched after a British man arrested in Amsterdam in 1989 claimed such a film existed, and Scotland Yard suspected nine other kids were murdered in this way.[325]

Perhaps this explains the obscure report on John Stamford found in a German tabloid from 1992, *"Scotland Yard, the famous London police, has a terrible suspicion: Stamford filmed 20 boys dying after sex orgies in England. On these perverse films: after the children have been repeatedly raped by men, they have been strangled, suffocated, strangled."*[326]

Near the end of July 1990 a teenager named Andrew Ash, who at the time was staying at the home of social worker Mary Moss as a victim of the *Elm Guest House*, *"claimed he was taken to Amsterdam in 1988 by a group of men from London, and forced to film in a warehouse where a 12-year-old boy was raped successively by 12 men, beaten with chains, run over by a motor cycle and his body dumped in a canal."*[327]

In October 1990 the obscene materials division at Scotland Yard then received information from multiple informants on a group of British pedophiles trafficking boys across the English Channel into Amsterdam, involved in the production of hardcore child pornography.

> "By October 1990, detectives on the old Obscene Publications Squad at Scotland Yard were picking up

worrying signals. An informant told them that someone called Alan Williams was trafficking boys into Amsterdam and that Williams had asked him to smuggle a child porn video back into the UK. Soon afterwards, another informant told how he had smuggled a dozen tapes in the opposite direction: they had been produced, he believed, in a house in North London, which was equipped with a bondage room for boys. He had delivered the tapes in Amsterdam to Boys Club 21, to 'Alan from Cardiff'. While he was there, this informant said, he had visited the Gay Palace across the road, where he had watched videos of boys in bondage, aged 11 to 14 years old, being buggered by masked men."

— 'When sex abuse can lead to murder', Nick Davies, The Guardian, November 27 2000

This had led to a joint investigation with Dutch authorities in the early 1990s into the production of snuff films in Amsterdam, called Operation Framework.

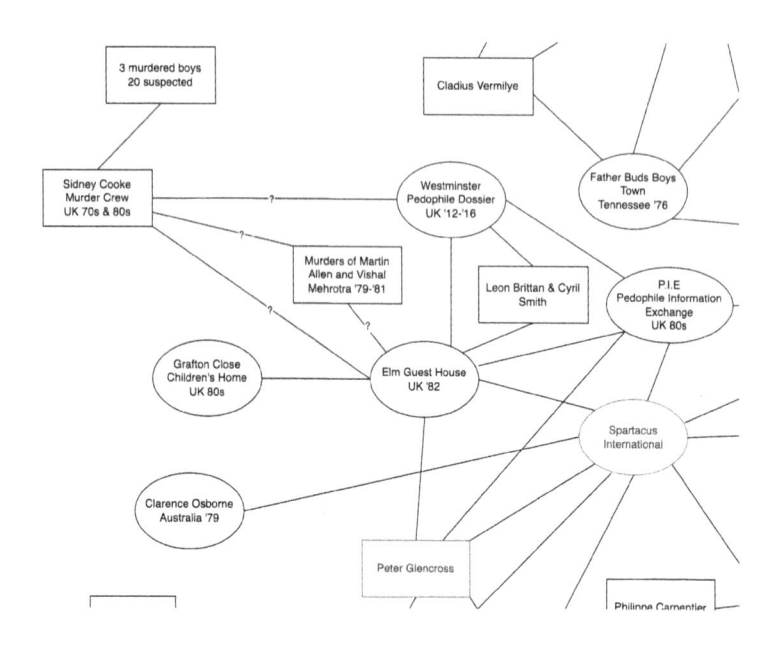

- 3 murdered boys, 20 suspected
- Cladius Vermilye
- Sidney Cooke Murder Crew UK 70s & 80s
- Westminster Pedophile Dossier UK '12-'16
- Father Buds Boys Town Tennessee '76
- Murders of Martin Allen and Vishal Mehrotra '79-'81
- Leon Brittan & Cyril Smith
- P.I.E Pedophile Information Exchange UK 80s
- Grafton Close Children's Home UK 80s
- Elm Guest House UK '82
- Spartacus International
- Clarence Osborne Australia '79
- Peter Glencross
- Philippe Carpentier

Operation Framework - Amsterdam 1992-93

Warwick Spinks & Amsterdam Snuff films

In 1992 the obscene materials division of Scotland Yard opened an investigation into a group of British pedophiles trafficking boys into Amsterdam boy brothels that masqueraded as gay nightclubs in the city's Spuistraat district. One of these was the *Gay Palace* managed by a child trafficker named Warwick Spinks, a pedophile involved in mail order boy prostitution and pornography through the 1980s and 90s.

> "Spinks had been running a mail order pornography business from Brighton, before he moved to Amsterdam, where he pioneered in the trafficking of boys as young as 10 – first, from the streets of London, and, after the collapse of the Soviet Union, from the poverty of eastern Europe. Having brought them to Amsterdam, he used these "chickens" himself, sold them into the brothels or through escort agencies and put them in front of the camera. Some resisted, some ran away, but most were made to comply through the removal of their passports and doses of drugs and violence."
> — 'When sex abuse can lead to murder', Nick Davies, The Guardian, November 27 2000

One facet of Spinks operation was to rent out apartments in European child sex hotspots to foreign pedophiles, who he then acted as a sort of concierge to. The same way Stamford's *Spartacus International* functioned with its host pedophiles around world, like Clarence Henry Osborne in Australia. Spinks name would also come up in connection to the *Elm Guest House* in 2013,[328] when it was learnt he'd known Russell Tricker, a close associate of *Spartacus International's* Peter Glencross.

> "Tricker also confirmed that he was a personal friend of Peter Glencross, who was commercial manager of Spartacus International. At the time, Spartacus International was used to attract members to the Spartacus Club, an underground paedophile network. A German company has since taken over Spartacus International, and transformed it into a respectable publisher of gay guides. Tricker also admitted a link with the notorious British paedophile, Warwick Spinks. Tricker said that he and Spinks "go back a long way."
>
> —'Man who tried to import video: I did not know what was inside', Exaro News, Mark Conrad and Mark Watts, 29 March 2014

A Scotland Yard informant claimed to have seen films screened at the *Gay Palace* which showed boys aged 11-14 being raped by masked men, and that Spinks, the clubs manager, was selling copies of a "special videotape" for £4000 of a boy being tortured. A different informant named "Frank" described another film Spinks had shown him. A snuff film shot inside a barn of a boy being tortured with needles then castrated and cut open with a knife. Another informant named "Terry" described a snuff film in which a boy had been killed in exactly the same manner—tortured, castrated, then cut open with a knife—only this one had been filmed inside an apartment not a barn.[329] Yet another informant named "Edward" later claimed to have seen at least five of these snuff films, which he alleged were produced by Spinks and his associates at a house in Hoofddorp and on a houseboat.

Spinks had used canal boats moored just outside of central Amsterdam as discreet locations for clients of his escort service,[330] and also rented boys to a convicted pedophile named Peter Howells, who ran a child pornography operation under the guise of a children's talent agency called *Bovver Boots*, located on a houseboat in central Amsterdam.[331]

Police raided a property Spinks kept in Hoofddrop but were unable to find any of the alleged films. However, an undercover officer posing as a client would manage to elicit the following admission from Spinks:

> " *'I know—I knew, some people who were involved in making snuff movies and how they did it was, they only sold them in limited editions, made 10 copies or something, 10 very rich customers in America, who paid $5,000 each, which is a lot of money to watch some kids being snuffed. I mean, I steer a wide berth from those people. I know somebody who was in a snuff movie and somebody got snuffed in front of him and he never knew it was a snuff movie. They had tied him up and done terrible things to him and killed him'*, *'Did they?'* asked the officer *'And he has been really petrified since, because he was like from Birmingham, middle twenties. I know the person who made the film. I felt sorry for this boy, it was a German boy.'*, *'How old?'* asked the officer, nudging Spinks along, *'About 13, 15. He thought he was going to make 200 guilders and ended up being dead.'* "
>
> — 'Britons killed boys in Dutch porn movies', The Guardian, April 5 1997

A Scotland Yard detective named Michael Hames who headed the investigation into Spinks, commented on the difficulty of actually obtaining a snuff film to the press in 1990 when investigating the suspected Sidney Cooke snuff films, *"Detective Superintendent Michael Hames, head of Scotland Yard's child pornography unit, said no snuff movies had yet been discovered. 'We don't know if they are being done here.' Such films would be expensive to buy and distribution exclusive. In America, the FBI went undercover to a meeting of people invited to watch a snuff movie with a view to buying a copy and the fee to attend the showing was $10,000."*[332]

Unlike other sting operations into illegal drugs or firearms, when it comes to human trafficking traditional law enforcement techniques run into a conundrum. If an undercover agent makes a purchase order for a person, and something happens to that people, say in transit as it so often does, the enforcement agency then becomes culpable. This predicament is even more pronounced when it comes to making a purchase order for what is effectively a murder.

As Spinks stated, the snuff films were "limited editions", which probably meant made to order. Selling them in this way, even as copies under the guise of this premise, not only inflates the prices of the snuff film, but prevents authorities from ever obtaining evidence through requesting one. The only way to obtain evidence of a snuff film from a producer aware of this predicament, would be through search and seizure in the hope one would be left lying around. When Operation Framework detectives did this they had no such luck.

What had begun in 1990 as a Scotland Yard inquiry into the possibility the murder of Jason Swift had been filmed by Sidney Cooke and his gang; later became a joint-investigation into snuff pornography with Dutch authorities in 1992 and 1993 targeting British foreign nationals in Amsterdam.

1993 was the same year Francis Shelden was named in an Amsterdam based child pornography investigation, alongside another British foreign national named King Tam Ang. As you may remember, this information had been used to verify some of the information provided by Richard Lawson during the OCCK cold case investigation in Michigan, who claimed Timothy King was killed in a snuff film financed by Francis Shelden.

"Today, the FBI in Washington D.C., forwarded a response they received from the Dutch police in Brussels in regards to our request. In this response, the Dutch authorities, state that they compared all the photographs of our OCCK victims to photos and films they confiscated during a large child porn sting in Amsterdam in 1993, with negative results. However, they state that Kim was identified in the 1993 investigation as Kim Tam Ang, born 4-16-1933, a British national from Selangor, Malacca, living in Amsterdam. Ang was well known to Dutch police for child pornography and sexual abuse of minor boys in 1997. The Dutch police, also provided that Francis Duffield Shelden, w/m", born 9-5-28, from Wayne County, Michigan, U.S.A. died 7-9-96, was also named in their investigation. Ang & Shelden were both mentioned in an investigation by the Danish police in 1993 concerning child pornography and sexual offenses against minors. This confirms Lawson's story."

— Casenotes of Det. Corey Williams, 2-7-07 entry

Furthermore, it was reported by a German tabloid Shelden's associate John Stamford was under investigation by Scotland Yard in 1992 for snuff pornography featuring boys murdered during orgies in the UK, assumedly the Sidney Cooke murders.

All these investigations appear to be interlinked through this motif of suspected snuff film production. Same place(Amsterdam), same time(1992-93), same business(Child pornography), proven associations(Spartacus International).

When John Stamford and Francis Shelden died within a year of each other in '95 and '96, Warwick Spinks had been in prison due to an incident a few years earlier.

In August 1993 a distressed British boy had shown up at the UK Embassy in Amsterdam. He'd just escaped through the bathroom window of a night club in the Spuistraat district called *The Blue Boy* and told embassy officials he'd been sold into prostitution by a man named Warwick Spinks.

The boy was a runaway from Hastings, who Spinks had picked up off the street and taken to his apartment. He'd kept the boy there for a number of days, drugging him with LSD and raping him at knifepoint, before taking him in a drug induced stupor to the port of Dover and he ferried him over to Amsterdam.[333]

Spinks had received a seven year sentence for this, that was reduced to five, of which he served little more than three and a half. Upon his release he immediately violated his parole and fled to the Czech Republic, where he linked up with former BBC Radio 1 DJ Chris Denning in exile.[334] Denning had of course been good friends with Jimmy Savile, and according to Czech police, head of an international pedophile network and running a child porn operation from his Prague apartment.

Denning had been arrested in November 1997 based on information Czech police received from Scotland Yard after Warwick Spinks went into exile there. The investigation into Denning would then serve as the genesis to on-going probes into a suspected child abuse ring linked to the BBC, that eventually culminated in the infamous *Operation Yewtree* investigation later in the wake of Jimmy Savile's death.

"A former Radio 1 DJ has been charged by Czech

police with the sexual abuse of young children. Chris Denning was arrested yesterday by detectives investigating an international child pornography ring. Police alleged he was the leader of the child sex ring and said he was arrested after cocaine had been fed to young boys in preparation for filming a pornographic video. The arrest came after a two-month surveillance operation in which Scotland Yard supplied vital information about Denning's movements to colleagues on the continent. Denning, who has a flat in Prague and runs a music and video production company from his home in Britain, was jailed for 10 weeks in February 1996 for possessing child pornography."
— 'Ex-Radio 1 DJ held over child sex ring', The Evening Standard, November 12 1997

Denning and three others, two Frenchman and an American, were charged with hooking boys as young as seven on cocaine to produce pornography they distributed globally online.[335]

A week after Denning's arrest British glam rock artist Gary Glitter, whose career Denning helped catapult to the *Top of the Pops* in the 1970s, was arrested aswell by British authorities after child pornography was discovered on a computer he had taken into a repair store.[336]

Denning alluded to a connection between the two during an interview he granted a journalist during his trial, in which he tried to present empirical evidence of his innocence by way of a hilarious adaptation of the polygraph test: *"A sexologist was then brought in to test Denning's sexuality by attaching a vacuum device, linked to a meter, to his penis. 'they gave me pictures of boys to look at. If your penis twinges they take a reading. Mine only twinged when I looked at an 18-year-old, so they said I couldn't technically be a paedophile, I was an ephebophile'* ," Denning then capped off the interview by asking the journalist,

"Tell me. Have you any idea what's happened to Gary?"[337]

Well, in regards to what happened to Gary Glitter it should be noted that the term 'child pornography', as it's reported in the press, can range anywhere from naked children artistically posed, right through to them being tortured. Using this as a 1-to-10 scale, the images found on Glitter's computer were a hard 10, featuring acts of torture on infants.

"Gary Glitter was jailed tonight for four months for downloading 4,000 sickening child porn images from the internet. It came after a sensational day in court which had seen him cleared of sexually abusing a besotted schoolgirl of 14, but reappear after two hours to admit the pornography offences. The 55-year-old pop star had created a 'vast library' of computer images which were described as *'about as hardcore, sick, and degrading as it is possible to conceive'* of children as young as two."

— 'Cleared of under-age sex then four months for child photographs', The Evening Standard, November 12 1999

Glitter had downloaded thousands of these images from specially encrypted members-only webservers.[338] Presumably one of these had been run by his old pal Chris Denning, who, if running around with Warwick Spinks in Prague coking up kids, assumedly produced child pornography on the harder end of the scale.

Glitter received a 4-month sentence in 1999 and with his music career over, went on a child sex tour of South-East Asia that eventually ended with his arrest in Vietnam in 2007 for the rape of two girls aged 10 and 11.[339]

During Glitter and Denning's trials in 1999, a BBC presenter for the series *Crimewatch* named Jill Dando was bizarrely assassinated on her doorstep in April. She was shot in the head at close range, in what was deemed a 'professional job'.[340] Years later a former friend and colleague for hers from the BBC would claim that in the mid 1990s, *"Dando tried to get BBC bosses to investigate an alleged paedophile ring in the corporation."*[341]

In March 2000 Denning was convicted of his '97 charges,[342] and the investigation into him in Prague led to another that year into an associate of his, another former BBC Radio One DJ named Jonathan King.[343]

> "The information which paved the way for King's downfall was first identified by the National Criminal Intelligence Service(NCIS), it emerged today. King first came to the attention of its Serious Sex Offenders Unit following a sex abuse case in the Czech Republic in 1997."
>
> — 'Jonathan King gets 7 years for sex crimes', Evening Standard, November 21 2001

In November 2000 King was charged with historic counts of child sex abuse(CSA) against boys based on allegations made by three men, who alleged King used them for sex in the 70s and 80s.[344] King would be charged with a total of 16 counts of CSA against boys(some reports stated 27 men came forward with allegations going back 32 years),[345] and he would be convicted for 5 of these in 2001.[346]

Following King's conviction investigators put in an extradition request for Chris Denning to face charges in the UK as well. This was rejected by a judge, though Denning was ordered to leave the Czech Republic.[347] He skipped about the Eastern European pedophile hotspots for a few years until he was deported back to the UK in 2005 to face 9 counts of historic CSA against boys in the 70s and 80s.[348]

The investigation into King and Denning in the early 2000s led to another, called Operation Arundel, into a suspected pedophile ring of BBC celebrities in the 70s and 80s who allegedly procured boys and girls from an underage nightclub called the Walton Hop Disco. This investigation led to the arrest of another BBC personality in 2003, but the charges against them were subsequently dropped.[349] One suspect in that investigation who was never arrested or charged had been a good friend and colleague of both Denning and King, BBC Radio One DJ Jimmy Savile.[350] Nothing came of this though. The case was closed and forgotten about for nearly a decade.

Then, after Jimmy Savile's death in October 2011, the floodgate of allegations against him opened. First a few, then many, and finally too many to ignore.

In December 2011 the BBC, under the stewardship Mark Thompson, killed a Newsnight report on allegations made against Savile by 10 women.[351] So the accusers went to another broadcaster ITV, who then announced their intentions to release an exposé documentary on Savile in September 2012.[352]

Well aware of the storm brewing on the horizon, the BBC that month started to discombobulate its upper hierarchy, which would confuse any incoming inquiry into its institutional accountability.[353] By then Mark Thompson had already timely announced his departure from BBC and had been jettisoned across the Atlantic ocean into the warm embrace of the New York Times.[354]

The allegations against Savile were aired publicly by ITV in early October 2012, which led to an investigation by Metropolitan police called *Operation Yewtree*. Now, this has been framed as an investigation into Savile, but remember, Savile was dead. This was actually an investigation into the BBC and his associates there who could still face prosecution. Much like Marc Dutroux, who we will get to, Savile is just a leaping off point into the deep end of the pool for whoever wants to take that dive.

Operation Yewtree investigated accusations of a highly organised pedophile ring at the BBC, which not only included its famous personalities, but operational level employees too.[355]

> "New victims of Jimmy Savile have gone to the police with complaints about a "very organised" paedophile ring operating at the BBC, it emerged today. The allegations relate to the DJ and several of his associates working at the corporation about 40 years ago. The victims say they were abused by the entertainer as well as other BBC staff who were not famous TV faces. Although some of the complaints about the alleged paedophile ring have been referred to Scotland Yard, not all of those making the claims have yet contacted police, their lawyer said. Liz Dux is leading a legal team dealing with more than 20 victims, most of whom allege they were abused by Savile, who died last year aged 84. Some were also victims of the "paedophile ring" at the BBC, she said"
>
> — 'Jimmy Savile: New victims say 'organised' paedophile ring operated at BBC', Evening Standard, October 24 2012

One woman abused by Savile as a ward at a group foster home called Duncroft, alleged she and two other girls from the home were driven to the BBC studios and sexually assualted in Savile's dressing room by Savile, Gary Glitter, and a third famous BBC personality.[356] As you can see with the mention of Gary Glitter, *Operation Yewtree* was very quickly circling back to the investigation into Jonathan King and Chris Denning.

Glitter was arrested in October 2012 and convicted of historic CSA related to *Operation Yewtree* charges. The arrest of Chris Denning followed in June 2013,[357] who was convicted of historic CSA against 24 boys, one of whom Denning allegedly raped at Jimmy Savile's house.[358] Jonathan King was then arrested and charged during an interlinked investigation in 2015 called Operation Ravine, though the charges against him would be dropped.

Other BBC personalities convicted during *Operation Yewtree* were former BBC Radio One DJ Dave Lee Travis(his convicted was mild - groping breast of female colleague), BBC presenter Stuart Hall, and by far the biggest scalp of all Rolf Harris. Others charged but who later had these dropped due to lack of evidence were BBC TV presenter Jim Davidson and BBC TV personality Freddie Star.

Perhaps one could argue *Operation Yewtree* was an investigation into the UK entertainment industry at large, as opposed to the BBC itself, which just happened to largely be the UK entertainment industry. If that is true, which it is, then why would anyone differentiate between the two other than in an attempt to remove accountability?

A counter narrative of 'the wrongly accused' that developed during *Operation Yewtree* was largely based on the two instances which led to successful defamation suits, both of which were against the BBC. Which is to say, the BBC are responsible for any claims of a 'media witch hunt' used to bring the investigation into the BBC child abuse ring into question.

In November 2012, at the very beginning of *Operation Yewtree*, the BBC paid out defamation damages to a prominent 1980s conservative politician named Lord McAlpine, who they'd falsely implicated in the investigation during a Newsnight report which aired claims by a victim who misidentified him as an abuser.[359]

The second case brought against them was by former BBC talent star Cliff Richards, who had been accused o abuse but never arrested. When police showed up at Richards home in June 2014, the BBC were lying in wait with a camera crew which aired breaking round the clock news coverage of police raid his home, even bringing out the helicopter for aerial shots. This little spectacle led to a £2m defamation settlement by the BBC in 2019.[360]

These 'slip-ups' balanced the media narrative more evenly between 'the accused' and 'wrongly accused', muddied the waters between the two, and I would imagine detracted attention away from a far more interesting aspect of the investigation into the BBCs own operational level employees. Where evidence of its true culpability can be found lurking around the limelight of its stars.

The very first suspect to be charged with a CSA count in *Operation Yewtree* had been a former BBC chauffer named David Smith. A convicted pedophile who'd driven for Savile and other BBC celebrities during the 1980s, and was used to 'transport guests' to and from the BBC studios. He was charged with the sexual assault of a boy he had driven to the studios in 1984.[361] Smith also would've been the first person brought to trial, if he hadn't been found dead of a herion overdose the day before it commenced.[362]

> "The BBC faced questions last night over how it came to employ a convicted paedophile as a chauffer in the Eighties. David Smith, 67, was found dead at his flat in Lewisham, south east London, on Monday, the day before he was due to go on trial accused of sexually assaulting a 12-year-old boy in 1984. He was the first person to face charges under Operation Yewtree, the police investigation set up after the revelations of sexual abuse by the BBC presenter, Jimmy Savile."
> — 'BBC face questions on paedophile driver', The Daily Telegraph, October 30 2013

While it's true pedophiles often kill themselves from the shame of being exposed, it's also true murders are often framed to look like suicides.

To that point, David Smith had been living with the shame

of 22 prior CSA convictions against young boys, the earliest of which dated back to 1966.[363] In spite of this, or perhaps because of it, he was gainfully employed at the BBC in the 1980s. The shame of this seems to have only finally struck him prior to his employment at the BBC coming under the scrutiny of a court trial.

See, as the BBC had worded things so very carefully at the time, they had *"not found any record of David Smith being employed by or working for the BBC."*[364] This was because the BBC employed Smith through a private company off the books, and used this to craftily infer he'd never worked there, *"Court documents say there is 'no evidence to suggest any connection' between Smith and Savile, though the former 'was contracted to work as a driver for the BBC in the relevant period', it added."*[365]

A month prior to Smith's arrest in December 2012, the head of employee tax at the BBC, coincidentally also named David Smith, which is how I stumbled upon this, admitted before a parliamentary committee, *"that 25,000 contracts covering around 1,500 workers had been issued on a freelance, off-books basis, but insisted the Corporation abided by the rules. He conceded, however, that the use of so-called service companies, particularly by on-air 'talent,' allowed the BBC to "cut [its] exposure" in cases where the HMRC ruled that the person involved was not a genuine freelancer."*[366]

To clarify this — the BBC had a history of paying certain employees assigned to 'on-air talent', 'off the books', 'to cut its exposure'. At first glance this appears to be for tax purposes, but two of David Smith's victims would forefeit their anonymity in April 2014 to publicly accuse, *"the BBC of covering up Smith's abuse after the corporation refused to admit he ever worked for them."*

> "A child sex victim of a driver who chauffeured BBC stars has told detectives he was abused by a paedophile ring linked to the pervert. Jason Little, 42,

said he was assaulted in the world famous Television Centre by David Smith during a number of visits with the convicted abuser. Jason said Smith got him a BBC pass and introduced him to scores of stars, including fellow paedophile Jimmy Savile...Jason and his childhood pal Lee Sullivan, 41 – also abused by Smith – have chosen to become the first victims to waive their anonymity in an effort to give hope to others. Both accused the BBC of covering up Smith's abuse after the corporation refused to admit he ever worked for them...They spoke out as solicitor Liz Dux revealed two of Savile's alleged victims have come forward to say they were abused by other men with Savile. One was a former BBC cameraman, who has now died. The other attack is alleged to have happened at the TV Centre in West London. Speaking at his home in Ramsgate, Kent, Jason said: *'He took me to parties with other men and kids. We were given drugs so they could attack us. Smith also took me to a big house outside Amsterdam where I was abused with other - children. At the time I didn't know what was happening to me.'* Smith used his BBC connections to groom children and even had a white Ford Granada with the number plate "372BBC". Jason said he took him to the set of Saturday Superstore and Top of the Pops. He said: *'I remember seeing Savile on quite a few occasions. Smith knew him and I saw them talking together.'* "

— 'I was abused by paedophile at BBC Television Centre: Victim's anger at Jimmy Savile friend's drugs suicide', The Mirror, April 3 2014

As you may recall from the previous chapter, David Smith was mentioned in a 2015 report regarding a private chauffer company in London allegedly investigated after the 1979 disappearance of Martin Allen, the son of the personal chauffer to the Australian High Commissioner. According to the boy's brother, *"it was standard practice for the high commission to supplement its regular drivers with stand-in and casual drivers from a particular chauffeur firm located just across the Thames,"* and, *"that this chauffeur firm had, at various times, employed Sidney Cooke, whose gang the "Dirty Dozen" would later be convicted and jailed for the torture and murder of three young boys in the 80s. Jimmy Savile's chauffeur, David Smith, who killed himself last year before standing trial on sex charges, is believed to have had links to the same car company in the late 70s."*[367]

In October 2015 a victim of Jimmy Savile named Georgina Martin stated she was frequently driven to his home by up to five different drivers, one of whom she said she was 'pimped out' to. These five drivers she said had been men other than David Smith.[368] An interesting thing to note on this point is one of the accusations now(2023) being made a decade later against Russel Brand from his time working at the BBC.

> "The BBC is facing urgent questions about Russell Brand amid allegations that he used its car service to pick up a 16-year-old girl from her school so that she could play truant and visit him at his home. The woman, who accuses Brand of grooming and sexually assaulting her when she was a teenager, remembers going to and from his home in north London in a chauffeur-driven car paid for by the corporation."
> — 'Russell Brand sent BBC chauffeur to pick up teenage girlfriend from school', The Times, September 18 2023

Alongside Brand, a former BBC Radio One DJ named Tim Westwood, who suspiciously left the company in 2013 during *Operation Yewtree*, is now(2023) under investigation as well. While these allegations are more reflective of the #MeToo era, it appears a culture comedic sadism persisted at the BBC right up until Savile's very last gasp.

The BBC archives are full of their stars jokingly alluding to what they were actually doing. Almost as if tacitly gaining the public's consent to do it through a confession disguised as a joke. And Savile's jokes got pretty dark.

Savile once held up a drawing of himself at a public event and laughed, *"It's a photofit for the Yorkshire Ripper"*, then quipped to a little girl in the crowd at the same event, *"I kidnap girls like you"*.[369] Saville then actually befriended the actual Yorkshire Ripper Peter Sutcliffe.[370] Haha Get it? Who murdered his third victim Irene Richardson in the park right behind Savile's penthouse. LOL! And in 1980 the police took moulds of Savile's teeth to compare with bite marks found on the victim's breasts.[371] Classic Savile!

Comedy is a powerful thing. There's a reason political pundits are comedians and comedians political pundits. It can disarm morality because it cuts through flimsy ideology into that semi-unconscious fear people have of not being taken seriously. That is—being laughed at for taking something seriously.

Let us return now to a statement made by David Smith victim Jason Little, and take it very seriously:

> *'He took me to parties with other men and kids. We were given drugs so they could attack us.* **Smith also took me to a big house outside Amsterdam where I was abused with other children**. *At the time I didn't know what was happening to me.'*
>
> — 'I was abused by paedophile at BBC Television Centre: Victim's anger at Jimmy Savile friend's drugs suicide', The Mirror, April 3 2014

According to a tabloid report a few months earlier in January 2014 entitled, *'BBC embroiled in further scandal as executive filmed Dutch child abuse movies'*, an anonymous source claimed a BBC executive was part of a child porn operation in Amsterdam during the 1980s.

> "DETECTIVES are investigating claims that a retired BBC executive abused young boys at his home in

Amsterdam. He is said to have owned a three-storey property near the city centre in the Eighties. Boys from British care homes were allegedly ferried there to take part in sex films. Police have been told that the BBC employee was involved in the abuse and played a key role in distributing the films."

— 'BBC embroiled in further scandal as executive filmed Dutch child abuse movies', Daily Express, January 26 2014

This is of particular interest because the first formal investigation into a BBC child abuse ring, Operation Arundel in 2001, arose out of an investigation which evolved from the one into Chris Denning in Prague, which in turn was based on information received from Scotland Yard after Warwick Spinks went into exile there.

After Denning went away, for some reason Spinks was left undisturbed in Prague for over a decade, until in November 2012 he was suddenly extradited back to the UK. This was just weeks into *Operation Yewtree* and a few months before *Operation Fernbridge* was launched into the *Elm Guest House*.[372] Perhaps some 'top men' sought a brief word with Spinks, as he was soon released and seen roaming free again back in Prague. When the UK Ministry of Justice was probed for answers, their response, *"We do not comment on individuals. Any convicted sex offender who breaches their licence conditions faces spending the duration of their sentence in prison."*[373]

A few months after Spinks was briefly summoned home, it was reported in March 2013:

"The most infamous alleged visitor to the Elm Guest House was Warwick Spinks, a violent paedophile who in 1995 was jailed for a series of sexual offences on boys, including buggery, taking a child without lawful authority and taking indecent images of children. Lewes Crown Court heard that he had he drugged a 14-year-old boy and "sold him" to a gay brothel in Amsterdam. Spinks denies ever having visited Elm Guest House and would have been no older than 16 when it closed."

— 'Police failings put dozens of children at risk from notorious paedophile ring', The Independent, March 3 2013

This report was then followed by another in December 2014. Though keep in mind this is after the investigation had been sullied by Carl Beech:

" Met detectives are now re-examining files on Spinks amid claims he was a regular visitor to Elm Guest House, where the alleged systematic abuse of children sparked the original VIP inquiry in 2012. Boys were allegedly taken to the guest house in Barnes, South-West London, and Dolphin Square flats near Westminster, to have sex with VIPs and MPs including Cyril Smith. Yesterday it emerged that police who investigated Spinks in the 1990s were told a boy had died at the club while the MP was present. A source said: *'Officers were told Spinks knew the MP and arranged a tour to Amsterdam. While there he went to the Blue Boy bar, where Spinks was running a brothel.' The MP was said to have been present when a boy died during an orgy which was being filmed. The information was not confirmed and the MP's identity never surfaced. However, clear evidence that boys were tortured was discovered.'* "

— MP 'was at snuff film lad's murder, The Sun, December 6 2014

Spinks actually sued the tabloid that reported this for libellous and the judge upheld the accuracy of their reporting and dismissed his case.[374] Though the information in it is presented here mostly to segue back into *Operation Framework* in Amsterdam.

Right across the street from *The Blue Boy* mentioned in the article had been another boy brothel investigated in *Operation*

Framework for trafficking in snuff films, called *Boys Club 21*. Its manager was a close associate of Warwick Spinks named Alan Williams, a convicted pedophile dubbed the "The Welsh Witch" on account of his violent rapes of boys in Cardiff, Wales during the 1980s. Alan Williams and two other Welsh pedophiles named John Gay and Lee Tucker setup a video production company in Amsterdam called TAG Films, and according to a Scotland Yard informant "Frank", the pair had produced a snuff inside a barn belonging to a German man who frequented the boy brothels managed by Williams and Spinks. This was one "Frank" claimed Spinks had shown him of a boy being tortured, castrated, and cut open with a knife. The same German man was identified by an informant "Terry" as one who'd murdered a boy in similar fashion—tortured, castrated, and cut open with a knife, in another snuff film.[375]

All this led to a raid by German authorities on a video distribution company in Dusseldorf linked to TAG Films called Gero-Video.[376] A company allegedly owned by elements of the German mafia according to an alleged dossier by a bookkeeper familiar with the operation.[377]

Many of the Operation Framework informants also gave the same description of a German boy named 'Manny' as a victim murdered in one of these snuff films. Warwick Spinks himself mentioned to an undercover officer a German boy was killed in a snuff film produced by people he knew, *"I know the person who made the film. I felt sorry for this boy, it was a German Boy. About 13, 15. He thought he was going to make 200 guilders and ended up being dead."*[378]

A close associate of Spinks at the time was a German child trafficker named Lothar Glandorf. He owned boy brothels in Rotterdam and ran an escort service there which fell under investigation in 1994 after the disappearance of a 12 year-old German boy named Manuel Schadwald.

- Australia '?

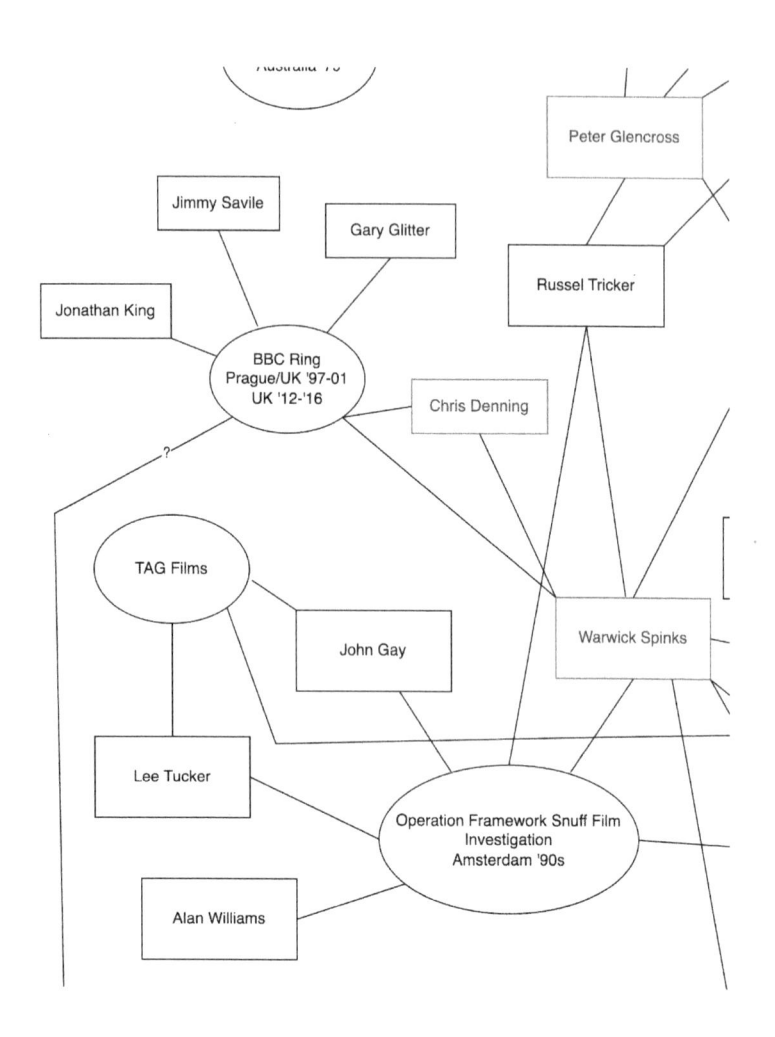

- Jimmy Savile
- Gary Glitter
- Jonathan King
- Peter Glencross
- Russel Tricker
- BBC Ring Prague/UK '97-01 UK '12-'16
- Chris Denning
- ?
- TAG Films
- John Gay
- Warwick Spinks
- Lee Tucker
- Operation Framework Snuff Film Investigation Amsterdam '90s
- Alan Williams

The HIK Report, Rolodex Affair & Joris Demmink - Amsterdam 1994, 1998

The HIK Report & Lothar Glandorf

In Germany, July 1993, a twelve year-old named Manuel Schadwald was reported missing, though little was done for over a year as he was considered a runaway. In 1994 two teenagers came forward complaining they'd been trafficked into the Rotterdam sex trade. The pair had been prostituting themselves on the streets of Hamburg and been approached by two Dutchmen who'd offered them large sums of money to travel to Rotterdam to film pornography. When they arrived however, their passports were seized and had been forced to pay off the cost of their travel, at an exorbitant rate, working in a brothel owned by a German man named Lothar Glandorf. There they met a boy who said his name was Manuel Schadwald, who matched the age and description of a boy of that name they'd seen on missing persons posters back in Germany. Not long after, a third teenager from Berlin told a similar story. He'd been taken to Rotterdam and forced to work in a brothel owned by Lothar Glandorf, and from a series of photographs identified Manuel Schadwald as another boy he'd met there.[379]

German authorities relayed this information to Dutch police in Rotterdam, who put together a task force in September 1994 to investigate Lothar Glandorf and find the missing boy Manuel Schadwald. A wiretap was placed on

Glandorf's phone and a surveillance team assigned to monitor his movements. Members of this surveillance team would then observe Glandorf in the company of a boy they identified as Manuel Schadwald, but inexplicably did nothing about it. Their observation was never reported to German authorities and would be left out of the final report compiled on their investigation, which would be called 'De Handel In Kinderen', or HIK report.

Their sighting of the boy had however been recorded into the raw surveillance logs kept at the time, which were included as an auxiliary document in their report, and was learnt about after the report was eventually leaked to the Dutch media in 1998, given what else it had contained.[380]

The investigation into Lothar Glandorf found he was smuggling boys from Eastern Europe into his Rotterdam brothels *Euro Boys* and *Young Boys*. He would then pimp them out to VIP clients of his escort service and to child pornographers. One of Glandorf's clients had been a particularly sadistic pedophile named Martin Smollners, who actually murdered a boy in 1986. It was found Glandorf had rented a boy to Smollners to use in a torture porn film in which the boy's testicles had been wired to a generator and the current slowly increased. Glandorf had also sold boys to the British pedophiles in Amsterdam, though this was apparently never reported to Scotland Yard.[381]

In November 1995 Lothar Glandorf had been convicted and sent to prison, but the investigation into the operation he'd been running then received renewed attention in 1998 when details of the classified HIK report were aired by the Dutch TV news network NCRV.

The HIK report included transcripts of conversations recorded from the wiretap placed on Glandorf's phone. In one of these a senior Dutch government official with the first name "Joris" had called Glandorf from Poland asking his advice on how best to smuggle a boy across the Dutch border. In another conversation "Joris" had asked Glandorf whether any new boys were available for sex, and mentioned the last one having had an STD.[382]

"Investigating Glandorf, the Rotterdam police found that British paedophiles were routinely using his brothels, but they never send a copy of their report to Scotland Yard. Glandorf had little fear of international policing. When a senior Dutch civil servant phoned him from Poland to say he was bringing back a boy, police phone taps recorded Glandorf saying *'When you get to the bridge at the border, let him out so he can go on foot so they can't catch you'* "
— 'When sex abuse can lead to murder', The Guardian, November 27 2000

There was some contention over the identity of "Joris". According to the researcher who provides the most thorough English language accounting of the incident in the article: 'Dutch Joris Demmink Affair Reveals Heroin, Cocaine and Pedophile Entrapment Affairs',[383] the "Joris" in question had been Joris Francken. A bureaucrat who worked in the Ministry for Health under Minister for Health Els Borst, who would later serve as Deputy Prime Minister of the Netherlands from 1998-2002,[384] and be viciously stabbed to death in the garage of her home in February 2014.[385]

This seemingly motiveless murder, bizarrely first reported as a possible suicide, occurred weeks after a Dutch court in Arnhem ruled to launch an investigation into historic allegations of child abuse against the former Secretary General of the Ministry of Justice of the Netherlands—Joris Demmink. the other "Joris" suspected to have been the senior government official from Lothar Glandorf's wiretap conversations.[386]

A Dutch author named Tomas Ross, who'd known Joris

Demmink personally, said Demmink had been a pederast but never acted upon the impulse illegally. According Ross, Els Borst was murdered over what she'd learnt during her tenure at the Ministry of Health in 1990s. Namely, reports of rampant child abuse by Dutch politicians and other prominent figures, which had flowed up to her office in reports received from social workers at various government care facilities under her supervision during that period.[387] A month after her murder, an investigation had in fact been launched, *"into the involvement of high-ranking people in sex parties with underage boys, in addition to the name of top civil servant Joris Demmink, those of three chief public prosecutors were also mentioned."*[388]

In 2012 Joris Demmink had resigned from his position as Secretary General, around the same time the U.S Helsinki Commission begun an inquiry into his connection to a 1997 investigation into an Amsterdam callboy service catering to Dutch Justice officials. A case known euphemistically as the Rolodex Affair.[389]

Amsterdam 1997 — A man who had been arrested for raping his girlfriend's daughter complained to police about a double standard allowing government officials to skirt their own child sex laws. The man had then provided them with information on a callboy service called *Bell Boys*, which he claimed catered to Dutch justice officials.[390] This service was operated by a child trafficker named Karel Maasdam, also known by the alias 'Alex Privee', who was an associate of Warwick Spinks and Lothar Glandorf and owner of a boy brothel in Amsterdam called *Festival Bar*.[391]

It was discovered a professor from the University of Amsterdam named Prof. Der Van Roon frequented the *Festival Bar*, and served as a reputable go between for high profile clients of Maasdam's *Bell Boys* service. The names and numbers of these clients were kept by Prof. Van Roon in a rolodex, which had been provided to police by the informant. In it were the private numbers belonging to at least three Dutch district attorneys named Henry Hans Holthuis, Henk Wooldrik and Jan Wolter Wabeke. Joris Demmink, who was a senior ministry of justice official at the time, would also be named in the investigation.[392]

A boy prostitute working in the *Festival Bar* at that time would later testify as a witness during a 2012 Helsinki Commission hearing into child sex trafficking in Amsterdam. The witness testified Karel Maasdam sold boys to Amsterdam child pornographers, some of whom were involved in snuff films.

> "In addition, we were rented out for escort services to private clients and parties. The same person who ran the brothel – who ran the brothel – also made child pornography films. I performed in three of those movies. I also knew people who made snuff movies. I was offered vast sums of money to perform – yeah. I was offered vast sums of money to perform in one of these movies, but refused, due to fact that at the end of the – of these movies, the actor is killed."
> — Commission on Security & Cooperation in Europe: U.S. Helsinki Commission, Listening To Victims of Child Sex Trafficking, Witness "Mr. B", October 4, 2012

The witness claimed they had been introduced to Joris Demmink at the *Festival Bar* by Professor Van Roon, and been instructed to have sex with Demmink inside his government car.

> "As escort, I worked for the same brothel owner and worked out of a bar called the Festival Bar, where I met Professor van Roon. Professor van Roon was the man who introduced me to Joris Demmink. We were sitting at a table and he said that I needed to go outside to meet Joris Demmink in his car. Joris wanted to

have anal sex with me, and I refused. I did have oral sex with him. The second time that we met, he wanted me to go with him to him home in Den Haag, Riouwstraat 13. I didn't want to go with him, as we were forbidden to leave the city of Amsterdam by our pimp."

— Commission on Security & Cooperation in Europe: U.S. Helsinki Commission, Listening To Victims of Child Sex Trafficking, Witness "Mr. B", October 4, 2012

It turned out back in the 1990s multiple complaints were lodged by drivers assigned to Joris Demmink's government car. One had come from a driver named Rob Mostert who complained Demmink had sex with boys in the backseat of his government car in his presence.[393] The driver died shortly his complaint was lodged, so it was never followed up on, but similar complaints were made by other drivers aswell:

"A prosecutor and an outside consultant who worked there told this newspaper. Justice officer Tjeerd Postma: *"I told the BVD about complaints from drivers about nightly visits to a club and about a business trip to Brussels, where Demmink had sex with a young boy in the back seat of the official car, while the driver saw everything through the rear view mirror"*...According to former Justice Manager John Moeleker, the top officials of the ministry were aware of a complaint that another driver, Rob Mostert, allegedly submitted about Demmink. Moeleker later learned that the case had not been investigated because Mostert died shortly after his complaint. Former Works Council chairman Rinus Bruël says that the complaint has been 'lost'. " [Dutch to English]

—BVD was gewaarschuwd over Joris Demmink('BVD was warned about Joris Demmink'), AD, March 29 2014

According to information provided to the Dutch current affairs program *EenVandaag* by an alleged bookkeeper of

Karel Maasdam named Richard Carl-Samson, Warwick Spinks frequently pimped boys to Joris Demmink and Henry Hans Holthuis.[394] While the source(Richard Samson) of this information is somewhat dubious, an article published in January 2014 entitled, *"BBC embroiled in further scandal as executive filmed Dutch child abuse movies"*, appears to suggest UK and Dutch authorities had actually explored this connection to the case, which may have been the reason why Spinks was briefly extradited back to the UK in late 2012:

"Demmink will be questioned over allegations that he raped the boys, aged between 12 and 15, while visiting Istanbul in the mid-Nineties. He denies the claims and says he was not in Turkey at that time. In 1998, his name came up during a Dutch inquiry, called the Rolodex Affair, into an Amsterdam paedophile network. The probe was shut down shortly afterwards, prompting accusations of a cover-up. A spokeswoman for the Office of Public Prosecutions in The Hague said the Demmink case might trigger a wider investigation into British paedophiles in Amsterdam. She said: *'The investigation will initially focus solely on the allegations made by the two Turkish boys. Whether the investigation starts to look at other things at a later stage, we don't know, it's too early to say.'* However, sources revealed Dutch and British police met last summer on the Isle of Wight."

— 'BBC embroiled in further scandal as executive filmed Dutch child abuse movies', Express.co.uk, James Fielding , January 26 2014

Further allegations were levelled against other prominent figures by nine witnesses who came forward during a 2016 court hearing in Amsterdam, with claims they'd been used as boy prostitutes by Prof. Ger van Roon and others in 1980s, including members of the Dutch Royal family,[395] *"Among those implicated are Prince Claus, the late husband of former queen Beatrix, the former finance minister and executive director of the international monetary fund Onno Rudding, and former Amsterdam mayor Ed van Thijn, the Algemeen Dagblad reports."*[396]

A detective who investigated the *Bell Boys* service, stated the case had been closed in 1998 with the arrest and sentencing of Karel Maasdam, shortly after senior government officials such as Joris Demmink had been implicated.[397]

According to Nick Davies, a journalist who investigated the network of British pedophiles in Amsterdam during the 1990s, a boy who worked at Maasdam's *Festival Bar* had seen the missing German boy Manuel Schadwald in one of Lothar Glandorf's Rotterdam brothels. And the rumour was the boy had been sold to child pornographers in Amsterdam's Spuistraat district, where Warwick Spinks and Alan Williams managed nightclubs:

"I found a man who looked like Fagin in a flat hat. His real name is Karel Maasdam but he is known here as Alex Privee, owner of the Bell Boys escort agency, producer of boy pornography, close friend of Lothar Glandorf. He is a clever man...And Manuel Schadwald. Well, he had never heard the boy's name until it started to come out in the Dutch press, but since then, he had heard a little bit about him. There was a boy – an escort who worked for Alex Privee's agency, Bell Boys – and he had mentioned that he had seen this boy in Glandorf's clubs in Rotterdam. And there were rumours that he had been used in videos, whether they had been made by Glandorf or by the people in Spuistraat. Perhaps that was a line worth following, he suggested, and carried on ironing."

— 'Paedophile network trafficks young boys across Europe', Nick Davies, Previously unpublished, October 1 1998, Researched on commission from the New Yorker.

A former boy prostitute of Lothar Glandorf's named Robbie Van Der Plancken, who'd since graduated to become an exploiter himself, would state Lothar Glandorf sold Manuel Schadwald to Warwick Spinks.

"Serving drinks at the Festival Bar, Ricky the transvestite said quite simply that he remembered the German boy coming in. In an unbroadcast section of his interview with Dutch TV, I found that Robbie van der Plancken had claimed that some time after being taken from Berlin by Lothar Glandorf, Manuel had been sold to the Englishman Warwick Spinks in Amsterdam. These English paedophiles had been the core investors in the Amsterdam branch of the industry."

— 'Paedophile network traffics young boys across Europe', Nick Davies, Previously unpublished, October 1 1998, Researched on commission from the New Yorker.

Robbie Van Der Plancken had been a central figure in yet another interlinked investigation into, at that time—1998, the world's largest online distributor of sadomasochist child pornography, served from a website called Apollo Bulletin Boards hosted in the Dutch seaside resort town of Zandvoort, just outside of Amsterdam.

It is here, in Zandvoort, where this interconnected network of child traffickers and pornographers investigated in the 1990s start to intersect in a downstream distributor of the materials they produced. But before we continue into the next chapter, let me clarify the three interlinked investigations in the 1990s which hint that such a network existed.

1. 1992-93: Operation Framework - A joint Dutch/Scotland Yard investigation into suspected snuff pornography produced by a group of foreign British nationals in Amsterdam with links to John Stamford's *Spartacus Network*. The key suspects were Warwick Spinks and Alan Williams, who managed the *Gay Palace* and *Boys Club 21* nightclubs located in Amster-

dam's Spuistraat district. In addition to these two were two other Welsh pedophiles named Lee Tucker and John Gay, who had a film production company called *TAG Films*. This production company was linked to a German distribution company named *Gero-Video*. And these men were suspected of producing snuff films which Spinks had sold, including one with a German man in which a German boy was killed.

2. 1994: HIK Investigation - An investigation by Dutch authorities in Rotterdam into a missing German boy named Manuel Schadwald and a German child trafficker named Lothar Glandorf. Glandorf was a business associate of Warwick Spinks, and Manuel Schadwald had last been seen with Glandorf by Dutch police, who also discovered Glandorf sold boys to British child pornographers in Amsterdam. It was also learnt Glandorf pimped boys to a VIP clientele, including at least one senior Dutch official.

5. 1997-98: Rolodex Investigation - An investigation by Dutch authorities in Amsterdam into a callboy service called *Bèll Boys*, operated by another associate of Spinks and Glandorf named Karel Maasdam from a nightclub called *Festival Bar*. It was learnt a professor named Der Van Roon served as a go between for VIP clients of this service, and his rolodex included the private numbers for Dutch justice officials and other prominent figures.

Then in 1998 it was learnt from a figure involved in yet another investigation into an online child porn distributor in Zandvoort, that Manuel Schadwald had been sold to Warwick Spinks.

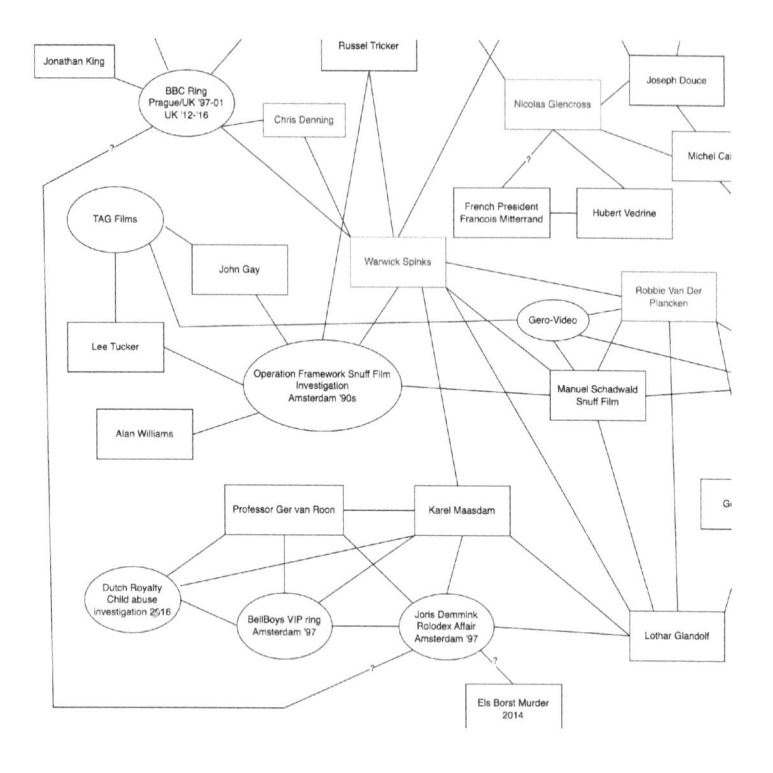

- Jonathan King
- BBC Ring Prague/UK '97-01 UK '12-'16
- Russel Tricker
- Chris Denning
- Joseph Douce
- Nicolas Glencross
- Michel Ca...
- French President Francois Mitterrand
- Hubert Vedrine
- TAG Films
- John Gay
- Warwick Spinks
- Robbie Van Der Plancken
- Gero-Video
- Lee Tucker
- Operation Framework Snuff Film Investigation Amsterdam '90s
- Manuel Schadwald Snuff Film
- Alan Williams
- Professor Ger van Roon
- Karel Maasdam
- Dutch Royalty Child abuse investigation 2016
- BellBoys VIP ring Amsterdam '97
- Joris Demmink Rolodex Affair Amsterdam '97
- Lothar Glandolf
- Els Borst Murder 2014

Apollo Bulletin Board - Zandvoort 1998

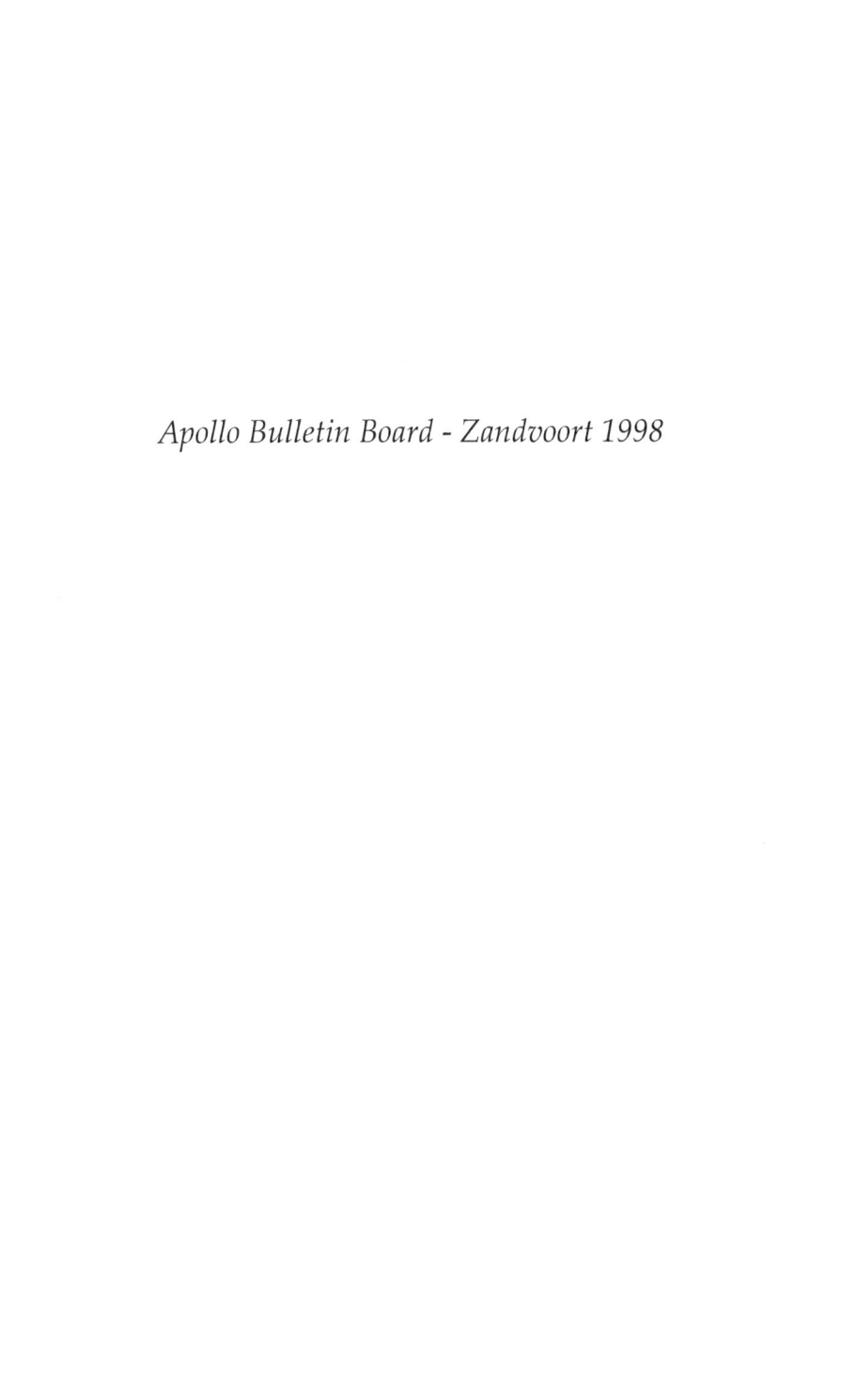

Gerrit Ulrich & Robbie Van Der Plancken

In the mid 1990s a private investigator named Marcel Vervloesem was investigating the disappearance of Manuel Schadwald for an NGO called the *Morkhoven Workgroup,* when he came across Lothar Glandorf's name in a 1992 police report detailing a raid on an underage sex party in the Dutch town of Wallre.[398]

The report stated Glandorf was arrested at the party in the company of a teenager named Robbie Van Der Plancken. Vervloesem managed to track this teenager down, now a young man in Amsterdam sometime in June 1998 and ambushed him with questions about Manuel Shadwald during a TV interview filmed by journalists from the Belgian public broadcaster RTBF.[399] During this interview Vervloesem's associates noticed an interested onlooker nearby, and followed them to the dutch seaside resort town of Zandvoort. This turned out to be a German associate of Van Der Plancken named Gerrit-Jan Ulrich, a 49 year-old computer technician who owned a computer store called Cube Hardware.[400]

Under circumstances not entirely clear, Gerrit-Jan Ulrich invited Vervloesem to meet with him at his apartment. Inside were many running computers dialed up to five phone lines, and the place was full of digital storage disks and networking equipment. Ulrich revealed himself to be the administrator of a child pornography website called *Apollo Bulletin Board Service*, and handed Vervloesem a collection of encoded disks which contained thousands of images and videos of violent child abuse, along with information on their producers and lists of those who paid to access them from around the world.[401]

Why Ulrich agreed to meet with Vervloesem and admit to all this is unclear, as are the exact circumstances under which they had met. One of Ulrich's neighbours would later say he had heart disease and not long to live. According to Vervloesem, Ulrich feared for his life and sought some kind of life insurance against a network of child pornographers who produced the materials he distributed online.[402]

Whatever his motivations may have been, a few days after this meeting Ulrich fled the Netherlands and called Vervloesem from Italy. He said he was frightened and hadn't long to live, and told Vervloesem about a cache of digital disks hidden beneath a floorboard of his apartment which contained information on his network of associates.[403]

A few days after he made this phone call, Ulrich's body was discovered in an Italian forest on June 20 1998. He had been shot multiple times and Italian police had arrested Robbie Van Der Plancken as a suspect in his murder.[404]

When Dutch police were notified of Ulrich's death they inspected his apartment and noticed obvious signs of a child pornography operation. A surveillance team was assigned to monitor the apartment and within a few days, upon also learning of Ulrich's death, Vervloesem was caught breaking in to retrieve the disks Ulrich told him were hidden beneath a floorboard. These, along with hundreds of others in Ulrich's apartment, were found to contain tens of thousands of images and videos showing extremely violent sexual abuse of children, and even infants.[405]

A child psychiatrist who inspected the materials stated, *"I've never seen anything like this. The pictures show very disgusting things, sexual abuse, violence, and the tying up of young children. There were children aged four to five, children aged eight to nine, and I saw one child about 18 months."*[406] Some films were described as *"almost killing,"* as *"very special, very aggressive, very hard, mechanically brutal."*[407]

The disks found beneath Ulrich's floorboard had been hidden alongwith bags of child sized clothing. These contained information on, seemingly, a network of suppliers involved in producing and selling these films and images. Two of those identified by Dutch authorities were Warwick Spinks and Lothar Glandorf. Warwick Spinks' name was also found in an address book belonging to Robbie Van Der Plancken.

> "Later he[Vervloesem] informs the police about the secret stash and on 28 June they return to the flat, carryout a thorough search, and find computer records under the floorboards, including a list of 300 names which is said to amount to an international Who's Who of suspected paedophiles. It includes Warwick Spinks, who was released from prison in Britain last July after being convicted of drugging and kidnapping a 14-year-old boy, and is now believed to be in Prague, and Lothar Gandolf[sic], a notorious German paedophile."
>
> — 'No kind of Hero', Tim Hulse, The Independent, September 13 1998

"Mr. Spinks name also appeared among the possessions of the Belgian Robbie van der Plancken, a leader of the ring which traded thousands of pictures showing sexual abuse of children and infants via the internet."

— 'Fugitive Briton linked to Dutch child porn hits at witch-hunt from Prague refuge', The Guardian, July 31 1998

What police hadn't seized however were the *Apollo Disks* Ulrich handed Vervloesem when the pair met in person. Vervloesem hadn't trusted Dutch authorities, so passed them on to a colleague in the *Morkhoven Workgroup*, who made copies before they were given to police. This was done by a woman named Gina Pardaens-Bernaer, a computer specialist who had worked closely with Vervloesem on the Manuel Schadwald case. On November 15 1998, a few months after she took possession of the *Apollo Disks*, her body was found inside the wreckage of her car, which had crashed into the concrete pillar of a bridge at full speed.[408]

Two days before her death, Gina sent copies of the *Apollo Disks* to the *International Committee for the Dignity of the Child*(CIDE) in Geneva, with a letter attached stating her life had been threatened. She had also filed police reports earlier that week regarding death threats she received and an incident in which her son had been run off the road by a car while riding his bike.[409]

"Gina Bernard, the Flemish children's rights activist who was responsible for the discovery of a large pedophilia network in Zandvoort in the Netherlands in the summer of this year, died in a traffic accident over the weekend. She crashed into a bridge pillar in Lembeek at quite high speed and died instantly. There's no indication of a murder. Police assume that Gina Bernard was driving too fast in the rain on a slippery road surface, which also explains why no skid marks were found. In the days and weeks before her death, Gina Bernard told several people that she had been receiving death threats. On Saturday she called Marcel Vervloesem twice about this from the Morkhoven Working Group, the non-profit organiza-

tion that received diskettes with 9,000 gruesome child pornography images in the summer. The contacts were then made by Gina Bernard, who had been searching for the teenage boy Manuel Schadwald who disappeared in Berlin in 1993. Vervloesem very much doubts that it was an accident and yesterday plainly spoke of "another murder". Several other children's rights activists in Brussels confirmed yesterday that Gina Bernard had been living in fear in recent weeks and openly said she feared for her life, although these statements were not always taken seriously."[Dutch to English Translation]
— 'Zaak-Morkhoven: ontdekster komt om in ongeval'('Morkhoven case: discoverer dies in accident'), De Morgen, 17 november 1998

According to friends and colleagues, Gina had spoken of a snuff film found on the *Apollo Disks* which showed a girl being murdered by an associate of a child trafficking network exposed during the 1996 investigation into Belgian 'serial killer' Marc Dutroux— *"Before her death, she tells friends about a video tape in which a girl is being murdered during a sex party. She believed one of the perpetrators to be an acquaintance of Nihoul."*[410]

"A judicial investigation is underway at the Brussels public prosecutor's office into the death threats that child rights activist Gina Pardaens received in the last days and weeks of her life, De Morgen has learned. The case is in the hands of investigating judge Edith Callewaert. She will try to determine what exactly is the meaning of the accusations that Pardaens herself made, about a second telephone line on her private number through which e-mail messages were allegedly intercepted, telephone threats and an incident in which her son was driven off the road. The woman was an employee of the RTBF program Faits Divers, helped the non-profit organization Morkhoven in its

investigation into the so-called Apollo network and, before her death, alluded to an important discovery that she had made on the sidelines of the Dutroux case." [Dutch to English Translation]
— 'Parket onderzoekt doodsbedreigingen Gina Pardaens'('Public prosecutor's office investigates death threats Gina Pardaens'), De Morgen, 11 december 1998

In February 2001 the *Morkhoven Workgroup* followed up on this lead and tracked down a transvestite in Amsterdam named Robert Jan Warmerdam, who claimed to have known not only Robbie Van Der Plancken, but also Marc Dutroux.[411]

The *Workhoven Group* compiled a dossier on information provided by Warmerdam, alongwith 20 CDRoms of files taken from the *Apollo Discs,* and sent it to a prosecutor named Michel Bourlet over seeing the Dutroux case in 2001. This dossier would be leaked to the press in the lead up to Dutroux's trial in 2004,[412] then later to the public via wikileaks in 2009.[413] The wikileaks release came after a Belgium court convicted Marcel Vervloesem for distribution of child pornography and sexual assault of three minors.[414] Make of that what you will, but perhaps read the following chapter before passing judgement on the rulings of Belgium courts in cases of child abuse.

According to this dossier, Dutroux had frequented a nightclub in Amsterdam called the *G-force* as well as two hardcore pornography studios called *Rex Productions* and *Roxanne Films*. *Roxanne Films* was located at 111 Admiraal de Ruijter Road in a building owned by a transvestite named Didier Pellerin.[415] Pellerin had been interviewed by investigators back in 1996 regarding Dutroux, and confirmed a woman named Marlene Decokere had worked there. Marlene Decokere was the mistress of Michel Nihoul, the ringleader of a child trafficking network Marc Dutroux would be linked to.[416]

According to Warmerdam, Dutroux had mentioned a nursery near *Roxanne Films* where infants were used for pornography.[417] Among the abuse materials seized from Ulrich's apartment had been videos and photos of this type, and a document found on the *Apollo Disks* was a detailed order list for accessing infants for sex.[418]

Just down the street from *Roxanne Films* was a nursery called Jenno's Knuffelparadijs' crèche, located at no. 74 Admiraal de Ruijter Road. In 2010 it would be discovered this nursery had been used by a pedophile named Robert Mikelson, dubbed "The monster of Riga" by he media, to procure babies for use in pornography distributed online.[419]

Warmerdam claimed Marc Dutroux and Robbie Van Der Plancken had been regulars at the *G-Force* nightclub in Amsterdam. According to the dossier, it was owned by an American identified as John Edward Mullaney, who could apparently be linked to John Stamford's *Spartacus Network* through a company called *Korper and Korver*, as well as Karel Maasdam through another company called *Adonis*.[420] Mentions of the *Spartacus Network* during the Dutroux investigation are covered in the following chapter.

This dossier served as the basis for a series of 2004 media reports, rather messily linking Dutroux to child traffickers in Amsterdam. However much of this was true is questionable, as what we are about to embark on is a fucking mess.

> "His accuser, public prosecutor Michel Bourlet, already has it. Marc Dutroux's connections to the international child porn scene are documented in investigation file 8257/01, which was leaked to the Berliner Morgenpost. It was created on behalf of Bourlet and is also available to the British New Scotland Yard and the Belgian Ministry of Justice. The analysis of the file

allows only the following conclusion: Dutroux worked together with a pederast ring that was active throughout Europe. The center of the ring is the red light scene in Amsterdam, where Dutroux was seen, according to several witnesses. Along with those men who are also suspected of kidnapping Berlin boys." [German to English]

— 'The ring of child molesters surrounding Marc Dutroux reached as far as Berlin', Berlin Morgenpost, August 3 2004

After he was arrested for the murder of Gerrit Ulrich, Robbie Van Der Plancken admitted to helping Lothar Glandorf transport Manuel Schadwald from Berlin to Rotterdam.[421] Then in an unaired interview he told Dutch reporters the boy had then been sold to Warwick Spinks in Amsterdam.[422]

"According to the detailed announcement from the Morkhoven Working Group, there has finally been a breakthrough in the file of the missing German boy Manuel Schadwald. In Venlo, representatives of the Working Group met one of the three boys who accompanied Manuel Schadwald on his trip to Rotterdam in July 1993. According to the Morkhoven Working Group, the boy's testimony puts the Belgian Robby Van der Plancken, who is currently imprisoned in Italy and suspected of the murder of the Zandvoort businessman Ullrich, and his associates LG and the British WASP[Warwick Spinks], in close shoes…Van der Plancken recently admitted to the RTBF that he was present when Manuel Schadwald was taken by LG from Rotterdam from the Pinoccio bar in Berlin, but that he himself did not participate." [Dutch to English Translation]

— 'Morkhoven houdt kroongetuige in zaak-Schadwald achter de hand("Morkhoven keeps a key witness in the Schadwald case in reserve")', De Morgen, 21 september 1998

Here things start to get murky as intelligence agencies from various countries strangely started to volunteer information on Manuel Shadwald's fate, which generally means state sponsored disinformation. There's a convergence of conflicting accounts, which seem to provide half-truths of twisted details. The following should be read as if squinting at the form of something vaguely familiar behind opaque glass. Everything fits nicely together into a familiar shape, but of details you can't quite make out.

During his trial, Robbie Van Der Plancken's father told the media, " *'If Robby spoke, the Dutroux case wouldn't be anything against it.' And he said that his son was in a movie where a child was dying. In an interview with this newspaper shortly afterwards, the father confirmed: 'There is a snuff video in which a boy from Berlin dies. I saw it and recognized my son as the actor in it'.* "[423]

The transvestite Robert Jan Warmerdam claimed in the dossier to have seen this film as well, *"And Robert Jan W. also describes scenes from this film. The investigation file from the Neufchâteau public prosecutor's office states that the video was filmed in a bungalow near Amsterdam. The then 13-year-old boy from Germany initially refused to satisfy the perverse desires of several men. But he was then forced to do so and suffocated. This statement is also available to the public prosecutor in Haarlem, Netherlands."*[424]

This was the same description given of a snuff film by the informant "Edward" during the Operation Framework investigation into Warwick Spinks, only the setting had changed, *"A man molests a boy on a boat. The child suffocates. Panic breaks out on board. The camera falls over."*[425]

Spooks had started to haunt the press reports on the Manuel Schadwald case soon after news of *Apollo Bulletin Boards* investigation broke in 1998. By this time Dutch journalists had traced Manuel Schaldwald's kidnapping back to a child brothel owned by Lothar Glandorf in Berlin, called

Pinocchio Bar. An associate of Glandorf's named Peter Goetjes, involved in trafficking boys across the Dutch-German border, said Manuel Schadwald's biological father had been involved; That the boy hadn't been kidnapped, but rather sold.[426]

The father's name was Reiner Wolf, and it turned out he'd been an intelligence asset for the Stasi during the 1980s. This much the man admitted himself, saying he'd been used to infiltrate various peace movements. However, a former liaison officer between the Stasi and KGB named Wanja Götz then stated in an affidavit, *"I was commissioned by the GDR secret service to psychologically assess this man. It was only much later that I found out that after his move to the Federal Republic of Germany in 1984, orchestrated by the Stasi, Wolf blackmailed Western Europeans with child pornography on behalf of the GDR secret service's foreign espionage service."*[427]

The former head of West German intelligence during this period, Bernd Schmidbauer, took the Stasi conspiracy theory one step further and suggested Marc Dutroux may have, *"also worked for a time on behalf of the Stasi"*, telling press:

" 'There were indeed indications that such information could be found in the Stasi material that was leaked to the American secret service, the CIA. The Belgian secret service would be well advised to evaluate these documents thoroughly,' says Bernd, former intelligence coordinator of the Kohl government Schmidbauer (CDU). During the turning point, the CIA was able to secure extensive material about the espionage department of the MfS reconnaissance headquarters. Because of the explosive nature of the information contained therein, also about Western European politicians, these documents are still withheld from the public."[428]

Later sources within Dutch intelligence agency AIVD provided more specific details. Apparently Manuel Schadwald had been killed on a yacht called "der Apollo" owned by Gerrit Ulrich and his business partner, a Dutch accountant named Leo Van Gasselt.[429]

> "If what several informants describe to the "Algemeen Dagblad" and the "Welt am Sonntag" is true, then something terrible happened on this boat. Then it was the place where a boy, Manuel Schadwald, lost his life. Then a few rich customers from politics and society gathered there to hold a sex orgy with several children in front of the camera. Then, after the crime, the ship was towed to a Dutch Navy military port and cleaned. It is unclear what became of the film footage. In fact, the suspicion was also confirmed by a Dutch intelligence officer who was willing to talk about the case just a few days ago. *"Manuel Schadwald died playing sex games on this boat,"* he says. This is also documented in the files of the Dutch secret service. The body was then sunk into the sea. And he also says that the case was covered up because high-ranking people were involved. He doesn't say why he's breaking his silence now."[German to English Translation]
> — 'Die verlorenen Kinder'('The Lost Children'), Welt, July 12 2015

You can never trust spooks, not really; especially to provide you with the information you've been looking for. German spooks seemed eager to finger the Russians, who are no doubt famous for their 'Kompromat' brand of espionage. It isn't surprising Germany would do this, since all roads do seem to led there. That is - West Germany. A nation at that time in the midst of sausage making itself into the core power within the European Union.

Claims made by a former German intelligence chief that Dutroux may have had ties to the Stasi are the give away.

Dutroux, as we shall soon learn, was a rather marginal figure on the periphery of a network that, if it had state-sponsored ties, they were almost certainly aligned with NATO interests.

Among the noted ties to Germany in the cases covered so far:

- The *Elm Guest House* was owned by a German woman who died suddenly after passing along evidence it was setup as a *Spartacus Network* child porn operation which produced compromising photographs and videos of British politicians who visited it.
- *Spartacus International* was absorbed by a German holding company in the 1980s called *Bruno Gmunder Verlag* after Stamford's child sex tourism operation was exposed.
- John Stamford fled to Germany after his estate was raided in Amsterdam, and then died suddenly before his trial into the *Spartacus Network* properly commenced.
- British child pornographers in Amsterdam accused of making snuff films owned a video production company called *TAG Films* linked to a German distribution company in Dusseldorf called *Gero-Video*.
- Lothar Glandorf was a German national operating child brothels in both Berlin and Rotterdam, and was pimping boys to at least one senior Dutch government official.
- Gerrit Ulrich was a German national administrating a child torture-porn distribution server, murdered soon after handing over information on his associates.

Marcel Vervloesem, the private investigator who took possession of the *Apollo Disks* from Ulrich, was convicted by an Antwerp court in 2008 for publication of child pornography and sexual abuse of three minors.[430] Regardless of whether the charges were genuine or contrived, this has since allowed for facts concerning the Apollo investigation, not just claims by Vervloesem but facts, to be dismissed *ad hominem*. Gina Pardaens-Bernaer, who took possession of the *Apollo Disks* from Vervloesem, died in a car crash a few months after receiving them.

Weeks before Gina's death journalists reported she claimed to be in possession of a film featuring Robbie Vander Plancken and Manuel Schadwald which the US secret service had been interested in:

"Gina Pardaens-Bernaer worked intensively on the Schadwald and Dutroux cases in the 1990s and wanted to prove a connection between the murders even back then. She sought contact with private investigators and journalists. Also told us about having the video with Manuel Schadwald. "You know, things are getting more and more dangerous. I get death threats. I was also approached by American secret service agents. They want to put the film and me into the witness protection program for it," said Gina Pardaens-Bernaer in her home in Herne in October 1998. Her husband stood next to her and said worriedly: "I'm afraid for her." A few weeks later, the woman drove along her car crashed into a bridge pillar without braking. One day before her death, on November 13, 1998, her house was broken into. Was it about the movie? A day after her death, she was scheduled to appear for questioning at the Belgian police."

— 'Die verlorenen Kinder'('The Lost Children'), Welt, July 12 2015

The video in question appears to have been distributed by *Gero-Video* and called "The Poison Dwarf".[431] It was reported in Germany that, *"the finds in Zandvoort have nevertheless brought Gero-Video into the spotlight. The alleged child molester*

Robby van der Plancken, who is imprisoned in Italy because he is said to have shot his partner Gerrit Jan Ulrich, **can be seen in at least five Gero films***. Tomek: "The films were bought by a Dutch production company before my time in 1993." To his knowledge, there were no personal contacts between Gero-Video and van der Plancken."*[432] The investigation into Warwick Spinks and TAG Films in 1993 led to a German police raid of a video distributor in Dusseldorf, where *Gero-Video* was located. *Gero-Video* changed hands that same year and is also identified as a child porn distributor in a dossier provided by Karel Maasdam's accountant to Dutch intelligence services.[433] All the evidence suggests Manuel Schadwald met his end with Warwick Spinks in Amsterdam.

Vermisster Manuel Schadwald

The Poison Dwarf, Gero-Video

Gina Pardaens-Bernaer had also told friends and colleagues of another film, a snuff film in which she claimed to identify an associate of the network linked to Marc Dutroux. And there's a context here yet to be touched on. When Gina ploughed her car at full speed into the concrete pillar of a bridge, she became one of more than twenty 'accidental' and 'sudden deaths' linked to the investigation of the Marc Dutroux case. This is not hyperbole and entirely mainstream knowledge. In 1999 a *New York Times* headline read, *"Prosecutor in Pedophile Case Kills Himself : Belgian Official's Death Puts Top Cases On Hold"*,[434] and in 2002 *The Observer* reported, *"Since 1995, there have been 20 unexplained deaths of potential witnesses connected with Dutroux."*[435] It is within this context of the dead, the case of Marc Dutroux is entered into.

1. July 4, 1995: Alexandre Gosselin, Bernard Weinstein's neighbour.[436]
2. August 25, 1995: Guy Goebels, gendarme investigating the disappearance of Julie and Melissa, committed suicide in his apartment with his service weapon
3. November 1995: Bernard Weinstein, Dutroux's accomplice, poisoned by Dutroux
4. November 5, 1995: Bruno Tagliaferro, poisoned scrap dealer who wanted to testify against Dutroux[437]
5. April 2, 1995: Jean-Pol Taminiau disappears, he had rented a garage near a hangar rented by Dutroux. One year after the disappearance a foot of Taminiau is found.
6. July 26, 1995: Francois Reyskens, run over by a train shortly before a hearing
7. February 21, 1996: Simon Poncelet, a policeman investigating the Dutroux car-jacking milieu and the son of a judge, was shot dead in his office during the night shift.[438]
8. August 22, 1996: Michel Binon, acquaintance of Marc Dutroux, suicide
9. December 5, 1996: Michel Poiro, nightclub owner who was acquainted with Michel Nihoul, shot dead before a meeting with the parents of Julie and Melissa
10. February 2, 1997: Christoph Vanhexe, journalist

investigating Dutroux case, dies in car crash.[439]
11. February 25 1997: Jean-Marc Houdemont dies in car crash. A child pornographer tied to the CRIES investigation.[440]
12. March 5, 1997: Joseph Toussaint, confessor of Michelle Martin, died of a heart attack
13. March 7, 1997: Christian Coenraets, inmate who was supposed to testify about his relationship with Weinstein but fled the day before testifying, is found dead a month later
14. April 25, 1997: José Steppe, dies two days before he was supposed to testify to a journalist and the gendarmerie
15. July 2, 1997: Virginie Pinon, almost-victim of Dutroux, dies of mucoviscidose
16. November 16, 1997: Gérard Vannesse, Gendarme officer and one of the runners of Nihoul, dies of a thrombosis
17. April 5, 1998: Brigitte Jenart, a friend of Michel Nihoul, commits suicide
18. April 7, 1998: Anna Konjevoda is found dead in the Maas (a river), the body shows signs of beatings and strangulation
19. December 18, 1998: Fabienne Jaupart, wife of Bruno Tagliaferro, burns to death in her bed[441]
20. July 13, 1999: Hubert Massa, a public prosecutor commits suicide[442]
21. August 15, 1999: Grégory Antipine, police officer, commits suicide by hanging
22. November 4, 1999: Sandra Claeys, Michel Lelièvre's ex-girlfriend commits suicide
23. March 1, 2001: Jean-Jacques Feront, paedophile hunter who dies of a heart attack
24. March 28, 2001: Nadège Renard, ex-girlfriend of Jean-

Pol Taminiau, dies in a car accident
25. May 17, 2001: Pierre-Paul "Pepe" De Rycke, acquaintance of Michel Nihoul, commits suicide

Most of these deaths were compiled from a list on the website of the *Institue for the study of Globalization and Covert Politics*,[443] which has published a collection of well researched articles on the Marc Dutroux investigation and others interlinked with it. While I have only independently verified some of these deaths listed, the details of many were also covered in a German documentary called *'Die Spur der Kinderschänder - Dutroux und die toten Zeugen'* by Piet Eekman, broadcasted by the German television network ZDF in 2001. This documentary also explored the circumstances surrounding Gina Bernaer's death.

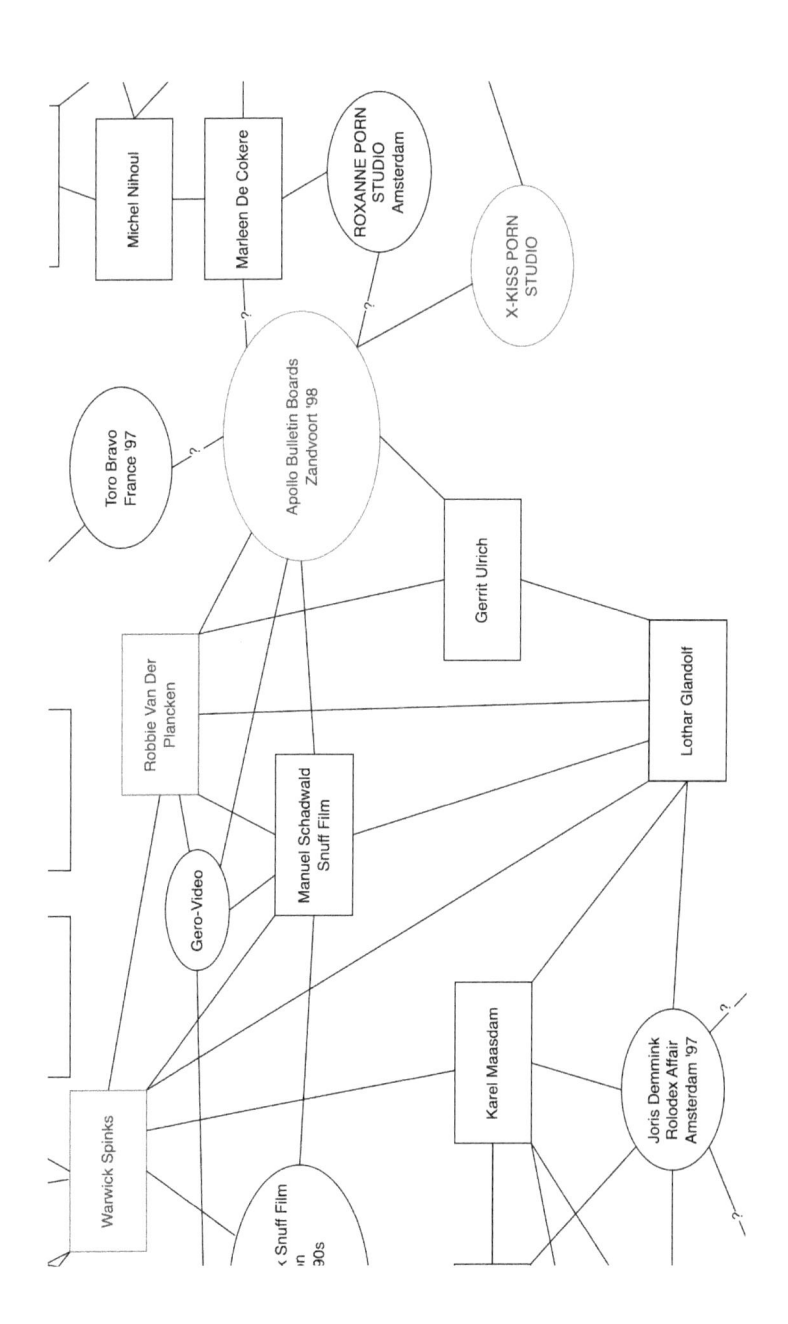

- Michel Nihoul
- Marleen De Cokere
- ROXANNE PORN STUDIO Amsterdam
- X-KISS PORN STUDIO
- Toro Bravo France '97
- Apollo Bulletin Boards Zandvoort '98
- Gerrit Ulrich
- Robbie Van Der Plancken
- Manuel Schadwald Snuff Film
- Gero-Video
- Lothar Glandolf
- Karel Maasdam
- Joris Demmink Rolodex Affair Amsterdam '97
- Warwick Spinks
- Snuff Film ... 90s

The X-Dossier - Belgium 1996-97

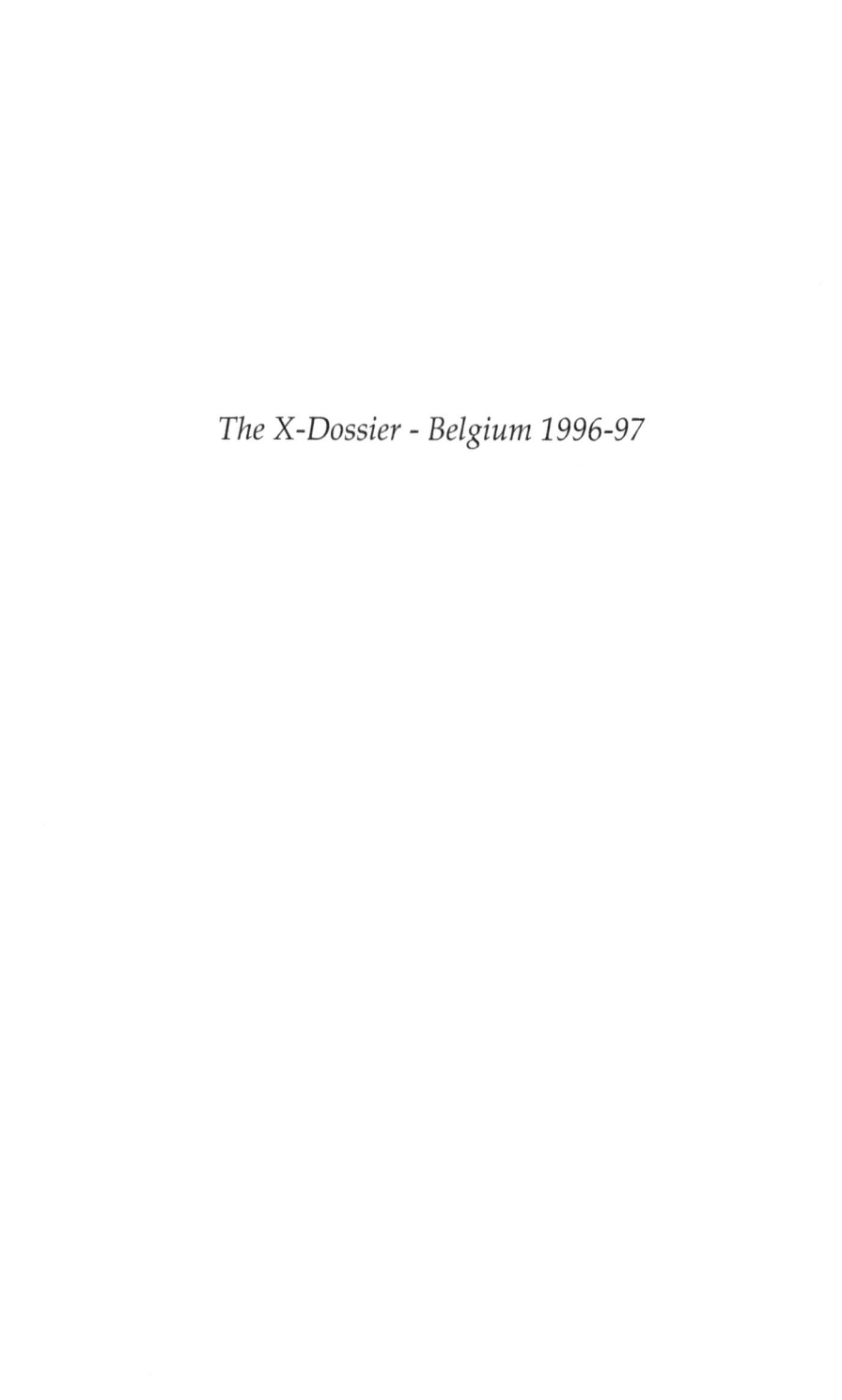

Marc Dutroux Kidnappings

Belgium, August 1995 — After the disappearance of two eight-year-old girls a month earlier in July, police in the city of Charleroi began surveilling one of seven properties belonging to an unemployed electrician named Marc Dutroux. A petty criminal named Claude Thirault had told them Dutroux hired him in 1993 to help renovate a section of his basement into a hidden dungeon which Dutroux said he intended to use to imprison kidnapped girls. Police had inspected these renovations at the time but accepted Dutroux's explanation he was merely installing a new drainage system.[444]

Two days after the disappearance of Julie Lejeune and Melissa Russo in July 1995, Claude Thirault reminded police of what he had reported back in 1993, and emphasised a remark Dutroux had made while they'd been working on the renovations when two high school girls had passed them, *"If you want to kidnap them, you'll make 150,000 franks. . .Grab them from behind, put a sedative drug under their nose, pull them into the car, and lock the doors."*[445] Dutroux hadn't been joking.

In 1986 Dutroux had been charged with the kidnap, torture, and rape of five girls between the ages of 11-19 for which he'd been sentenced to 13 and half years.[446] However, in 1992 he'd been granted an early release by a justice minister named Melchior Wathelet, who was soon after appointed to the European Court of Justice.[447]

Surveillance of the house belonging to Dutroux commenced on August 10 1995 under the auspices of an investigation led by a police inspector named Rene Michaux called Othello. At the time Julie Lejeune and Melissa Russo had in fact been imprisoned in the basement of this house.[448]

On August 22, while under surveillance, Dutroux had then kidnapped two more girls and taken them to the house. These were 17-year-old An Marcha and 19-year-old Eefje Lambrecks. Two friends who disappeared after being hypnotised on stage at a casino during the performance of a magician named Rasti Rostelli. Since his basement dungeon had been occupied, Dutroux tied the girls up in a bedroom of the house and kept them there for a couple of weeks. He'd then removed them from the house and taken them somewhere they were murdered. Police surveillance somehow failed to notice any of this.

A few months later in early December 1995 Dutroux was arrested and jailed on unrelated auto theft charge. He and an associate named Bernard Weinstein had kidnapped and drugged three teenagers who'd stolen a truck for them, one of whom escaped and told police.[449] As a result, Dutroux's home was searched twice in December 1995 by members of the Othello investigation team. On one of these occasions both a locksmith and the lead detective Rene Michaux heard children's screams coming from the basement, where at the time Julie Lejeune and Melissa Russo were still being held.

A search of the basement failed to locate the two girls, who were locked within cells hidden behind a removable plywood partition disguised as shelving. The screams were deemed to be coming from children outside of the house, and as a result the two girls would supposedly be left to starve to death while Dutroux served four months in jail on the auto-theft charges.450

Investigators had however discovered the following items in Dutroux's basement, which were booked into evidence: Videotapes, a speculum, vaginal cream, chains, and chloroform. The videotapes contained footage of Dutroux raping a number of girls as well as footage of him constructing the hidden cells in his basement. All these items, including the videotapes, were returned to Dutroux's wife shortly after they'd been taken as evidence. When it was later revealed what had been on them, the police claimed to have never viewed the tapes, despite the fact they had taken them along-with other items which effectively constituted a rapekit.451

In January 1996, while jailed on the auto theft charges, Dutroux was eliminated as a suspect in the disappearances of Julie Lejeune and Melissa Russo. Then two months later in March he was released for "humanitarian reasons". So in May Dutroux kidnapped another girl, twelve year-old Sabine Dardenne. And then on August 9 another, 14 year-old Laetitia Delhez. During this abduction, a witness spotted a white van driving suspiciously around the time and place of Laertitia Delhez's disappearance and had provided police with a partial license plate number. A match was returned on a white van owned by Marc Dutroux, who was arrested along with his wife and another accomplice named Michel Lelievre.452

This breakthrough led to the rescue of Sabine Dardenne and Laetitia Delhez who were found in Dutroux's basement dungeon, starved but still alive. The two girls he'd abducted in July 1995, Julie Lejeune and Mélissa Russo, were found buried on another of Dutroux's properties. The bodies of An Marcha and Eefje Lambrecks, who'd been abducted in August 1995, were also found buried on another of Dutroux's properties, along with Dutroux's former associate Bernard Weinstein, who Dutroux had killed in November 1995 just prior to his auto theft charges.[453]

This is generally where the story ends in many accounts. With the arrest of a serial killer after a series of police failures that fuelled a series of conspiracy theories which culminated in a massive hoax targeting Belgium's political class. But this is really where the story begins.

Marc Dutroux was not a serial killer in any of the definitions provided by behavioural scientists. He was a profit driven and rather marginal figure on the periphery of a particularly brutal child sex trafficking network.

The best place start among the generally forgotten facts would probably be with the fact Dutroux somehow managed to accrue enough wealth as an unemployed electrician to own seven properties. Soon after his arrest it was revealed he had around ten bank accounts across Europe, and large sums had been transferred into and between these accounts over a period of ten years, and large lines of bank credit had been made available to him.[454]

Part of Dutroux's income was explained almost immediately, when videotapes of child rapes were seized from his properties:

> "In the meantime, gendarmes and police officers are taking a grim inventory of the clues accumulated over the past few days. And, among other things, view the hundreds of seized tapes. These videocassettes are beginning to reveal their secrets. They are labeled with the name of "normal" films: Laurel and Hardy, "Gone with the Wind". And on the first meters of tape, it is indeed the announced film that we see. Then, suddenly, the vile invades the screen. Very often, we unmistakably see Dutroux in the images. One or two accomplices - who we are not sure have correctly identified - accompanied him in his crimes.

Their victims: young girls obviously drugged or force-fed with medication. . .Gendarmes and police officers no longer have the slightest doubt: Dutroux was (at least) at the center of videocassette trafficking from which he probably derived a significant part of his income. Was he "the leader", did he have a sponsor? Various theses confront each other on this subject. " [French to English Translation]
— 'Les Cassettes Livrent Leurs Secrets'("Cassettes Deliver Their Secrets"), Le Soir, August 22 1996

The bodies of Julie Lejeune and Melissa Russo, who supposedly starved to death, had in fact been horribly mutilated, and video equipment connected to a computer belonging to Dutroux was recovered from his property.[455] Dutroux would later write one of the girls father claiming he had kidnapped them for an organised 'snuff orgy'.

"The convicted child murderer Marc Dutroux also writes about such films in his letter to the father of the murdered Julie Lejeune. Julie and her friend Melissa were kidnapped by a gang who needed the girls for an orgy and for these so-called "snuff recordings". The children were held by Dutroux until all of the "guests" could agree on a date. There was already a pit for the children's bodies." [German to English]
— 'Auf den Spuren der verlorenen Kinder'('On the trail of lost children'), Dirk Banse & Michael Behrendt, Welt, July 12 2015

Apparently no such films were among those retrieved from Dutroux's properties, though a rather strange report stated an FBI child abuse center in America had received from authorities in Charleroi, Belgium, *"around fifteen cassettes seized (several months ago[that is - prior to Dutroux's arrest]) in a sauna or a video club, including two cassettes of snuff movies (representing torture and a real assassination) and a few pedophile cassettes."*[456]
In October 1996 a Belgian Senator named Anne-Marie Lizin

had visited this FBI affiliated *Center for Missing Children* in Washington D.C., which received child abuse materials from around the world to identify victims and perpetrators in photographs and videos. According to the Senator during their visit:

> "The managers of this center ("semi-public", in which FBI officers collaborate, among others) assured him[Lizin] that, according to their contacts in the investigation carried out in Belgium, a certain number of cassettes seized during Marc's arrest, Dutroux reproduces rapes of unidentified children committed in front of potentially identifiable spectators. The camera, which the Americans believe is manipulated by Michelle Martin, explains Anne-Marie Lizin, films the act of rape and, from time to time, the rapist. But at the end of the sequence, she would linger at length on the spectators who numbered ten to fifteen per session. In all, around fifty people would thus be potentially identifiable. Anne-Marie Lizin thus explains that her interlocutors are convinced - referring to their own sources and the analogy with the cases they deal with over the years - that some of the identifiable people are magistrates, senior officials (or who were) of certain security services, such as the gendarmerie, or politicians."[French to English Translation]
>
> —DUTROUX: ON S'ACHEMINE VERS UN DESSAISISSEMENT("Dutroux: We are moving towards a divestment"),
> Le Soir, October 11 1996.

Reports on the tapes recovered from Dutroux's properties were mixed and very much the subject of speculation. However, that Dutroux made and sold rape tapes with accomplices was a widely reported fact in newspapers globally in 1996. You will find articles on this in the New York Times,[457]

The Chicago Tribune,[458] or any run of the mill newspaper of record. Dutroux's associate Bernard Weinstein also for a time worked as a video copier at a tape cassette processing company called *SPRL Video Promotion,* perhaps making copies of tapes Dutroux had produced.[459]

The evidence suggests Dutroux's main source of income came from selling girls he kidnapped on to wealthy clients of an underworld business figure named Michel Nihoul. Something which was learnt during a concurrent investigation into reports of men driving white Mercedes-Benz's following and photographing school girls in the same locations Dutroux was kidnapping them.

Investigators learnt these men were part of a network which put together catalogues of prospective kidnapping victims for clients. A client could pick a girl by her photo and for a fee she would be snatched off the street and delivered to them. This is supposedly how Lothar Glandorf's scheme had operated in Germany, only targeting boys.

These white Mercedes were found to be company cars registered to a secondhand car exporting business called, *Achats Services Commerces*(ASCO), owned by a man named Michel Nihoul and run by associates of his.[460]

> "Asco's manager was the Frenchman Jean-Louis Delamotte, an old acquaintance of Nihoul from the Brussels sex party scene. Other founders were Michel Forgeot, manager of the bar Le Dolo, which was much discussed in the Dutroux case, and Marleen De Cokere, Nihoul's life companion. After only four years, financial difficulties arose, which led to bankruptcy in October 1995. Delamotte had long since packed up his things and in the year and a half before that, Nihoul apparently played manager there, a position he was no longer allowed to hold due to a series of previous convictions for fraud…The compa-

ny Asco was briefly in the spotlight at the end of '96 because, a year before Marc Dutroux was arrested, the La Louvière police had indications that this company, which had a number of white Mercedes through a branch, might have played a role in a number of attempted child abductions. That is why the public prosecutor's office in Neufchâteau and the Verwilghen committee attached great importance to Nihoul's precise function. And also because the name of the curator's husband appeared in Marc Dutroux's private administration." [Dutch to English Translation]
—'Nihoul vrijuit in faillissement duister autobedrijfje'('Nihoul free in bankruptcy dark car company'), De Morgen, November 29 1999

Michel Nihoul was a quasi-underworld figure who brushed shoulders with prominent figures of the 'clean professions' at a nightclub called *The Dolo*. He'd been a well-known libertine during the 1980s, known for hosting socialite sex parties at a chateau, sex parties Nihoul supposedly filmed, *"He was known in the 1980s for his lavish parties — supposedly attended by prominent businessmen, lawyers, doctors and government officials — at a magnificent rented chateau in the Ardennes. These events are said to have included 'carnality shows' and, often, orgies that were regularly videotaped by Nihoul."*[461]

Both Michele Martin(Dutroux's wife) and Michel Lelievre(accomplice) would state Dutroux had kidnapped his victims based upon orders received from Michel Nihoul.[462] Dutroux would later admit this as well during his 2004 trial.[463]

"LELIEVRE'S HEARING. When they were looking for a girl she had to comply with the order. DUTROUX asked NIHOUL for places to employ girls in BELGIUM. NIHOUL said yes, that he could bring

some back from SLOVAKIA. DUTROUX came into contact with people in SLOVAKIA and CZECHIA. DUTROUX said it was easy because there the girls were often alone in the evening by bike. DUTROUX said he raped one and abandoned her on the spot near TRENCIN. editor's note: check if young girl raped and murdered near TRENCIN. A man came to SARS with MERCEDES 190 old model. DUTROUX was scared - the man demanded money from him. Editor's note: DUTROUX hearing on this subject. He already saw this man in the cafe at SARS. It was a little after the kidnapping of AN and EEF. He saw AN and EEF naked. DUTROUX said that like that she couldn't escape. He also saw one of the two cleaning the tiles. Afterwards he said that the people who ordered came to see the girls but they were not interested in them." [Flemish to French to English Translation]
— PV 100.225 HEARING of Michel LELIEVRE, X-Dossier summary, 1235 pages, 2005, published by Wikileaks in 2009.

Phone records from early August 1996, around the time of Laetitia Delhez's kidnapping, showed Nihoul had made over twenty calls to Marc Dutroux, *"On August 13 at 1 p.m., Dutroux, his wife Michelle Martin and Lelièvre are arrested. Their telephone traffic is being monitored. One song stands out. In the days just before and just after the kidnapping, Dutroux and Nihoul called more than twenty times."*[464]

Nihoul was charged as an accomplice in the kidnapping of Laetitia Delhez on August 16 alongwith two of his associates.[465] These were a disbarred lawyer named Annie Bouty and Nihoul's girlfriend Marleen De Cokere, who was linked to the hardcore child porno studio in Amsterdam called *Roxanne Films/Rex Productions*, mentioned in the previous chapter.

From Nihoul's home police seized hundreds of videotapes of violent child pornography, some which had allegedly featured prominent people,[466] *"Following Nihoul's arrest in August, the police searched his residence and secured 300 videos, some said to contain footage of high-society figures and others of child pornography. Last autumn, segments of one such video -- showing a middle-aged man beating a 9-year-old -- were broadcast on the European satellite network RTL."*[467]

Nihoul would himself openly boast of having sexual blackmail on powerful individuals during an interview he granted the German newspaper *Der Spiegel* in 2001, in the lead up to his trial:

"Then he talks about the past. How he and Marleen threw group sex parties 'but in style!' attended by influential politicians and officials. In the Le Dolo club or in the Faulx-Les-Tombes rental castle near Namur. There should be photos and film recordings of these amusements. Nihoul likes to flirt with his guest list. One of the first sentences was: *'I have the government in my hands'*, He's just a trader. He deals in everything he can get his hands on. With fish, with pills, with women and lately with stories. An interview costs 1,000 marks: *'Add another 20,000 and I'll send you an incumbent minister who is involved in a murder.'* Allegedly everything can be proven: *'I know the murderer and have him call the minister. You're listening, okay?'*. Then Nihoul asks to turn off the recorder and lowers his voice. There's another special offer. For a six-figure sum. *'Because then I would have to leave Belgium. I give you the photo of the then Prince Albert jumping on a 16-year-old girl. Naked. Recorded on the second floor of the Mirano Club 20 years ago'* " [German to English Translation]

—'Im Netz der Dossiers'("In the network of dossiers"), Der

Spiegel, October 14 2001

In late August 1996 a senior detective named Georges Zicot who headed the auto theft division of Charleroi PD was arrested and charged for insurance fraud and document forgery regarding a stolen truck. The detective had been an associate of Bernard Weinstein, the accomplice of Marc Dutroux who'd been killed in November 1995 just prior to Dutroux's arrest on auto theft charges, which had involved the kidnapping of three teenagers and a stolen truck.[468] A further nine Charleroi police officers were questioned over suspected links to either Dutroux or Nihoul, and another from the city of Dinant was detained and questioned over their association with Nihoul as well.[469]

The judge initially assigned to oversee the investigation into Marc Dutroux, and by extension the network linked to him, was Jean-Marc Connerotte. A magistrate who'd established a reputation as a crusader during a prior investigation into the 1991 assassination of a former Belgian deputy prime minister named Andre Cools. Connerotte had been removed from that case in 1994 in a move widely seen as having been a cover-up of his findings by his higher-ups.[470]

These political overtones carried over into the Dutroux investigation when the family of Andre Cools accused the Minister of Justice Melchior Wathelet, who ordered Dutroux's early release in 1992, of having played a role in the cover-up of the investigation into Cools assassination.[471] The accusations came after a motorcycle matching the description of one used by the assassins was excavated from the grounds of one of Dutroux's properties(or one linked to him) in September 1996 during the searches for his victim's bodies.[472]

Given the evidence of Dutroux's connection to Nihoul, and Nihoul to sex parties involving powerful people, Judge Connerotte appealed for victims of a suspected child sex trafficking network catering to a powerful clientele to come forward, and having demonstrated his willingness to investigate the matter, eight people identifying themselves as victims did. These became known as the X-witnesses.[473]

In September 1996 Connerotte assigned a team led by a prosecutor named Michel Bourlet to investigate the voracity of X-witness claims. Over a matter of months this team compiled x-witness statements and their findings from investigations into these, within a highly classified dossier known as the *X-Dossier*.

A month after the *X-Dossier* investigation began, Judge Connerotte was replaced as the overseeing magistrate in October after eating a plate of spaghetti at a public function held in support of Dutroux's victims. His removal sparked a series of large scale protests known as the White Marches. Up to 300,000 Belgians dressed in white took to the streets in protest of what was viewed as a coverup of connections discovered between a criminal network linked to Dutroux and powerful individuals. These demonstrations included wide-spread labor union strikes and spectacles such as firemen hosing down the courts of justice with their trucks.[474]

When these protests subsided the *X-Dossier* team were accused of fabricating evidence and silently replaced as well. However, the classified *X-Dossier* they had compiled was then leaked to Flemish journalists in 1997, who released details of it within a 1999 book entitled, *The X-Files: What Belgium Was Not Supposed to Know About the Dutroux Affair*.[475] Another book published on the *X-Dossier* in 2001 led to a lawsuit brought against its publisher by the head of the Belgian monarchy King Albert.[476] The same monarch Michel Nihoul boasted having a photo of jumping on a naked 16 year-old.[477]

A summary of the *X-Dossier* was then compiled by court order for the eventual trial of Marc Dutroux in 2004. A copy of this highly classified summary document, dated from 2005, was then leaked to Wikileaks, who released it to the public without redaction in April 2009.[478] [Extensive footnote for those interested]

> "The recent publication of secret documents on Wikileaks is causing trouble in Belgium: Sensitive investigative files from the case of the convicted child molester Marc Dutroux have been uploaded to the disclosure portal. Liège Attorney General Cédric Visart de Bocarmé told Belgian broadcaster RTBF on Wednesday that he was "unhappy because the documents come from trial files that are still classified." [German to English]
> — 'Enthüllungen sorgen für Ärger'("Revelations cause trouble"), Suddeutsche Zeitung, August 25 2010

Much of what the *X-Dossier* contains is hard to believe. It describes allegations of extreme acts of sexual violence against children, and I do mean extreme, committed by some of the most high profile individuals in Belgium at the time. Politicians. Magistrates. Royalty. Some it reads like literal excerpts from libertine pornography written by Marques de Sade, particularly his novel *120 Days of Sodom*. Which was adapted into an Italian film called *Salo* by director Pier Paolo Pasolini.

Pasolini's film is about four leaders from institutions within the fascist Republic of Salo in Italy; a Bishop, a Magistrate, a Duke, and a President; who meet at a palatial estate in the twilight of WW2 to solidify their alliance through marrying each others daughters during a black mass ritual involving the torture, rape and murder of a group of kidnapped youths. Pasolini had made a point of dressing the guards of these fascist leaders in uniforms of the *Decima Flottiglia MAS*, a former regiment of the Italian Navy commanded by Junio Valerio Borghese. This was an aristocrat known as the Black

Prince of Borghese descended from the Borghese family of the Italian black nobility.

In 1943 Mussolini established a Nazi puppet state in Northern Italy tucked up underneath the breast of Germany, called The Republic of Salo. The Black Prince and his *Decima Flottiglia MAS* were a prominent piece of the army there that continued to fight the allies in the northern territories under the Republic's administration, right up until the very end of WW2.

Unlike some fascist collaborators strung up beside Mussolini in the Piazzale Loreto, Junio Borghese had been chaperoned to the sanctuary of Vatican City by OSS spook James Angleton. Borghese then became the primary OSS(CIA) asset in establishing the Italian branch of Operation Gladio's stay-behind network, designed to quash left-leaning political movements there. Because of this the Black Prince lived on to become a figurehead of Italy's post-war fascist movement.

Paolo Pasolini made *Salo* in response to an Italian fascist coup attempt in 1970, orchestrated by Junio Borghese and carried out in his name, known as the *Golpe Borghese coup*. After it failed, Borghese had fled to Spain where he died in 1974, possibly poisoned.

A year after, and just prior to *Salo's* theatrical premiere, Pasolini was murdered horrifically in 1975. Film reels from another production Pasolini was working on were stolen, and he reportedly went to meet with the thieves who demanded payment for their return. His partially burnt remains were found on a dusty beachside football pitch, with most of his bones broken and his testicles smashed in with a blunt object.[479]

If you read film analysis on *Salo* you'll generally get a lot of *Salo is a metaphor for this or that*. However, perhaps Pasolini's intent had been to show something quite literal.

In 1981 a fascist secret society called P2(*Propaganda 2*),

linked to the *Golpe Borghese coup* attempt a decade earlier, was uncovered after a membership list fell into police hands during the raid of a villa belonging to an Italian financier named Licio Gelli.

> "The list of names, some of which had been leaked to the press in preceding weeks, included three Cabinet ministers, two under secretaries, 30 members of parliament including the leader of the Social Democratic Party, 170 top military officers, the Foreign Ministry's highest ranking diplomat, scores of high-ranking civil servants and public officials, magistrates, industrialists, university professors, policemen and journalists, including the editor and publisher of Italy's most prestigious daily newspaper, Corriere della Sera."
> — 'Scandal Erupts Over Italian Masonic Lodge', The Washington Post, May 26 1981.

The most notable P2 member was future Italian Prime Minister Silvio Berlusconi, who would later be prosecuted for hosting underage sex orgies at his palatial estate in 2010.[480] Another was Alessandro Moncini, a member of Italy's old money industrialist establishment in the seaport city of Trieste.

In 1988 Americans casually eating breakfast would read about this member of the P2 Lodge,[481] traveling to the United States to purchase a 10 year-old Mexican girl for a ritual seemingly similar to the one Pasolini had "explored as a metaphor" in his film *Salo*.

> "An Italian businessman was arrested at Kennedy Airport after a California undercover cop promised him a 10-year-old girl for a weekend of sadistic sex, authorities said yesterday. Alessandra Moncini, 47, owner of a tire company in Trieste and the married father of a 20-year-old daughter, was nabbed in New York last week in a trap set by federal prosecutors in

Los Angeles...Authorities said Moncini, in tape-recorded telephone conversations, expressed a desire to either rent or buy a 10-year-old girl in the U.S for hard sex. The tapes, which were not included in the indictment, are part of an active probe by California officials into Moncini's affairs. Moncini described in lurid detail what he planned to do with his intended victim, authorities said. *'He told him about whipping her, putting spikes into her body and forcing her to eat excrement and to drink urine,'* Assistant U.S Attorney Dave Shapiro told U.S Magistrate Carol Amon yesterday during a detention hearing at Brooklyn Federal Court...Shaprio said Moncini also had told the undercover cop about a prior encounter with a 13-year-old Brazilian girl he had rented. He said the businessman told the cop: *'It was hard sex, but not very hard sex —she didn't die,'* He also told the agent that he had a snuff videotape of the real murder of a young girl after sex. Lawyer Jonathon Marks said Moncini was 'flabbergasted' over the allegations. *'He's well-respected in his country and he cannot believe that anyone would take this seriously,'* Marks said. *'To him, all this is pure fantasy'*."

— 'Sex trap nets exec: He bit on offer to buy a girl, 10',
Ruben Rosario, Daily News, March 24 1988

Trieste was part of the former Republic of Salo, and being a seaport city had strong left-leaning labor union movement after the war. This had made it one of the first targets in *Operation Gladio* using former *Decima Flottiglia MAS* operatives under Borghese's direction in 1953.

Like the film *Salo*, the *X-Dossier* contains accounts of youths being tortured and murdered at orgies attended by prominent members of Belgian society. Politicians. Magistrates. Barons. Royalty. Ones closely linked to Europe's neo-fascist movement and *Operation Gladio*.

The reason why some parts of the *X-Dossier* should be taken seriously is largely to do with verified accounts provided by the first witness to come forward, known as X1, whose identity was leaked to the press as a woman named Regina Louf.

It should be mentioned X1 suffered from a condition called *Dissociative Identity Disorder*(Multiple Personality Disorder), which is almost exclusively diagnosed in those who experience extreme trauma in early childhood. This is touched on later in greater depth, as it would be used to discredit her. In my opinion X1's testimony is both credible and unreliable, and should be considered with the following maxim in mind:

"it is the mark of an educated mind to be able to entertain a thought without accepting it."

X1 claimed she was raised as a child prostitute by her grandmother and in her early teens sold to a pimp named Tony Van den Boggaert, a friend of her family. She was leased out as 'entertainment' at what she described as 'abuse parties' organised by Michel Nihoul during the 1980s, and claimed Marc Dutroux had attended these parties where he functioned as a sort of caterer, suppling attendees with drugs, girls, and other kinds of vice.[482] As she grew older she learnt these parties served a pragmatic purpose of bonding loyalties through sexual blackmail, and explained how the business aspects of Nihoul's operation worked in a book she published on her experiences in 1998:

> "In Brussels in the Avenue Louise there was a mansion with a room equipped with built-in cameras. Even during the seventies these cameras were so silent that only the people operating them and the child prostitute knew where they were. We were informed because it was our job to position the cus-

tomer in such a way that he was very' visible for the camera lens. The cameras couldn't zoom in or change position because this could be heard...I understood also why sex was not the most important factor. The contracts signed between the abusers were arranged and discussed, before I went to bed with them, when I was having dinner with them. I was the carrot held in front of the donkey to make him move. It also happened that the parties agreed to sign the contract after the sex. Appetizer or desert, this made no difference to me, to them it was a way to make them keep their promises, unwritten agreements with an enormous binding power. From the moment one has had sex with a child, one is chained, unless all parties involved keep their mouth shut. And then, nothing tastes sweeter than a child, I once heard from one of the abusers. Contracts between business and the political world, contracts among business people, cheating with subsidies or permits, the establishing of fake companies, criminal contracts, and illegal arms trade, nothing was impossible. And it always ended with sex and children. When the deal was good, the other party got the services for free. They then were allowed to do all kind of immoral things with one or more children, for free. Pictures were taken, jokingly, to keep both parties to their contract. I'm convinced that these compromising photographs must have abruptly wiped the smile off many men's faces, when they were discretely, in an envelope, put on their office desks, a long time after the effects of booze and the euphoria were finished." [Flemish to English]
— 'Zwijgen is voor daders - De getuigenis van X1' ('Silence is for perpetrators - The testimony of X1'), Regina Louf, 1998

According to X1, a higher and higher intensity of violence

against child prostitutes would be gradually encouraged to further solidify these bonds, *"Step by step, customers who at first were very careful in bed with me were pushed to become more violent. I was ordered to facilitate this because the combination of sex and violence is extremely compromising. No offender could afford to break silence after he had done this. They became partners in crime with strong ties to each other. None of them was inclined to conclude contracts with outsiders. The penalty for this could be extremely high but that was way over my head."*[483]

According to X1, as these children got older they became a liability and were made available to murder for a fee. What X1 called the final stage, *"I pretended to like their advances, I fought back when they wanted me to, I played their games. That way I remained important and didn't end up in the final stage. Because hidden very well from the outside world, children did die at the request of customers who could afford the money. The child prostitutes knew this very well and the longer they had been part of the network, the more threatening it became. The risk that children would break the code of silence increased with their age indeed."*[484]

X1 testified children would usually be killed in one of three ways. At an abuse party, at a factory used as a snuff film studio, or during something called a 'hunt':

> "The hunts were generally organised during the official hunting season which is in October - November, although they sometimes did it during summer too. The number of tourists in the Ardennes is low in the fall and the sound of gunshots is normal in that period of the year. In the area close to Namur the hunters only used crossbows. That was more silent. In the other area East of Bouillon they also used shotguns because the area is very remote. The rules of the hunt were basically the same as in Knokke. The children had to run into the woods and the hunters tried to catch them. At the boundary of the area in which

the children had to stay, guards with dogs were posted so no one could run away. If a child got caught it had to take off a piece of clothing and was hunted again. When it was totally naked the hunter who had paid for it could do whatever he wanted with it, depending on the amount of money paid. Usually two sometimes three children were killed during a standard hunt." [Flemish to English]
— 'Zwijgen is voor daders - De getuigenis van X1' ('Silence is for perpetrators - The testimony of X1'), Regina Louf, 1998

X1 gave accounts of many victims murdered in these ways, but four in particular led to the reopening of cold case murders by *X-Dossier* investigators who interviewed her.

One of these was a detailed account X1 gave of the torture and murder of a girl named "Chrissie" at a factory farm in 1984. The details X1 provided matched those of the murder of 14 year-old Christine Van Hees, whose body had been discovered on an old mushroom farm in 1984. X1's description of the crime scene, unavailable to the public nor published in any newspaper, matched those of the cold case file so precisely that even those who would later discredit X1's testimony were forced to claim the *X-Dossier* investigators had fed her this information as part of a conspiracy against the accused. The victim's body had been badly burnt and bound with ligature fixed to the neck running down to the ankles, one wrist had a penetration wound caused by a metal nail-like object.

X1 claimed she'd witnessed a group of men torture Chrissie in this way in the basement of a factory on the farm and then set her on fire. Those she accused of having participated in this were: Michel Nihoul, Marc Dutroux, Bernard Weinstein, and a lawyer named Michel Vander Elst.[485] This lawyer had ties with Nihoul and the video processing company where Dutroux's associate Bernard Weinstein had worked.[486]

When investigators checked the cold case files they discovered it was noted back in 1984 Christine Van Hees often visited locations also frequented by Michel Nihoul and Marc Dutroux at that time. As it was reported in 1998:

> "An analysis of the old file shows that there is a real chance that they both crossed paths with Christine Van Hees at the beginning of 1984. Nihoul was active at the free radio station Radio Activité, located above the swimming pool where Christine Van Hees used to swim every week. The old file contains a never-exploited testimony against Nihoul's stamface Le Dolo. In 1984, witnesses also talk about a friend of Christine Van Hees who drives an American car with an eagle on the hood. Nihoul drove such a car. Francis H., the companion with whom Marc Dutroux went to harass girls at the skating rinks - including Michelle Martin - was active at the time at a free station: Radio Arc-en-Ciel in Schaarbeek. A certain Philippe M. also worked there, whose name was found in the personal telephone book of Christine Van Hees. The girl would have regularly skipped school to spend time with him. At the end of 1983, H. and Dutroux often went skating on the Poseidon in Woluwe. Christine Van Hees came there every week." [Dutch to English]
> — 'Who did not kill Christine Van Hees?', DeMorgen, September 22 1998

Investigators then discovered the judge who'd been assigned to Christine Van Hees' murder case in 1984 was a magistrate named Jean-Claude Van Espen, who turned out to be a close friend and business partner of Michel Nihoul.

When the Christine Van Hees' case was reopened under the auspices of the X-Dossier investigation in 1996, now with

Michel Nihoul as a prime suspect, Van Espen hadn't recused himself until after his conflict of interest was brought to light by a journalist two years later. And had in fact interfered with the investigation.

"For 12 years the unsolved murder of Van Hees gathered dust in the Brussels files under the direction of Judge Van Espen. Two years ago a Belgian journalist revealed the close relationship between Judge Van Espen and Nihoul and his then wife. As a lawyer, Van Espen had represented Nihoul's wife. Van Espen's sister was the godmother of Nihoul's child. Yet, when Louf accused these two of the murder, Judge Van Espen saw no conflict of interest, no reason to resign. Nor was he sacked, as Connerotte had been. Instead he was allowed to order the police officers to stay out of the case. Van Espen only resigned as the judge in charge of the mushroom factory investigation in early 1998 after his relationship with Nihoul was exposed."
— 'Belgium's silent heart of darkness', The Observer, May 5 2002

X1 detailed the death of another girl named "Clo", a girl she said had gotten pregnant at one of Michel Nihoul's sex parties. X1 said she was taken to a house in 1983 and found Clo locked inside a room on the brink of giving birth. She helped deliver the baby, which had been taken, and Clo was left in the room bleeding. X1 believed Clo died giving birth. After this X1 said she had been gang-raped by a group of men, among whom she identified: Michel Nihoul, the lawyer Michel Vander Elst, and Count Leopold Lippens. The latter of the accused was a longtime Mayor of Knokke-Heist from a prominent family with a controlling interest in Belgium's most powerful financial institution, Societe Generale de Belgique.[487]

X1 provided the name of a school she thought "Clo" had

gone to and was presented with a yearbook from the class of 1981-82. From the photos she identified "Clo" as a student named Carine Dellaert, who went missing in 1982 and whose body was found in 1985 inside a septic tank. It was reported the autopsy report on Carine Dellaert's body at the time had stated, *"At the level of the pelvis is a piece of tender woody tissue. It is a piece of a laminaria stick, an ancient medicine used to enlarge the cervix in order to easily do the conception. The drug is used very little, as it causes a lot of pain to the mother." - "Presence on a cup of a rectangular piece of gauze, indicating swelling of the breasts and fluid loss. This is common in nulliparous women." (note: nulliparous are women who give birth for the first time)."*[488]

X1 then identified a second girl from another photo in the yearbook as one who was murdered in a snuff film during an abuse party sometime in 1982. Those present at the party X1 said were: Carine Dellaert, her father Emile Dellaert, Michel Nihoul, and two brothers named Joost and Albert Bert who owned a cinema company called *Decatron NV*.[489]

The photo X1 identified was of a girl named Veronique Dubrulle who died of cancer in 1983. Her father had been an administrator of *Decatron NV* named Jacques Dubrulle, who later became chairman of the International Film Festival of Flanders.[490] Veronique Dubrulle's death certificate listed her cause of death as given by two neurologists, who X1 identified as abusers in Nihoul's network.[491]

A fourth victim X1 had identified from a series of photographs of murder victims thought to have been used in child pornography. This was a girl named Katrien de Cuyper who disappeared in 1991. X1 said the girl was murdered during a party at a Castle, later identified as one belonging to a Baron named Philippe de Caters. According to the cold case file, Katrien de Cuyper was last seen making a phone call from inside a building that housed a Dutch porn studio called X-Kiss, which was linked to Gerrit Ulrich's operation in

Zandvoort:

"The last sign of life that Katrien De Cuyper gave was a phone call from a café on the Antwerp Yzerlaan. She informed her parents that she would be home a little later. The cafe was called 'Les Routiers'. The Belgian branch of a Dutch porn company was located on the top floor. The name of the same company has repeatedly cropped up in the investigation into the Zandvoort affair in the Netherlands. Bank certificates were found in Gerrie Ullrich's private records showing deposits to the same porn company. The pocket diary of Ullrich's life partner (and alleged murderer), the Belgian Robby Van der Plancken, contained the company's name and Dutch telephone number." [Dutch to English]

— 'Is dit Katrien De Cuyper?'('Is this Katrien De Cuyper?'),
De Morgen, June 22 1999

Members of the *Morkhoven Workgroup* believed they had identified Katrien de Cuyper in pornographic photos found on the *Apollo Disks*.[492] Which served as one of the major suspected connections between the Dutroux investigation and a web of snuff pornography rings interlinked with *Apollo Bulletin Boards*.

X1 spoke of many more murders, but only those four were traced to cold cases and investigated before the initial *X-Dossier* team started to be replaced in early 1997.

Many of these other victims X1 claimed had been killed at a factory on the outskirts of Brussels used as a snuff porn studio. According to the book *Les X-Dossiers,* written by the journalists the *X-Dossier* was leaked to, *"At the time, she talked about a secret studio where snuff movies were recorded. On the E40 Brussels-Link she had pointed to exit Sterrebeek. From there she made the inspectors drive until a crossing. 'Go left here', she said. A few miles down the road she made the car stop. That's it, 'the factory'. De Pauw looked and saw a large board with a name on it."*[493]

In her own book X1 explained how she'd accurately described the factories interior, *"I also explained how they made child porn and snuff movies, many times with dogs, in the factory that I would recognise a little later when Danny, one of the detectives, look me on a tour in Zaventem near Brussels. I described very accurately the inside of the building and the awful smell of the cleaning product, I guess it was Detol, they used to clean the bloodspots."*[494]

The factory belonged to *ASCO Industries NV*, an aerospace company owned by a military industrialist named Roger Boas, a close associate of politicians, lawyers, and financiers orbiting Belgium's *Parti Social Chretien* (Christian Social Party - CSP). This was a political faction, at its fringes aligned with Belgium's neofascist movement and *Operation Gladio*, a post-WW2 effort by NATO bloc spy agencies to tamper the dialectic swing away from fascism towards left-leaning political movements.

In Belgium a bulk of industrial firms were controlled by a holding company called *Societe Generale de Banque*(*Society General*), the largest financial firm in the country controlled by a fraternity of families who provided most of the funding for CSP political campaigns. A group of prominent figures involved with this political party, and this financial firm backing it, were identified in the X-Dossier as powerful figures in a network of child abusers linked to Michel Nihoul. Among these X1, and later other x-witnesses, would name or identify two former Belgian Prime Ministers affiliated with the CSP, Wilfried Martens and Paul Vanden Boeynants; a director of *Society General* named Baron Benoit de Bonvoisin; a chairman of *Society General* named Count Leopold Lippens, and his brother Count Francois Lippens; a magistrate named Melchior Wathelet, who served on the European Court of Justice;

and a powerful Brussels attorney named Jean-Paul Dumont, a close associate of many of the above and Michel Nihoul.[495]

It is through Jean-Paul Dumont a link to the *Spartacus Network* was made during the *X-Dossier* investigation. According to the leaked *X-Dossier* summary, Jean-Paul Dumont had acted as the attorney for a number of high profile individuals implicated in a child porn operation housed in the headquarters of UNICEF in Belgium during the 1980s.[496]

In June 1987 the head of UNICEF in Belgium and another employee were arrested for using the basement of the UNICEF HQ as a child pornography studio and using computers there to share these materials internationally.

"The scandal erupted last week, when the Belgian police arrested Jos Verbeek, 63 years old, the director of Unicef's Belgian committee, and charged him with inciting minors to debauchery. The arrest followed the discovery of a secret photographic studio in the basement of the Brussels building where the committee's offices are housed. The studio was used to take pornographic photographs of children, many of whom were of North African origin, the police said. The police said more than 1,000 such photographs were seized, along with a mailing list of some 400 names in 15 European countries that had been prepared on the Unicef office computer."
— 'CHILD SEX SCANDAL ROILS UNICEF UNIT', New York Times, June 25 1987

According to an investigator named Andrew Rogge, the UNICEF computer system was used to serve clients of 'a network', and a police commissioner named Yves Zimmer told him, *"You can drop this affair. We will not be able to go further. Some of the clients are highly placed."*[497]

This network was uncovered months earlier in March, after

the arrest of a former justice ministry official named Philippe Carpentier,[498] who was found operating a VIP child prostitution ring using a front organisation called *The Centre for Research and Information on Childhood and Sexuality(CRIES)*, "*The Government was highly embarrassed by the news that a former justice ministry, Philippe Carpentier, was one of those arrested, together with a close associate, a top government official working on highly sensitive anti-terrorist legislation.*"[499] CRIES claimed to help pedophiles deal with their sexuality and was located within a diplomatic neighbourhood of Brussels. A number of parents were found to be prostituting their children to pedophiles linked to the center, who were also taking them to the UNICEF building to be photographed.

Philippe Carpentier was partners with a Belgian priest named Joseph Douce,[500] a former NATO corporal with a psychology degree who founded a similar group in France called the *Centre du Christ Liberateur(CCL)*, which also fell under investigated in 1987.[501] This was a *very* progressive religious organisation that supported sexual minority groups such as sadomasochists and pedophiles, headquartered in an old porn theatre in central Paris.

In the late 1980s Douce distributed and managed the subscription list for a pedophile magazine called *Gaie France* produced by a Neo-Nazi child pornographer named Michel Caignet.[502] The magazine, and others like it published by Caignet, mostly dealt in softcore child pornography; photographs of naked children, but posed artistically, at times scantly dressed in the attire of Hitler Youth.

In 1995 it was discovered Caignet and two of his associates, Philippe Desnous(alias 'Bernard Alapetite') and Jean-Manuel Vuillaume, were producing films in Colombia distributed through a company called *Toro Bravo*, "*showing very young children gagged, tortured and raped.*"[503] Customer lists for these videos led to large scale search and seizure raids across France as part of an operation called *ADO 71* in '96 and '97, resulting in a spate of suicides among those arrested or questioned.[504]

"In a dawn sweep across France yesterday more than 2,500 gendarmes brought in for questioning at least 800 men suspected of selling or buying pornographic videos and other material involving young boys. Last night 345 were still in custody. The raid coincided with the start of the trial in Paris of 71 men and woman accused of trading in videos of children involved in sexual acts. The prosecution linked the trade with a neo-Nazi activist, Michel Caignet, publisher of the outlawed Gaie France magazine, which combined photographs of male adolescents with Nazi nostalgia."
— 'Hundreds held in swoop on French child porno suspects', The Guardian, June 18 1997.

"The inquiry began in 1994 when police raided the home of Daniel Waillez, who had advertised for under-aged contacts. His collection of films and magazines led them to La Moutte, a Paris company. Michel Caignet, its director, and Michel Meignez de Cacqueray, its treasurer, were arrested. Caignet said the films had been made in Colombia using boys hired by Toro Bravo, a Bogota company headed by Jean Manuel Vuillaume. Caignet claimed that the films were shot in Vuillaume's house and were then brought to France and duplicated for sale by mail order…Vuillaume, who was arrested at Roissy airport in 1995, has denied all connections with Toro Bravo, but prosecutors claim 38 pornography videos, sado-masochistic material and a child-sized toreador costume seen in one of the films were found in his house in

Bogota."
— '70 on trial in French child porn ring case', The Daily Telegraph, June 17 1997

A prior investigation into Michel Caignet and his *Toro Bravo* associates in 1989 led to the arrest of a British-born French pastor named Nicolas Glencross, who was using his rectory in the French commune of Saint-Leger-des -Vignes to take softcore child pornography photos of the type Caignet had published in *Gaie France*.[505]

Nicolas Glencross wasn't just any ordinary priest. He was the uncle of Peter Glencross, the commercial agent for John Stamford's *Spartacus International*, responsible for turning the *Elm Guest House* into a *Club Spartacus* spabath.[506] He was also politically connected all the way up to the French Presidential Palace. President Francoise Mitterrand had sent his most trusted advisor, Hubert Vedrine, to live at Glencross's parish to help establish him as a municipal candidate in Saint-Leger-des-Vignes and kickstart his political career.[507]

The connection between Nicolas Glencross and the *Toro Bravo* Neo-Nazi pornographers was through Pastor Joseph Douce.[508] After Glencross was charged in early July 1990,[509] a bookstore operated by Joseph Douce called *Autres cultures* was placed under surveillance, *"to discover possible links with pedophile networks, in particular with a network based in Holland."*[510] Douce had made frequent business trips to the Netherlands,[511] and a lead detective stated, *"My superiors asked me to investigate the possible existence of a pedophilia network which revolved around the bookstore run by the pastor. My real target was not the pastor, but a certain JS, an individual already involved in a pedophilia case and who frequented the place."*[512]

Joseph Douce then disappeared on July 19 1990, and his body was discovered in a forest a few months later. After his disappearance it had been reported Douce, *"was preparing to give names of people controlling the child trade,"*[513] and it was learnt an illegal wiretap countersigned by the Prime Minister's office had been placed on his bookstore.[514]

A strange series of events to digest no doubt. Perhaps 'JS' stood for John Stamford, who Douce would've been connected to given his other contacts with Edward Brongersma and Fritz Bernard, contributors to Francis Shelden's *PAN*, published under the *Spartacus* umbrella.[515] Not to mention Douce's connection to Philippe Carpentier and the CRIES/UNICEF investigation, which, as we shall learn, was connected to the *Spartacus Network* in other ways.

In the *X-Dossier* compiled some years later, a pedophile named Serge Heylens, who had been convicted of sexual crimes against children in 1989, provided investigators with a list of names which contained the following three in consecutive order:

"MEIER Beat. Creator of the pedophile publication LIBIDO.

BRONGERSMA. Ex-Dutch Senator.

CARPENTIER Philippe (deceased). Friend of DOUCE. Ex-president of CRIES."

— PV 102.712/96, Interview of Serge Heylens, X-Dossier summary, 1235 pages, 2005, published by Wikileaks in 2009, page 1031

As you may remember, Edward Brongersma was the Dutch Senator who was made trustee of Francis Shelden's offshored estate. The name listed just above his, Beat Meier, was the honorary President of the *Swiss Paedophile Association*, and a particularly sadistic child pornographer who published a pedophile magazine called *LIBIDO*.[516]

In late January 1987, just prior to the CRIES arrests later in March, Meier was caught smuggling a kidnapped 3 year-old boy from Belgium into the UK with another man named

Roger Lawrence, a close associate of Francis Shelden credited as an editor of *PAN* under the penname Roger E. Hunt.[517]

"The April 1986 issue of BLW contained a glowing tribute to Frank Torey[Francis Shelden] for his advice and support. The editor of that issue was listed as Martyn Simons. Simons had previously edited PAN magazine using the name Roger E. Hunt. Neither was his real name. Simons, aka Hunt, was born Roger Lawrence on 25 February 1946...He left Spartacus in January 1986 after a row with the organisation's leader, John Stamford. He went on to edit PAN and BLW. Just over a year later he met up with a Swiss paedophile named Beat Meier; together the two men packed a car and, on 24 January, drove it on to the midday Ostend-to-Dover ferry. As the car drove off the ferry and up to an immigration checkpoint officer, Mike Staunton of the Dover Harbour Board, police stepped forward and asked to see Meier's papers. Meier handed over his Swiss passport and Lawrence his British one, but Staunton noticed something in the back of the car, covered by a blanket. He asked Meier to show him. Dimitri Thevenin owes a great deal to Officer Staunton."

— 'Child Pornography: An Investigation', Tim Tate, 1990

"Police are poised to smash an international child-porn ring following the arrest of a man wanted in four countries. He was held at Dover after trying to get a kidnapped three-year-old boy into Britain. Both the middle-aged man and little Dimitri Thevenin were in a car driven off a ferry from Belgium three weeks ago. The man, thought to be leader of the evil child-sex organisation, produced papers which he claimed gave him legal custody of the boy. These were found to be forged."

— 'Police Smash Child-Sex Ring', Daily Mirror, February 16 1987

In addition to the child, customs agents discovered a large amount of child pornography in the car,[518] including a photograph in Meier's possession which showed a baby girl, no more than 8 months-old, being tortured with a speculum.[519] It was later learnt Meier had been taking boys from Britain to Zurich throughout the 1980s, with their parents permission, to be used in sadomasochist pornography with other men. *"The video films he made were found at another address in Zurich, along with a huge amount of films and photographs of sexual activity— including some of an even more serious nature involving a young child and a baby,"*[520] and, *"a court heard yesterday that other men were also expected to face serious charges in connection with sexual assaults on many youngsters—one a girl only six months old, shown being attacked in video films."*[521]

Similar videos were found at the UNICEF headquarters months, and a Swiss member of the CRIES network was later arrested for attempting to sell these films in the UK, *"Police in Britain are helping to uncover the secrets of a child-sex ring run from a cellar under the Brussels offices of the United Nations children's organisation. A man, believed to be Swiss, has been arrested in Manchester for organising the sale of pornographic films to wealthy British clients. The youngest child in the films was an eight-month-old baby, and the oldest only 12."*[522]

In the mid 1990s Beat Meier then became a suspect in Scotland Yard's snuff investigation. In 1993 two British pedophiles named Richard Mercer and David Barry were caught returning from Amsterdam in possession of 9 video tapes. One tape showed a young girl being beaten, raped, and tortured with needles. Another showed the brutal bondage rape of a boy around age 9 by two masked men. Investigators managed to identify the victim of this film as one of the British boys Beat Meier had taken to Zurich in the 1980s.[523]

Scotland Yard then received information from Interpol in Luxembourg a convicted pedophile imprisoned there named Jean Michel Klopp had information on British children killed in snuff films. Klopp was an associate of another Swiss pedophile named Karl Hobi, who was a founding member of the *Swiss Pedophile Association* with Beat Meier. Klopp claimed Meier had been involved in the rape and murder of a 4 year-old English girl, and Karl Hobi had shown him a snuff film featuring a British boy in 1989. A portion of the transcript from the interview of Jean Klopp by a Scotland Yard detective named Bob McLachlan is as follows:

"Mr Klopp, are you willing to be interviewed about matters relating to paedophilia in England?"

—*"Yes"*

"Are you prepared to give an account of the facts to the best of your knowledge and belief?"

—*"Yes. In my opinion the facts I am going to reveal are so horrific that the people responsible should be punished."*

"You saw a film in which a child was killed?"

—*"When I was staying with Karl Hobi about 5 years ago [1989], Hobi showed me in confidence a video cassette in which a boy was tortured, mutilated, and probably died afterwards from what was done to him."*

"Why did he show you the film?"

—*"He showed it to me because he thought I might be able to find some customers for the film; I had already found customers for other films"*

"How much were you going to sell the film for?"

—*"About 40,000 Luxembourg francs [£650]."*

"Was it a video cassette?"

—*"Yes"*

"Was the film made with a video camera or a normal old type of camera; was the quality good or bad?"

—*"No, it was a video camera. You could tell that from*

the grain. The quality was average, and you could see it was a copy and not the master tape."

"What did Hobi say to you before you watched the film?"

— "He said it was a new kind of film for a new clientele and this type of film could make a lot more money because of what was in it."

"Tell us what you saw in the film, from beginning to end."

—[Scotland Yard detective omits this portion of the interview in his book, but notes, *"Klopp described the violent death of a small boy at the hands of his masked killers. From time to time, he would make reference to detail within the images captured on the film, which suggested to us that, although he had never been here, the events had taken place in England."*]

"Was there sound on the film?"

— "No."

"What where you told about the boy and the men?"

— "Hobi told me he was a boy the men didn't know; he had been picked up in the street. After the film, I asked Hobi a lot of questions about where it was made, about the child and the adults. He told me he only knew that Meier had organised it."

— Monsters and Men(also published under title 'The Hunt for Britain's Paedophiles'), Bob Long & DCI Bob McLachlan, Hodder & Stoughtonpage(2003), page 81-82

Karl Hobi and Beat Meier, both in prison at the time, refused to be interviewed regarding the allegations.

It appears Beat Meier's arrest with his *Spartacus/PAN* associate Roger Lawrence in late January 1987 is what had led to the arrests of his *CRIES* associates later in March, and then finally those at UNICEF in July.

To repeat an except from a news report on *CRIES* from July

1987, *"The Government was highly embarrassed by the news that a former justice ministry, Philippe Carpentier, was one of those arrested, together with a close associate, **a top government official working on highly sensitive anti-terrorist legislation.**"*[524] This close associate in question was a translator at the Ministry of Justice's anti-terrorist division named Michel Decre,[525] who received a seven year sentence as, *"one of the organizers of 'special evenings' where child prostitutes from Cries appeared."*[526]

In October 2001 Michel Decre was arrested once more, this time in relation to the seizure of 15 cubic meters of CDRoms, photographs, and video cassettes from the home of a former gravedigger named Jacques Delbouille, who had also been arrested during the *CRIES* investigation but released without charge.[527]

Rather bizarrely, it was reported by the Belgian newspaper *Le Soir* that Delbouille was 'believed' to have been an associate of Marc Dutroux's accomplice Bernard Weinstein, whom Dutroux had drugged and buried alive sometime in November/December 1995.[528]

> "At his home too, the investigators, greeted by Delbouille who brandished a sword, had got their hands on images of a pedophile nature, but he had managed to secure part of his collections. The investigators were also confronted in the sixty-year-old's cellar with two coffins containing the corpses...of two of his dogs. Delbouille is a strange character. A public writer, he is believed to have connections with Bernard Weinstein, Dutroux's murdered accomplice, whom he allegedly helped to write several letters and administrative forms."
>
> — 'Justice Plus de 15 m3 de documents saisis Les archives des pédophiles'("Justice More than 15 m3 of documents seized Pedophile archives"), Le Soir, October 2 2001

That Jacques Delbouille had apparently handled Bernard

Weinstein's mail correspondance is stranger than fiction. This is because a note found in a cabin belonging to Weinstein was used as the basis for a police raid on the *Abrasax Institute*,[529] an organisation involved in, "*the study and experimental research of human psychological and psychotronic faculties, as well as the development of alternative techniques in psychotherapy*"... among other things.[530] The cult name 'Anubis' used by institute's leader, a man named Francis Desmedt, was found signed on the note addressed to Bernard Weinstein, which read:

"Bernard, don't forget that the feast is nearing and that the high priestess expects her present, Anubis."

Now this gets into something I'd usually ignore as a red herring, however it's relevant to understanding the connection between the Dutroux investigation and John Stamford's *Spartacus Network*. Before continuing it's important to understand religious cults are often used by criminal organisations at the operational levels of drugs, weapons, and sex trafficking. This is a well-documented phenomenon since at least the 1960s. An example around the time of the Dutroux investigation would be the *Order of the Solar Temple's* involvement in arms trafficking and money laundering, which ended in a spate of well publicised 'murder-suicides' in the 1990s.[531] A more contemporary example would be the cultivation of *Santa Muerte* death cults by new-age Mexican drug cartels.

Basically, the *Abrasax Institute* was a Satanic cult, or gnostic sect if you like, which briefly became the center of attention during the Dutroux investigation around December 1996, much to the media's delight. Details of the investigation into the cult were leaked to journalists, who circulated reports of satanic child sacrifices, the *Abrasax Institute* was raided, nothing was found, and the credibility of the investigation was harmed. However, it turned out a few police officers were members of the *Abrasax Institute*,[532] and its leaders were tipped off to the investigation prior to the searches.[533]

A member of the *Abrasax Institute* named Armand Van Ghysegham appears to have been the primary focus of the investigation, not the institute itself. Ghysegham was a book publisher under the name Aba-Vangh, the owner of two esoteric bookstores in Brussels who seemingly spent much of his time in Thailand. Police went to search one of his bookstores during the *Abrasax* raids in December 1996 but found the property vacant with a 'for rent' sign.[534] It was learnt Ghysegham's publishing company declared bankruptcy in 1995, the same year John Stamford faced trial in Belgium, and the *X-Dossier* contains summary interviews with three of Ghysegham's former employees.

All three said Ghysegham was a pedophile who frequently visited Thailand for this purpose, one even stating he'd been involved in child trafficking. All three said he participated in black mass rituals held at the *Abrasax Institute*. And two mentioned Ghysegham had a wealthy benefactor named Dessy, who was his mistress.[535] This was identified as Suzanne Dessy, a member of a wealthy industrialist family who owned a controlling interest in a steel production plant called Forges de Clabecq.[536]

A few months earlier in the investigation, in November 1996, two members of the Dessy family are named by an anonymous witness in the *X-Dossier* as close associates of the lawyer Jean-Paul Dumont, who sent us off on the CRIES tangent.

In this part of the *X-Dossier* it is stated Dumont had been the lawyer for individuals under investigation in the CRIES case, including the brother of a former executive of the *Bank Brussels Lambert* named Georges Dessy. According to this witness, Georges Dessy's brother, who is only identified as

DESSY, was *"a member of the homosexual network SPARTACUS,"* and *"pays a lot of money for pedophile cassettes (tortures) and/or children."*[537]

Shortly after the interviews with Armand Van Ghyseghem's employees, which were conducted between December 21 1996 and January 14 1997, a note appears in the *X-Dossier* dated January 16 1997 linking John Stamford to Ghyseghem:

"Report PJ TURNHOUT dated 01/16/97

Anonymous witness says the STAMFORD file is linked to DUTROUX-NIHOUL

STAMFORD dossier = worldwide dissemination of the pedophile idea

And on the sidelines: trafficking in organs of foreign children

Witness hands over a copy of a VLAN advertisement for ABA VANGH (= VAN GYSEGHEM and GULDFUSCH)

According to info: VAN GYSEGHEM = friend of STAMFORD"

— 16/01/97 PJ TURNHOUT, X-Dossier summary, 1235 pages, 2005, published by Wikileaks in 2009

It appears prior to his death, Stamford was suspected, not only of producing snuff films, but trafficking in child organs. Which if you think about it, go hand in hand if one were to dismally reduce a life to the most amount of money that could be extracted from taking it. Apparently in Belgium they say, everyone knows everyone.

The real question remains, how did X1, through her family, come into the orbit of this lawyer Jean-Paul Dumont and other these powerful figures she claimed murdered children. And how much of her explanation for this was corroborated by others she grew up with.

* * *

X1 explained she had known these powerful men through her grandmother, a woman named Cecile Beernaert, who was married to a former police commissioner in the Belgian municipality of Knokke-Heist. Apparently her grandmother had been a brothel hostess named Madame Cecile, who operated a hotel-villa which catered to the perversions of Nazi officers during WW2. After the war she had become a widower and continued to run a brothel at another hotel-villa, which became a haunt for politicians and businessmen involved in Belgium's neo-fascist movement.[538]

X1 said she'd been used as a child prostitute at this hotel-villa, frequented by members of a nearby golf course called the Royal Zoute golf club. According to the *X-Dossier*, X1's grandmother lived in a house at the address, Golfpad 4, 8300 Knokke, Knokke-Heist, which was tucked discreetly behind a large hotel-villa located at Elizabetlaan 83, Knokke-Heist, located right on North-Western boundary of the Royal Zoute golf club.

This golfclub had belonged to a noble Belgian statesmen and banker named Count Maurice Auguste Lippens in the early 20th century, through whom it was granted a Royal title in 1925 by the Belgian monarchy. As such, the club became patronised by an exclusive mix of nobles and business elites, many with ties to the bank *Society General*, and the clubs custodianship remained within the Lippens family through one of Lippens' sons, who served as the Mayor of Knokke-Heist.[539]

It was here, in a hotel villa on the boundary of the Royal Zoute golf club, X1 claimed she'd been raped and tortured by clients of her grandmother, among whom she identified: Paul Vanden Boeynants, Maurice Lippens, and Michel Nihoul. This was how, according to X1, she'd ended up in Michel Nihoul's blackmail sex party circuit when she was older.[540]

A childhood friend of X1 identified as Natalie(or witness

X7) was interviewed by investigators and exhibited clear signs of trauma from sexual abuse in early childhood. Natalie and X1's parents had known each other, and Natalie thought something had happened to her as a child but couldn't clearly recall her own memories, only stating her father had been a sex maniac with a photo processing laboratory setup in their house she wasn't allowed into. Natalie only recalled having known X1's pimp Tony, and that this man had some kind of sexual relationship with X1 from an early age.[541]

Another childhood friend of X1 interviewed was identified as Chantal Storme. Chantal said she'd been prostituted to men at X1's grandmother's hotel-villa as well. She said she was taken there with X1 in early childhood, where the pair were forced to have sex with each other infront of men, who then took them to private rooms and raped them. She stated that when they misbehaved they were beaten with a metal ruler and often times threatened with a gun.[542]

> "She remembers having suffered violence in the house of the grandmother. She remembers a short old woman. The facts always took place in the same two rooms. She knew which room she had to go to. Description of the two rooms. In one, the facts were often committed with two children. In the other she called quick pleasures because men did not undress completely and always quick and painful sexual relations. Sometimes she was tied to the bed by X1 or her grandma. She also tied X1. The grandmother watched to see if she was obeying the customers. The grandmother has two faces. After the facts the grandmother consoled her. When X1 and her refused, the grandmother threatened them with a gun. X1's grandmother had contact with her grandmother. She remembers rapes until she was in 4th grade in the X1 class. She remembers rapes when she was already

wearing a bra. The facts generally related to oral sex following which she was going to vomit and sometimes to anal intercourse. She remembers two positions for anal penetrations - she describes. When she was tied, her nipples were pulled. She had forced gay sex with X1. She witnessed a rape of X1. When they refused to make a customer the grandmother hit their fingers with an iron ruler. On one occasion she pointed the barrel of a revolver at the temple of one of the two." [Flemish to French to English]

—150.817 20/03/97 -FINDINGS STORME HEARING of 02/25/97, X-Dossier summary, 1235 pages, 2005, published by Wikileaks in 2009.

Chantal's family knew X1's, and the *X-Dossier* stated her parents had operated a Tea-Room called *The Navy* which was shutdown in the 1980s, *"for acts of morals, sexual orgies, taking pornographic photos."*[543]

Another witness who came forward, known as X4, identified both these childhood friends of X1, that is — both Natalie and Chantal, as girls she'd been forced to perform with in child pornography. X4 hadn't known X1, but stated similarly she'd been sold by her parents into a child prostitution ring in Knokke through a pimp named Jacques V.[544]

Another witness, identified as X2, claimed to have been the mistress of a magistrate named Karel during the 1980s. X2 claimed she'd accompanied this magistrate as his guest to high society sadomasochist child sex parties around Belgium, and identified some of the same hotel-villa's surrounding the Royal Zoute golf club as venues where these were held.[545]

Among the attendees to these parties X2 identified: Baron Benoit de Bonvoisin, Jean-Paul Dumont, Maurice Lippens, Leopold Lippens, as well as various other prominent figures X1 hadn't identified.[546] One of these had been a Belgian politician named Karel Van Miert, who'd succeeded <u>Leon Brittan</u> of *Westminister Pedophile Dossier* infamy, as the European Commissioner of Competition in 1993.[547] And in 1996 Miert oversaw the approval of a government bailout for the aforementioned Dessy family's *Forges de Clabecq* steel factory.[548]

X2 had also been familiar with the *Dolo* nightclub and Michel Nihoul,[549] While X2 did not remember X1 from these parties, X1 identified X2 from a selection of photos as a slightly older girl than the others who attended the same 'abuse parties' as her.[550] X2 had also described the same 'child hunts' X1 talked about, though hadn't seen or taken part in them herself.[551] But did claim some rather extreme things were going on at the estates of the Belgian monarchy.

"Orgies in EINDHOVEN in 1988. An underage girl used to the place was abused and then never seen again. This girl told X2 that all the men she suffered were sick. She spoke of a castle in Brussels where she went to Easter 1987, to a madwoman named LILIANE. She said we should go back to the garden. X2 understands that bodies could be buried there. X2 is thinking of Liliane DE RETY...End of year celebrations 85/86. KAREL brings X2 to the MIRANO. She went back 4-5 times afterwards. Each time: orgies with distribution of coke. Presence of minors aged 12-15 made available until 03.00-04.00. Generally: about ten children - 25-30 adults including 5-6 women aged 50 and 3-4 girls aged 18-20. The orgies were started by older women. X2 had sex with one of these women who masturbated and sodomized her with a dildo - she will spread the Jew's sperm on X2's body. After the X2 parties was brought back to LEVI. Present at the MIRANO orgies: BONVOISIN

BOURLEED LEVI PHILIPPE (French from Prince ALEXANDRE) Princes PHILIPPE and LAURENT but never active - they watched while masturbating until ejaculation. strangers and strangers." [Flemish to French to English]

— 118.384 13/12/96 AUDITION of X2, X-Dossier summary, 1235 pages, 2005, published by Wikileaks in 2009

"Description of the 16 year old girl who disappeared after a sado-maso session. The oldest girls were the mistresses. She had a specific role. Check that the girls drink alcohol and take the drug (coke) prepared by the female teachers (in the form of sniffettes). Once the little girls are used, it is the mistresses-wives who serve. X2 was a mistress. Variable dose of coke according to the partners and their expected violence. One of the most violent was LIPPENS's friend - He has a penis 22 cm long and 5.5 cm in diameter - when he is erect his penis remains vertical and the glans is curved downwards. Her fantasy was to dry sodomize X2 then to make her perform a blowjob while she was taken by another. KAREL has a penis of 18 cm - he has very little hair on his chest and pubic hair is pale red - strawberry blonde. Description of the man with whom the girl went up for the sado-maso session. DE BONVOISIN only practices sodomy while being sodomized himself and so on in the chain (4-5 men). DUMONT is rather sadomasochistic." [Flemish to French to English]

— 118.376 11/12/96 - FOURTH HEARING of X2, X-Dossier summary, 1235 pages, 2005, published by Wikileaks in 2009

Allegations were also made against the Belgian Royal family by the witness X3. X3 testified her family had sold her into a child prostitution network around age twelve which catered to the Belgian monarchy from between 1950 to 1962. During this period, I shit you not, Francis Shelden's first cousin

Frederick M. Alger Jr. served as the US Ambassador to Belgium(1952-1956),[552] and regularly played golf with the royal family there.[553]

The testimonies of X3 were by far the most wild. They concerned high society events, hellscapes really, held at the castle estates of Prince Charles (Belgium 1903-1983), King Baudouin (1930-1993), and King Albert(1934-*). Among the attendees X3 identified Paul Vanden Boeynants, who'd also been accused by X1. The acts allegedly committed at these parties on children involved body mutilation torture, murder, necrophilia, beastiality, and grotesque combinations of these. For further details see the footnotes as it's difficult to present these claims seriously without further evidence, as they originated from another era.[554]

The testimonies provided by X1 and her two childhood friends, alongwith X4, appear to suggest families in Knokke-Heist were selling their children into a child prostitution ring during the 1970s and 80s. The testimony provided by X2 also corroborated X1's further claim she graduated into a more extreme sadomasochist sexual blackmail network operated by Michel Nihoul. The testimony of X3 then thematically aligned with the accounts given by both X1 and X2 and identified one of the abusers X1 had accused. The *X-Dossier* is also full of many more witness accounts than just the handful dealt with here.

However, even if all this were to be dismissed as a hoax, the accounts then provided by X1 on at least two of the three cold case murders investigated by the *X-Dossier* team, that of Christine Van Hees and Carine Dellaert, are so precise that X1 was either truthfully recalling events from memory or having information on the case fed to her by the *X-Dossier* investigators. Which is what they were accused of doing, and this had been used to justify their removal and replacement during the early to middle months of 1997.[555]

Either way you look at it, the *X-Dossier* investigation is a massive conspiracy, either to cover up the investigation into the network linked to Marc Dutroux, or to frame those accused for political reasons by linking them to it.

There is some evidence to support the notion of a police conspiracy against the accused, which isn't to say they were innocent. Police frame people for crimes they are guilty of all the time. The witness X2 had been a junior police officer who came forward, assumedly, only after being made aware of at least some aspects of the investigation. Which pollutes her testimony. In addition to this, some key figures involved in the investigation early on were also involved in a previous investigation into the assassination of Anthony Cools, which some of the accused in the *X-Dossier* were suspected of involvement.

In my opinion it's probable the *X-Dossier* investigators may have forced some things to get results. Though I personally believe the overall 'thesis' of their investigation is truthful. That is — that Marc Dutroux was linked to a powerful network of people, powerful enough to have the team put together to investigate them charged for fabricating evidence:

"In 1997, a judge charged Mr. De Baets with concealing the fact that Mrs. Louf had incorrectly identified the photograph of a murder victim, which would have seriously undermined her evidence. In fact, the authors said, the videotape of the interrogation showed that Mrs. Louf was deeply averse to looking at the photographs. It was later established that the missing piece of evidence, known as a proces verbal, had been in the files all along. Mr. De Baets was exonerated this year. In November, two journalists from Le Soir Illustre, who were judged to have defamed him and four colleagues, were ordered to pay the gendarmes 2.2 million Belgian francs ($55,000), plus

costs. Mr. De Baets and his colleagues, however, remain on leave."
— 'Belgium Pedophilia Scandal / Did Authorities Cover Up Its Scope?: Book Revives Fear of Grand Conspiracy', New York Times, December 16 1999

Soon after the *X-Dossier* team were replaced in 1997, X1's identity was leaked to the Belgium press as Regina Louf. She was then publicly discredited as a fantasist who suffered from 'false memory syndrome' and a media narrative was built around Marc Dutroux being a lone 'serial killer'. The X-witness accounts were all dismissed as a hoax, and on these grounds were prevented from testifying at the trials of Marc Dutroux and Michel Nihoul, which were held in 2004.[556]

Dutroux received a life sentence for the murders of the four girls found buried on his properties. Michel Nihoul was convicted by a jury as an accomplice to kidnapping, but the judge then acquitted him and instead he received a 5 year sentence for a criminal association with Marc Dutroux and drug trafficking. Nihoul was then granted an early release in April 2005.[557]

At the trial, the examining magistrate who'd been removed from investigation testified that attempts were made on his life:

> "Jean-Marc Connerotte choked in tears on the fourth day of the trial, describing the bullet-proof vehicles and armed guards needed to protect him against shadowy figures determined to stop the full truth coming out. 'Never before in Belgium has an investigating judge at the service of the king been subjected to such pressure,' he said. 'We were told by police that [murder] contracts had been taken out against the magistrates. As the danger mounted, emergency measures were taken' "
> — 'Judge tells of murder plots to block Dutroux investigation', The Telegraph, March 5 2004

***

While there isn't much doubt Marc Dutroux was supplying kidnapped girls to a broader network involving Michel Nihoul, the other aspects of the case built on top of this are much more uncertain, and complicated by the fact Regina Louf, the key witness, suffered from Dissociative Identity Syndrome(DID), also commonly known as multiple personality disorder.[558]

This is a disorder almost exclusively diagnosed in adults who have suffered severe trauma in early childhood. While it could be used as evidence of mental instability, it could also be used as evidence of severe trauma suffered in early childhood.

An academic movement which begun in the early 1990s pointed towards the exponential growth in child sex abuse allegations as being the result of people recalling false memories. I do believe that methods used in memory recall, such as hypnotherapy, need to be validated with real world evidence before being taken seriously. However, proponents of the false memory theory ignored the real world evidence gathered to validate the X-witness memories, and developed the term 'false memory syndrome'(FMS) to simply discredit them.

Both DID and FMS explanations for Regina Louf's condition do however converge to agree on the following point. That hypnotism can be used to access repressed memories, or implant false ones, within splits of the human personality.

The theory of DID posits trauma suffered from a very early age invokes a dissociative state, or catatonic blank slate personality, split off from the core personality developing within a child to protect it from the experience of suffering. That when this dissociative state is invoked, repeatedly through repeated abuse, it can develop into an ulterior personality alongside the core personality of the child, in which the experiences and memories of the trauma suffered become compartmentalised.

These trauma-invoked dissociative states are similar to the ones which can also be induced in certain people through hypnosis. The personality shuts off and they fall under the control of the hypnotist, who invokes this state through relaxation. Which demonstrates, quite often on stage before an audience, that the minds of people in dissociative states can be controlled.

For instance, in the hours before they were kidnapped by Marc Dutroux both An Marchal and Eefje Lambrecks had been hypnotised on stage during the performance of a hypnotist named Rasti Rostelli.

> "On the evening of the kidnapping, An and her girlfriend Eefje Lambrecks, who was also murdered by Dutroux, had attended a Rostelli hypnosis show in Blankenberge on the coast in August 1995. Father Marchal initially insisted on Rostelli coming as a witness, because he thought that the girls were still lured by Dutroux under the influence of hypnosis. He also bases this on statements made by friends of An and Eefje, who were on holiday with the girls on the Belgian coast at the time of the kidnapping. According to a friend, who testified in court in Arlon on Tuesday, An *'was a tigress when attacked; she would never just go along with a type of Dutroux'*. This strengthens Quirynen's conviction that the girls must have been confused or weakened by the hypnosis... Rostelli had put the two girls under hypnosis. Both were on stage in Blankenberge for almost two hours. The similarly hypnotized friends say it took them hours to fully recover from the hypnosis." [Dutch to English]
>
> — 'Rasti Rostelli no witness at Dutroux trial', deVolksran, April 6 2004

This performance was recorded on video and described in a Dutch magazine article critical of Rasti Rostelli's techniques.

"Eefje shrinks and remains lying on stage. An runs away screaming and has to be brought back by an assistant. He speaks to her a little later in his lingering, compelling voice: *'You are going to feel everything I do with this doll in your body.'* Rostelli smiles his sadistic smile. He hammers the head of the rag doll with a hammer. He puts a stick between the buttocks and kisses the cloth lips. An puts two hands in front of her face and screams something unintelligible. Nobody laughs. He lets An sleep for the rest of the show...He tells Eefje that she must seduce him. Giggling, she asks Rostelli, *'Are you coming to the beach?'* Nice and romantic. Now the audience is laughing. After the show, the security video camera records how An and Eefje wander around the casino in a daze. An eats from an imaginary lemon. Eve rubs her eyes. The same night they probably fall into the hands of child rapist Marc Dutroux...*'What he(Rostelli) is doing is simply irresponsible,'* says Johan Vanderlinden of the Association for Autogenic Training and Hypnotherapy. *'His methods always run the risk of resurfacing past trauma and people who have been hypnotized going home emotionally confused.'* According to psychologist Piet Vroon, it is not yet really clear what happens in the brain during hypnosis. *'One says it's pure role play, with the hypnotized playing along; others believe it goes further.'* Vroon believes that hypnotists should at least study their professional literature carefully. *'Hypnosis as entertainment is playing with fire. It's just not clear what kind of fire is being played with.'* " [Dutch to English]

— 'Rasti Rostelli', De Groene Amsterdammer, August 21 1996

The *X-Dossier* states Dutroux hypnotised a girl he raped in 1994,[559] and an item marked "hypnosis equipment" was seized from the house where he kept An Marchal and Eefje Lambrecks for two weeks prior to their murder.[560]

When Sabine Dardenne and Laetitia Delhez were rescued from the basement of this house, they had been conditioned to believe Dutroux was their protector, *"The Belgian investigating judge who ordered Marc Dutroux's arrest in August 1996 described yesterday how two young girls hid from their rescuers and embraced their torturer when they were freed...When Dutroux escorted police to the specially-built cellar where Sabine and Laetitia were held, they didn't want to come out and tried to hide from their rescuers, Connerotte said. They thanked Dutroux. It was absolutely terrible. They kissed him. That shows how much he had conditioned them,' he said."*[561]

Dutroux's accomplice Michel Lelievre had explained to investigators, *"DUTROUX said he conditioned girls to be docile and submissive for clients,"*[562] and that, *"He saw AN and EEF naked. DUTROUX said that like that they couldn't escape. He also saw one of the two cleaning the tiles. Afterwards he said that the people who ordered them came to see the girls but they were not interested in them."*[563]

The association between dissociative states and the development of ulterior personalities within them was written about by a Canadian-American psychologist named George Estabrooks as early as 1943 in his book *'Hypnotism'*. In it Estabrooks recalled the first known clinical treatment of a patient with multiple personalities in a woman named Christine Beauchamp by a physician named Morton Prince, who wrote of his experience in a 1906 book entitled, *'The Dissociation of a Personality'*.

"We would wish to make a point before we proceed, since we wish later to show more clearly how and why hypnotism is of such use in these cases; in reality they are caused by a form of hypnotism in the first place! We will see that emotional shock produces exactly the same results as hypnotism, that hypnotism may in reality be a form of emotional shock. We are not clear on this point, but we do know that shock gives us all the phenomena of hypnotism and vice versa. If we read over the Beauchamp case or most other such cases we will see that the condition has been caused by some severe emotional strain. What actually happened in the Beauchamp case appears to have been somewhat as follows. A very severe period of fear in childhood ending about the age of seven in a bad fright received from the father. This "split" the personality into the Sally, or Bill and the BII parts. Sally remained the childish creature she was at that time as a "co-conscious" personality, while BII continued her development. Then around the age of eighteen came another great shock, this time in connection with her love life, when BII split into BI, the Angel, and BIV, the Woman."

— 'Hypnotism' by George H. Estabrooks, published in 1943

Estabrooks, a prominent figure in the evolving field of 20th century hypnotherapy, believed hypnotism and emotional shock produced the same resultant state of dissassociation. In 1959 he applied to *The National Institute of Mental Health* for funding of his proposed study: *"Hypnotism in Juvenile Delinquency"*.[564] This institute at the time had been a cutout used to fund MKUltra research into various prospective methods of mind control, some of which involved children.[565] And in August 1961 Subproject 136 of the MKUltra program was approved for funding, entitled: *'Experimental Analysis of Extrasensory Perception'*.[566]

While this research was carried out under the auspices of

ESP and telepathy, the following details are found in the projects objective statement.

"In working with individual subjects, **special attention will be given to disassociative states**, which tend to accompany spontaneous ESP experiences. Such states can be **induced or controlled to some extent with hypnosis** and drugs. Some of this work will make use of qualitative stimuli, such as drawings and ideas with special associations...The experimenters will be particularly interested in disassociative states, from the abaissment de niveau mental **to multiple personality in so-called mediums, and an attempt will be made to induce a number of states of this kind, using hypnosis**...The data used in this study will be obtained from group ESP experiments which have yielded significant results, high scoring subjects from special groups such as psychotics, **children** and mediums, and from psychological and educational tests in which answers are of the multiple choice type. "

— Project MKULTRA, Subproject 136, Memorandum, 23 August 1961

A reasonable summation of the subproject's agenda was to, at least in part, induce dissociative states in children through drugs and hypnosis to create multiple personalities. It had been known such states could be induced in children through trauma leading to the development of ulterior personalities. Which aligned perfectly with MKUltra's mandate — The discovery of effective methods of mind control to create brainwashed operatives, able to to carry out their objectives unwittingly, thus obtaining perfect operation security in human intelligence assets, especially assassins.

If you find the concept of mind control assassination ridiculous, you should consider the fact you may already inadvertently accept that a vagrant of limited resources named Charles Manson managed to accomplish such a feat and was convicted of it in court.

According to correspondance published in the British Journal of Psychiatry, children had been used in these experiments with little ethical consideration.[567] And in his study proposal, Estabrooks had written of the especially high levels of susceptibility children had to these techniques, *"It is quite likely that in a large proportion, say, 50 per cent, of the cases classed as juvenile delinquents, hypnotherapy offers a promising approach. While one out of five adults are good hypnotic subjects, four out of five children fall in this category."*[568]

While it's unclear whether Estabrooks had been involved with MKUltra, he claimed in an article entitled 'Hypnosis comes of age', published in a 1971 edition of Science Digest, to have successfully created multiple personalities through hypnotic techniques in officers of the US Army's intelligence division during WW2.

But what if hypnosis had failed to produce in children what it was known trauma could. Would the behaviorists stop for ethical reasons? There is one theory. That when MKUltra ended in 1973 this line of inquiry had been continued off the books. Elements within the CIA turned from academics to 'alternative lifestyle' communities, pedophile rings and cults, as conduits to carry out trauma-based mind control research. And we do find overlap between all these things in a 1987 case called The Finders.

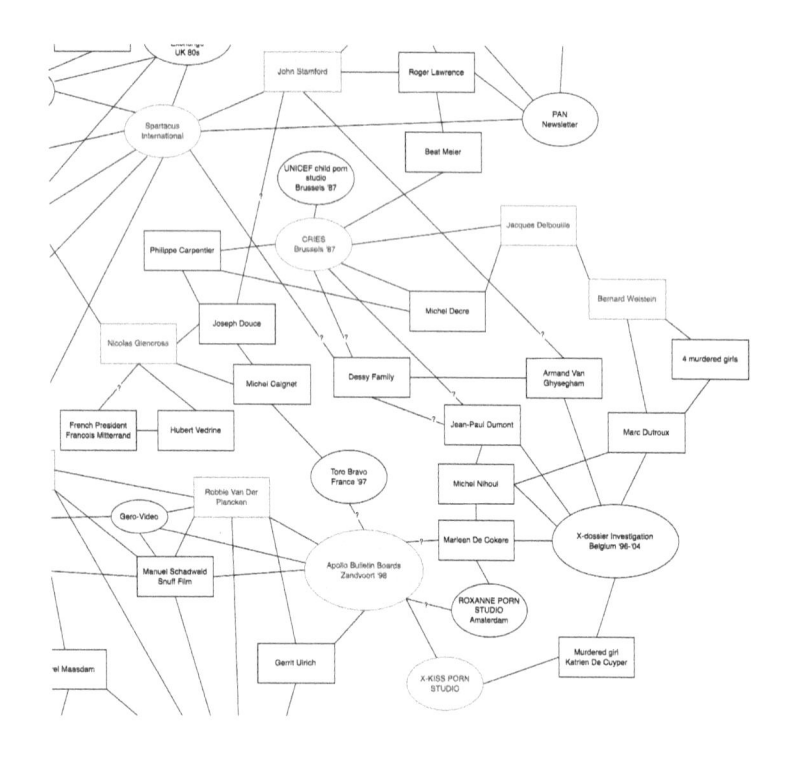

- UK 80s
- John Stamford
- Roger Lawrence
- PAN Newsletter
- Spartacus International
- Beat Meier
- UNICEF child porn studio Brussels '87
- CRIES Brussels '87
- Jacques Delboulle
- Philippe Carpentier
- Michel Decre
- Bernard Weinstein
- Joseph Douce
- 4 murdered girls
- Nicolas Glenerose
- Michel Caignet
- Dessy Family
- Armand Van Ghyseghem
- French President Francois Mitterrand
- Hubert Vedrine
- Jean-Paul Dumont
- Marc Dutroux
- Toro Bravo France '97
- Michel Nihoul
- Robbie Van Der Plancken
- Gero-Video
- Apollo Bulletin Boards Zandvoort '98
- Marleen De Cokere
- X-dossier Investigation Belgium '96-'04
- Manuel Schadwald Snuff Film
- ROXANNE PORN STUDIO Amsterdam
- Maasdam
- Gerrit Ulrich
- X-KISS PORN STUDIO
- Murdered girl Katrien De Cuyper

The Finders & The Odyssey Network

On February 4 1987 police in Tallahassee, Florida received a call from a member of the public concerned about six dishevelled children in a park seemingly under the supervision of two well-dressed men. The men were members of a 60s style commune/cult called *The Finders*, and the children those of women belonging to this group. The children were dirty, malnourished, and after being taken into police custody, one had shown signs of sexual abuse. The children demonstrated an unfamiliarity with the 'outside world' and stated the men had been their teachers taking them to a special school in Mexico for brilliant children. When asked who their parents were they replied they'd been weaned from their mothers and were under the control of the "game caller". The Tallahassee PD report stated, *"[name redacted - one of the children] said they would go to peoples houses and babysit. She stated that this was fun because they got to eat what was there, and do what those people wanted them to. She would not elaborate"*.[569]

The *Finders* men had been transporting the children in a white van registered to a warehouse in Washington D.C., *"During this process [name redacted - one of the children] saw the van registration on this investigator's pad. she stated that the address which the van was registered to was 'the warehouse'. She stated that they would go there sometimes."*[570]

This information was relayed to U.S customs officers and Metropolitan Police in Washington D.C who discovered they had preexisting information from an informant on file stating, *"That a group of people calling themselves, the 'Finders', were conducting brainwashing techniques at [redacted]"*, and that, *"The source reported children were used in rituals by the groups."*[571]

Search warrants were secured for the warehouse and a nearby duplex house owned by *Finders* leader Marion Pettie, which were raided the following day on February 5. Inside the warehouse was discovered: hot tub and sauna facilities, various film sets, a video screening room, a library containing books on mindcontrol, and a room full of networked computer equipment with a satellite link on the roof.[572]

According to a U.S Custom's official who conducted the raids named Ramon J. Martinez, a member of *The Finders* named Stuart Miles Silverstone had been found inside a computer room at the duplex home, which had also been hooked up with a satellite link. And files on the computers Silverston had been operating detailed various methods for acquiring children, *"SILVERSTONE was located in a room equipped with several computers, printers, and numerous documents. Cursory examination of the documents revealed detailed instructions for obtaining children for unspecified purposes. The instructions included the impregnation of female members of the community known as Finders, purchasing children, trading, and kidnapping."*[573]

According to the customs agent, other files seized during the raids contained printouts of messages sent and received through an electronic mail system called telex to other networked computer terminals across the United States and abroad. One such telex message had been a purchase order for two children in Hong Kong to be arranged through an official at the Chinese Embassy. Others detailed activities such as "bank secrecy" and "interests in high tech transfers" in London, Europe, and Africa. Most curiously, one recently received message, found in the possession of Silverstone, provided a detailed summary of the arrests of the two Finders members in Florida the day prior, and included a set of instructions, *"to move 'the children' and keep them moving through different jurisdictions, and instructions on how to avoid police attention"*.[574] MPD suspected members of *The Finders* had, *"cleaned the area, since they had notice captioned subjects had been arrested"*.[575] No children had been found in either the warehouse or duplex, though large amounts of children's clothing had been, along with photographs of children, including one described as, *"a child 'on display' and appearing to accent the child's genitals."*[576]

Among *Finders* documents seized from warehouse had been, *"a looseleaf binder with the names of presidential candidates on the dividers"* which contained *"newspaper articles relating to the candidates,"*[577] and *"intelligence files on private families not related to the Finders. The process undertaken appears to be have been a systematic response to local newspaper advertisements for babysitters, tutors, etc. A member of the Finders would respond and gather as much information as possible about the habits, identity, occupation, etc., of the family. The use to which this information was to be put is still unknown. There was also a large amount of data collected on various child care organizations"*.[578]

A summary of the findings provided by Special Agent Martinez later in a U.S Customs report reached the following conclusion:

> "On Thursday, February 5, 1987, Senior Special Agent Harrold and I assisted the Washington D.C. Metropolitan Police Department (MPD) with two search warrants involving the possible sexual exploitation of children. During the course of the search warrants,

numerous documents were discovered which appeared to be concerned with international trafficking in children, high tech transfer to the United Kingdom, and international transfer of currency."
— Report by U.S Customs Investigation report, USCS Special Agent Ramon J. Martinez, 04/13/87

On February 6, the day after these raids had been conducted, the FBI took over the investigation and subsequently possession of all computer equipment and floppy disks seized from both the warehouse and nearby home, as well as from the white van found transporting the children in Florida. The FBI then classified all MPD reports related to *The Finders* investigation "Secret". According to one of these dated February 19 1987, which has since been released through FOIA, an MPD Detective reported speaking with a CIA official who'd told them *The Finders* investigation had been, *"treading on their toes"* and that the CIA, *"apparently have a vested interest in [redacted] and/or group"*.[579] In a heavily redacted section of this report it then states a "Disc" had been sent to Europe by someone who, *"Did not know that the person he turned the information over to in Europe was a source of this office and is not aware that the Source brought the Disc back to this office. [redacted] actually transferred the disc in London. Det [redacted] then turned the Disc over to WFO(?)/FBI, Counter Intelligence office for analyzation. We have not been apprised of the results of that alaysis[sic], nor do we expect to be. Regardless of what type operation they may be engaged in, there will be no justification for the way the children have been treated, and the matter will be addressed in Family Division, Superior Court."*[580]

A photo album found during the warehouse raid had contained pictures of men and children from *The Finders* group dressed in robes slaughtering goats. When news of *The Finders* investigation was picked up in the press by *The Washington Post* on February 7, they went with the headline '*Offi-*

cials Describe Cult Rituals in Child Abuse Case,' and reported:
> "D.C. police, who searched a Northeast Washington warehouse linked to the group, removed large plastic bags filled with color slides, photographs and photographic contact sheets. Some photos visible through a bag carried from the warehouse at 1307 Fourth St. NE were wallet-sized pictures of children, similar to school photos, and some were of naked children. D.C. police sources said some of the items seized yesterday showed pictures of children engaged in what appeared to be "cult rituals." Officials of the U.S. Customs Service, called in to aid in the investigation, said that the material seized yesterday includes photos showing children involved in bloodletting ceremonies of animals and one photograph of a child in chains. Customs officials said they were looking into whether a child pornography operation was being conducted".
> — 'Officials Describe Cult Rituals in Child Abuse Case', Saundra Saperstein & Victoria Churchville, The Washington Post, February 7. 9187

The satanic cult aspect of the investigation was left to circulate in the national press for about a week before the FBI declared their investigation had uncovered no evidence of a federal crime, *"spokesman for the FBI's Washington field office, said the FBI investigation was 'pretty well winding down. . . At this point we have not uncovered any evidence of federal violations.' He said this included no evidence of kidnapping or using children for pornographic purposes."*[581]

The newspapers of record swiftly realigned themselves and became the voice of reason, debunking their own coverage of the investigation as a hoax reminiscent of the satanic panic. An Op-ed in the Washington Post informed its readers, *"When the satanic dust settled, all the Florida police had on the two men they'd arrested were six children who appeared to be unkempt, hungry and bug-bitten, a condition the Tallahassee gendarmes had apparently never before encountered. They were shocked beyond belief, and thus began the 1987 Salem witch hunt, aided and abetted by newspapers and TV."*[582]

The six children in Florida were returned to female members of *The Finders* identified as their mothers, some sooner than others, and both male members who'd been found transporting them were eventually released.

So far as the official narrative went, *The Finders* had been an alternative lifestyle community with some pretty bizarre but legal practises which law enforcement authorities had misconstrued as satanic, and this had led to hysteria in the press. The CIA aspect never become public and the incident soon slipped away into the transience of the news cycle, forgotten about for a number of years.

In October 1991 MPD officers had then observed suspicious activity of well dressed men accompanied by children at late hours of the night, coming and going from a building they thought had been raided during *The Finders* investigation back in '87.

> "On October 22, 1991, the undersigned received a telephone notification from Officer [redacted] 5th District Uniform, midnight section, home telephone number [redacted](PROTECT) Officer [redacted] advised that he and two footman, Officers [redacted] have observed activity which they believe is suspicious in nature. The officers have observed numerous well dressed males, who operate rental cars and expensive luxury type models, enter the building located at [redacted] at late and early morning hours. The subjects and their vehicles do not 'fit' the area in which this building is locate, namely the market area of N.E. On at least one occasion, the officers have observed adult males with a young male child enter

the building. This occurred after the midnight section had reported for duty on the street. On another occasion, Officer [redacted] stopped a van after it was observed leaving the building in the early morning hours. The van displayed tags which were not listed to a van. The operator identified himself as [redacted] He told Officer [redacted] that he did research 'stuff'. He also stated that he baby sat children for diplomats. Officer [redacted] advised the undersigned that the building and the neighbourhood is not fit for baby sitting activity, especially after midnight. The subject's story was very suspicious to Officer [redacted]. The van is listed to [redacted] white male [redacted] The vehicle is described as a [redacted]. Officer [redacted] advised that to the best of his recollection, this building is the same building which was raided by the police approximately [redacted] years ago for some type of child pornography."

— Metropolitan Police Department Investigation Report, 10/22/91, FIO/PA# 1412188-000 (TheFinders FBI Vault release 2of4 - as of August 2023)

Then in 1993 the Department of Justice received a copy of the aforementioned memo compiled by U.S Customs agent Ramon J. Martinez on the raids of *The Finders* properties, and launched an internal inquiry into CIA involvement with *The Finders* group and a potential cover up of the groups operations by the FBI in 1987. Details on this were leaked to the *Washington Times*, which published an article in December 1993 citing both the U.S Customs memo and the MPD report on CIA involvement. The article reported, *"A Metropolitan Police document dated Feb. 19, 1987, quotes a CIA agent as confirming that his agency was sending its personnel to "a Finders Corp., Future Enterprises, for training in computer operations."*[583]

The leader of *The Finders*, whom the children called "the game-caller", was a former Air Force Master Sergeant named

Marion Pettie. It turned out his late wife had been a CIA employee named Isabelle Pettie, and one of his sons had worked for Air America, a CIA cutout used to traffic herion in the golden triangle region during the Vietnam war. It was also learnt *Future Enterprises* had provided software training for CIA employees, and that an employee of the company named Robert Garder Terrell was a member of *The Finders* let go in February 1987.[584]

Curious minds were left to stew on all this for thirty years, prodding and poking with various FOI requests to get a peak behind the curtain. Then in 2019 the FBI starting dumping their trove of heavily redacted case files on their investigation into the *The Finders*, including the follow up inquiry into a suspected coverup in 1993.

Buried among these releases, sprinkled with red herrings such as Ted Gunderson's diagrams of the McMartin preschool tunnels near the beginning of the first batch, were three documents of instantaneous interest to anyone who knew what they were looking at. It turned out a list of names and addresses had been found on *The Finders* men caught transporting the children through Florida.

On February 9 1987 the FBI reported:

"Deputy Sheriff [redacted] Leon County Jail, Tallahassee, Florida, provided a two-page list of names and addresses of individuals both within the United States and various foreign countries, which was seized from the property of [redacted] and [redacted] Several of the last names are identical with members of the 'Finders' organisation, and are believed to be possibly relatives to those members. A copy of this list is attached."

— FBI Memorandum, field file 7-1248, Released in FIO/ PA# 1412188-000 (TheFinders FBI Vault release 4of4 - as of August 2023), p.168

The FBI field office that received the list then put through the following request on February 13:

"Enclosed for the Bureau and WFO is a two page list of names and addresses. The enclosed list was recovered from subject [redacted] and [redacted] by jail authorities at the time they were booked into the Leon County Jail, Tallahassee, Florida, by the Tallahassee Police Department. Bureau is requested to search and index all names appearing on this list and to advise Jacksonville and WFO of results of indices search."

— FBI Memorandum, field file 7-1248, Released in FIO/PA# 1412188-000 (TheFinders FBI Vault release 4of4 - as of August 2023), p.101

The response to this request took almost a month, but on March 10 it finally came through with the following information matched to three names on the list:

"The name [redacted] is reflected in Buffalo file 145C-663 entitled:
[redacted] ALLEGED MEMBERS OF NORTH AMERICAN
MAN/BOY LOVE ASSOCIATION (NAMBLA);
ITOM - SEOC - POSSIBLE MURDER.

The name [redacted] is reflected in Dallas file 145-0 entitled:
[redacted] **ODYSSEY FOUNDATION DALLAS, TEXAS;**
ITOM - CHILD PROSTITUTION"

The name [long redaction] appears as a member of the **ODYSSEY FOUNDATION**, in Dallas file 145-0."

— FBI Memorandum, field file 7-1248, Released in FIO/PA# 1412188-000 (TheFinders FBI Vault release 4of4 - as of

August 2023), p.133

The two *Finders* men had been found transporting 6 children in a van "to Mexico", with a list of addresses for, one individual named in a case of NAMBLA members suspected of murder, and two named in John Norman's *Odyssey Network*.

Whatever happened to John Norman? Last we heard of him he'd been imprisoned in Chicago in 1978 and his young accomplice Phillip Paske had gone onto to work for John Wayne Gacy.

By 1983 Norman had been free and arrested again in a Pennsylvania for using boys to produce pornography circulated in a publication called *Handy Andy*. He'd been released on bail in 1985 and fled the state. Then in 1986 it was reported Norman was, *"wanted in at least five other states on similar charges. A jailhouse lawyer, Norman successfully filed a writ to have his bail reduced. After posting $7,500 in cash he skipped bail. He is still at lagre."*[585]

A crime stoppers article mentions Norman was still at large during *The Finders* investigation in February 1987.[586] He was then apprehended not long after in Illinois in late July 1987 after police received, *"a tip about a man who was involved in homosexual child pornography. When police checked his apartment they found a computerised publishing operation which was being used for pornography."*[587]

A 20-year-old named Erik Kimble found harbouring Norman in the apartment had then attempted to kill himself a few days later in his jail cell by opening his veins with his teeth.[588]

Norman received a six year sentence and spent the rest of his life in and out of prison, enrolled in various parol based rehabilitation programs in-between, until his eventual death in 2011.

There is little doubt in my mind John David Norman had been an intelligence asset. Wittingly or otherwise.

Goodbye.

Simon Dovey

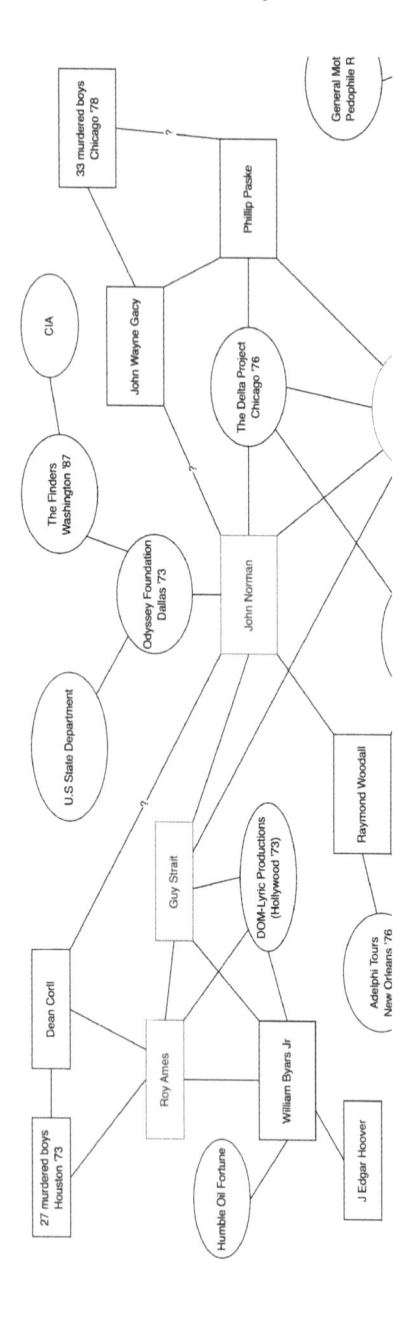

- 33 murdered boys Chicago '78
- Phillip Paske
- General Mot Pedophile R
- John Wayne Gacy
- CIA
- The Delta Project Chicago '76
- The Finders Washington '87
- Odyssey Foundation Dallas '73
- John Norman
- U.S State Department
- Guy Strait
- DOM-Lyric Productions (Hollywood '73)
- Raymond Woodall
- Adelphi Tours New Orleans '76
- Dean Corll
- Roy Ames
- William Byars Jr
- 27 murdered boys Houston '73
- Humble Oil Fortune
- J Edgar Hoover

258

[1] www.snopes.com/fact-check/a-pinch-of-snuff/

[2] The Family: The Story of Charles Manson's Dune Buggy Attack Battalion, Ed Sanders, published 1971 by E.P Dutton and Co., Inc, p. 214

[3] Ibid, page 211. According to Sanders, it was rumoured these films ended up in the possession of Paul Kaufman.

[4] Ibid, page 211

[5] 'Snuff sex films end with actual murder of females', Arlington Heights Herald, Illinois, October 3 1975

[6] 'The Cleveland Experiment', The Times Leader, Pennsylvania, June 22 1977

[7] 'Son of UN official jailed in slaying of masked student', The Reporter Dispatch, March 23 1985

[8] 'Boy Devastated by body won't testify at S & M trial', Daily News, August 28 1985

[9] 'Jury clears Crispo but can't agree on captive count', Daily News, October 17 1988

[10] 'Calm him down or kill him - Murderer Legeros testifies in torture trial', The Journal News, October 1 1988

[11] During the early 1980s a New York journalist named Maury Terry investigating the Son of Sam killings turned up evidence the motive behind the sixth and final murder had been the production of a snuff film. Terry outlined the evidence and reasonings for his findings in a book entitled *The Ultimate Evil* published in 1987, though had touched on many of the details in a series of newspaper articles published in the early 1980s. David Berkowitz, the alleged "lone gunman" who these murders were attributed to, would eventually confirm speculation he'd belonged to a Nazi satanic cult called the Process Church of the Final Judgement, one Ed Sanders had also linked to the activities of Charles Manson in his book *The Family*. If Maury Terry is to be believed, members of the Process cult were being used as hitmen in a murder for hire service operating in various 20-person cells across the United States. These interlinked cells operated as a multi-faceted criminal organisation, involved in everything from drugs and arms dealing to child sex trafficking, and used satanic and occult ideology to recruit members and secure their

loyalty. Maury Terry puts forward the theory that the cult had been responsible for ordering some of the six murders in New York in 1976 and '77, known as the Son of Sam killings. Some of these had been contract killings while others had been randomly selected victims to cover up the targeted ones. Berkowitz stated some of the victims he had killed himself while in others he'd been just an accomplice. The latter role he said he played in the sixth and final murder of Stacy Moskowitz, one of the random victims who'd been unlucky enough to be inside a car parked directly beneath a street light. Waiting close by with a perfect vantage of the parked car had been a yellow Volkswagon van, which would be seen leaving the scene shortly after she was murdered. Inside had allegedly been a photographer named Roger Sisman who had filmed a cult member walk up to the car and shoot Moskowitz in the head. Sisman had then been linked to Roy Radin.

[12] The Ultimate Evil, Maury Terry, 1989 Bantam Books . p. 619

[13] Declaration of Bernard J. LeGeros Signed under penalty of perjury at Dannemora, New York on the 2nd day of June, 1994.
Found in an archive on a section of the Carnegie Mellon website of affidavits made against an attorney and associate of Andrew Crispo named Graham Berry, www.cs.cmu.edu/~dst/Krasel/aff/aff_bl.html

[14] 'Man Who Murdered Two Young Women in Desert Sentenced to Die', Los Angeles Times, April 1985

[15] 'Two men charged in snuff killings', The San Bernardino County Sun, August 6 1983

[16] Fred Berre Douglas, Petitioner-appellant, v. Jeanne S. Woodford, Warden, of Rswl California State Prison at San Quentin, Respondent-appellee, 316 F.3d 1079 (9th Cir. 2003), https://law.justia.com/cases/federal/appellate-courts/F3/316/1079/581758/

[17] Pasadena PD Supplementary Offense Report, J-12,345, August 8th 1973.

[18] Pasadena PD Supplementary Offense Report, J-12,345, August 8th 1973.

[19] Houston PD Offense Report, D-68905, September 3rd 1973.

[20] Houston PD Offense Report, D-68904, August 9th 1973.

[21] Pasadena PD Supplementary Offense Report, J-12345, August 9th 1973

[22] Houston PD Supplementary Offense Report, D-68904, Progress Report - August 11th 1973.

[23] Pasadena PD Supplementary Offense Report, J-12345, 20 September 1976."
[24] Houston PD Supplementary Offense Report, D-68904, Progress Report - August 13th 1973.
[25] Dallas PD Prosecution Report, August 15 1973.
Reported, 'Alleged Homosexual Ring Found In a Raid on Apartment in Dallas', New York Times, Aug. 16 1973.
'Police seek tie between killings, homosexual ring', Independent (Long Beach CA), August 17 1973
[26] 'Alleged Homosexual Ring Found In a Raid on Apartment in Dallas', New York Times, August 16 1973.
[27] 'Chicago is center of national child pornography ring', Chicago Tribune, May 16 1977.
John D. Norman was arrested in Dallas multiple times in 1973, each time index cards had been discovered by police. Reportedly 5,000 in March, then 35,000 in August. This confusion was touched upon in a Senate hearing investigating in child pornography in the united states.
[28] 'For Money or Love: Boy Prostitution in America', Robin Lloyd, 1976, page 82
[29] 'Police Investigating Call-Boy Operation', Fort Worth Star-Telegram, August 16 1973
[30] Alleged Homosexual Ring Found In a Raid on Apartment in Dallas', New York Times, Aug. 16 1973.
[31] Alleged Homosexual Ring Found In a Raid on Apartment in Dallas', New York Times, Aug. 16 1973.
[32] 'Chicago is center of national child pornography ring', Chicago Tribune, May 16 1977.
[33] Protection of Children Against Sexual Exploitation, Hearings before the Subcommittee to Investigate Juvenile Delinquency of the Committee on the Judiciary United States Senate, Ninety-fifth Congress. Letter from Department of State Washington D.C, June 27, 1977, written by Douglas J. Bennet Jr, Assistant Secretary for Congressional Relations. Copy of the letter found on Page 119 of the report.
[34] FBI Freedom of Information Act Request for Documents on Phillip Paske. FOI/PA# 1352511-001, https://vault.fbi.gov/philip-paske/philip-paske-part-01/view
[35] Ibid

[36] Houston PD Supplementary Offense Report, D-68904, August 31st 1973.
[37] Houston PD Supplementary Offense Report, D-68904, August 31st 1973.
[38] Houston PD Supplementary Offense Report, D-68904, August 31st 1973.
[39] Houston PD Supplementary Offense Report, D-68904, August 31st 1973.
[40] '2 arrested for using boys as sex actors', The San Bernardino County Sun (San Bernardino, California), 3rd September 1973.
[41] 'For Money or Love: Boy Prostitution in America', Robin Lloyd, 1976, page 84
[42] '14 Men Indicted in Sex Movies Featuring Boys Ages 6 to 17', The Los Angeles Times, 26 October 1973
[43] '14 Men Indicted in Sex Movies Featuring Boys Ages 6 to 17', The Los Angeles Times, 26 October 1973
[44] 'Official and Confidential: The secret life of J Edgar Hoover', Anthony Summers, 1993
[45] '14 Men Indicted in Sex Movies Featuring Boys Ages 6 to 17', The Los Angeles Times, 26 October 1973
[46] THE PEOPLE OF THE STATE OF ILLINOIS, Plaintiff-Appellee, v. GUY STRAIT, Opinion filed November 22, 1982.
"On May 13, 1976, Guy Strait (hereinafter "defendant") was charged with the March 3, 1972 offense of indecent liberties with a child. Steven Kavadas (hereinafter "Kavadas") was 14 years old at the time of the incident in question."
[47] 'His only regret: I got caught', Chicago Tribune, May 17, 1977
"Strait said he knows John Norman, who ran a national male prostitution ring employing young boys and helping put together a neater package to attract customers"
[48] Protection of Children Against Sexual Exploitation, Hearings before the Subcommittee to Investigate Juvenile Delinquency of the Committee on the Judiciary United States Senate, Ninety-fifth Congress, page 25
[49] 'For Money or Love: Boy Prostitution in America', Robin Lloyd, 1976, page 86
[50] Houston PD Offense Report, D-68904, August 9th 1973
[51] Houston PD Offense Report, D-68904, August 9th 1973
[52] Houston PD Offense Report, D-68904, August 9th 1973

[53] Houston PD Supplementary Offense Report, D-68904, Progress Report December 22 1973.
[54] 598   STATE v. SMITH   Feb. 1991 60 Wn. App. 592, 805 P.2d 256
"According to officials from the U.S. Postal Service, in December 1973, a search was made of a warehouse belonging to Roy Clifton Ames in Houston, Texas. Postal Inspectors seized over four tons of child pornography materials. In 1975, a second search was conducted of Ames' warehouse by Houston police officers. In this search, over two tons of child pornography were seized."
'Children becoming commodities in pornography world', Fort Worth Star-Telegram, 1st May 1977,
"In 1974, postal authorities in Texas arrested Roy Ames and found 4 tons of magazines and films in a Houston warehouse. Ames was charged with recruiting children off the Houston streets and paying them $5 for posing for photos and $5 for sex acts. He was sentenced to 12 years imprisonment on federal charges of sending obscene material through the mails."
[55] 598 STATE v. SMITH, Feb. 1991 60 Wn. App. 592, 805 P.2d 256,
"In the letters seized during both searches, officials found correspondence from R.D. Smith, 16704 - 72nd Avenue Northeast, Bothell, WA 98011. In numerous letters that were seized, Smith described his receipt of various items of hard-core child pornography, including depictions of young boys engaging in sexual intercourse with older boys, and scenes of children in sexual bondage. In one letter, Smith wrote that he had been buying this explicit material for about five years. In another letter, Smith commented that a particular child pornography film would have been better if the manufacturers had "tossed in a stiff 14-year old." In another letter, Smith wrote that he possessed 650 slides of hard-core sexual activity involving children and "who knows how many B & W sets, all of which are enjoyably reviewed from time-to-time." Officers also recovered order forms with Smith's name and address, personal checks from Smith, and a release form signed by Smith indicating that he is not offended by sexually oriented material."
[56] 598   STATE v. SMITH   Feb. 1991 60 Wn. App. 592, 805 P.2d 256
"Postal Inspectors seized over four tons of child pornography materials. In 1975, a second search was conducted of Ames' warehouse by Houston police officers. In this search, over two tons of child pornography were seized."
'The select committee on Child Pornography: Its related causes and control', Texas House of Representatives, Sixty Sixth Legislative Session, page 72.

"Four and one quarter tons of porn and equipment were initially confiscated. Later two additional tons were seized by Houston Police Department. Roy Ames and his associate, Leonard Edward Cunningham, recruited boys from the Houston area and paid them to perform homosexual acts with each other and with adults while Ames filmed and took still photos of them in local residences and motels."

[57] 'Youths pictured in sex material', Wichita Falls Times, 28 Feb 1975.

"Juvenile officers say 11 boys who were victims in the Houston mass murders case are pictured in sex material seized in what police called a homosexual ring.

. . .The case became public last week when four men were charged with sexual abuse of a child. They are Bryant A. Burch, 31, Leonard E. Cunningham, 29, John Jennings, 40, and Alfred Van dyke, 35."

'Houston-Los Angeles Link Discussed In Mass Killings', The Napa Valley Register, 23 Sept 1976.

"Juvenile Lt. H.A Contreras said Detective John St. John and a partner met with officers Wednesday about the case of photographer Roy Clifton Ames, convicted in 1975 for using the mails to distribute obscene material. Ames was sentenced to a Springfield Mo., federal prison after photographs of 11 Houston area victims of the mass murders were seized following the arrests and murder convictions of Elmer Wayne Henley Jr. and David Owen Brooks. 'We knew that they were shipping kids – boy prostitutes – back forth to the West Coast in the Ames deal,' Contreras said.

. . .It was some sort of shuttle service. Ames and some of his people were engaged in this. They would send California kids here and Houston kids to California."

[58] 'Youths pictured in sex material', Wichita Falls Times, 28 Feb 1975

[59] 'Texas' Toll of Boys Rises to 27 In Nation's Biggest Slaying Case', New York Times, August 14, 1973.
David Owen BROOKS, Appellant, v. The STATE of Texas, Appellee, May 16, 1979

[60] 'Jury blasts handling of murder case', Brownwood Bulletin, 2 November 1973.

[61] 'Man facing Kid Porn Charges', Waco Tribune-Herald, March 25 1981

[62] Homewood, Illinois PD Investigation Report, Case Numbers 20219-20238, October/November 1973

[63] Porno-ring suspect fired by city, published in the Chicago Tribune, Chicago Illinois, 16 August 1977

[64] FBI FOI/PA# 1352511-001, FBI FOI, https://vault.fbi.gov/philip-

paske/philip-paske-part-01, page 66

[65] Letter from Department of State Washington D.C, June 27, 1977, written by Douglas J. Bennet Jr, Assistant Secretary for Congressional Relations. Copy of the letter found on Page 119 of the report.

Protection of Children Against Sexual Exploitation, Hearings before the Subcommittee to Investigate Juvenile Delinquency of the Committee on the Judiciary United States Senate, Ninety-fifth Congress.

[66] Chicago is center of national child pornography ring, Michael Sneed and George Bliss, Chicago Tribune, Chicago Illinois, 16 May 1977

FBI FOI/PA# 1352511-001, FBI FOI, https://vault.fbi.gov/philip-paske/philip-paske-part-01, page 52

[67] FBI FOI/PA# 1352511-001, FBI FOI, https://vault.fbi.gov/philip-paske/philip-paske-part-01, page 33

[68] Police seek '77 killing link to slain youths, Philip Wattley & Patricia Leeds, Chicago Tribune, Chicago Illinois, 28 February 1979

[69] 'Federal agents raid porno book stores', Chicago Tribune, May 18 1977

[70] 'Parolee arrested in child porn raid', Chicago Tribune, June 17 1978

[71] 'Bodies of three teens found in car; throats cut', Chicago Tribune, February 26 1979

[72] 'Porno ring suspect fired by city', Chicago Tribune, August 16 1977

[73] WGN9 TV NEWS report, June 21 2016.

The TV broadcast aired footage of the actual payslips and other documents, which were verified by the district attorney Terry Sullivan, who inspected them during an interview with the WGN host, Larry Potash.

[74] 'Parents of Missing Youths Hope, Fear — and wait', NYTimes, December 31 1978

[75] Des Plaines PD, Supplementary Report, December 13 1978

[76] Ibid

[77] Des Plaines PD Case Files, Property Inventory Report 78-35203, December 13 1978

[78] Des Plaines PD Case Files, CID Report, 78-35203, page 4

[79] Ibid

[80] Des Plaines PD Case Files, CID Report, 78-35203, page 14

[81] Des Plaines PD Case Files, CID Report, 78-35203, page 16

[82] Des Plaines PD Case Files, CID Report, 78-35203, page 9

[83] Des Plaines PD Case Files, CID Report, 78-35203, page 3

[84] Des Plaines PD Case Files, CID Report, 78-35203, page 5
[85] Des Plaines PD Case Files, Supplementary Report, December 18 1978
[86] 'New podcast on serial killer John Wayne Gacy raises questions about police investigation', Chicago Sun Times, July 26 2021
[87] Des Plaines PD Case Files on John Wayne Gacy, 1of6, page 12
[88] Des Plaines John Wayne Gacy Police Interview December 22
[89] People v. Gacy, Supreme Court of Illinois, June 6 1984
[90] 'Murder suspect Gacy acted alone, official says', Des Moines Register, January 2 1979
[91] 'Missed Gacy Leads', WLS Channel 7 Eyewitness News, February 13 1979
[92] 'Victims sister slain in 1972', Chicago Tribune, January 29 1979
[93] 'Boys Enter the House: The Victims of John Wayne Gacy' by David Nelson, book published in 2021
[94] 'Trail's end: Gruesome clues led to an attic alter', The Chicago Tribune, October 12 1987
[95] WGN9 TV NEWS report, June 21 2016.
The TV broadcast aired footage of prison notes Gacy made on Phillip Paske, which were verified by the district attorney Terry Sullivan, who inspected them during an interview with the WGN host, Larry Potash.
1992 interview clips with John Wayne Gacy, featured in the 2021 Peacock documentary 'John Wayne Gacy: Devil Disguise'
[96] CBS2 Chicago, May 15 1992, Walter Jacobson interview with John Wayne Gacy.
[97] WGN9 TV NEWS report, June 21 2016.
[98] 'JOHN WAYNE GACY COLLECTION!! HOUSE PAINTING 1 OF A KIND!!' , https://www.youtube.com/@andymatesi850, April 23 2012, https://www.youtube.com/watch?v=byq8rsavFrw
That this is the same recording referenced in the 1994 article is based on the repeated reference in article quoting "12 keys to the house" and the recording stating "12 keys to the house". These statements also align with other statements Gacy made in video interviews.
[99] HUMAN TRAFFICKING, HOMICIDE AND CURRENT PREVENTION EFFORTS IN THE UNITED STATES OF AMERICA, Steven W. Becker, October 2022.
Author references, "People v. Gacy, Case No. 79 C 69 et al., State's List of Witnesses, at 4, April 24, 1979

(on file with author); People v. Gacy, Case No. 79 C 69 et al., Defense's Second Supplemental
List of Witnesses, at 21, January 24, 1980 (on file with author)"
[100] Clip of interview with John Wayne Gacy, featured in Peacock documentary: John Wayne Gacy: Devil in Disguise(2021)
Originally clip from Robert Ressler interview series with John Wayne Gacy in 1992.
[101] Household inventory filed and received by Clerk of the circuit court Criminal Division, Morgan M. Finley, April 23 1979. Posted to the website of Tracy Ullman, producer of documentary:John Wayne Gacy Devil in Disguise, https://www.unlimitedbliss.net/post/gacy-s-arrest-and-important-details-that-were-never-publicized
[102] Ibid
[103] 'Success, Public Service Masked Gacy's Dark Past', The Wichita Eagle, 28 December 1978.
[104] 'Gacy shows multiple personalities: laywer', Chicago Tribune, December 29 1978.
[105] "Why didn't Gacy Kill Me?", Chicago Tribune, December 24 1978
[106] 'Gacy, Rosalynn Carter Had Picture Taken Together', Arizona Daily Sun, January 22 1979
[107] "Why didn't Gacy Kill Me?", Chicago Tribune, December 24 1978
[108] The exact month of Norman's bail in 1976 has been calculated based on the number of months he was credited for having already served in December 1976. If Norman went to jail in November 1973 and was credited for serving 23 months between then and December 1976, that means he was released on bail no later than January 1976. The same month Phillip Paske was paroled. However, this is a best effort assumption on the information available to me.
[109] It is also interesting to note the first three victims attributed to Gacy had been three of the seven victims to disappear during the five year period. Robert Piest, John Szyc, and John Butkovitch.
The boy responsible for reporting Norman to police in July 1978, who was then murdered in February 1979 before he could testify at Norman's trial, was Michael Salcido. Michael Salcido had been a ward of the state removed from his family by the Illinois department of children and family services and placed into the custody of The Maryville Academy, a large campus-like Catholic group home for delinquent youths in Chicago run by Father John Smyth. The academy had a high school placement program during the 1970s which would send boys in its custody to affiliated catholic high schools in

the area. And Salcido had been been put in this program.
There were only four high schools involved in this program - Sacred Heart, Notre Dame, Maine East, and Maine West High school. And of these four, Maine West High appeared to be the most involved with wards of the Maryville Academy. Gacy's political connections were throug the Cook County school superintendent Robert Martwick. Maine West High was the high school attended by Robert Piest and John Syzc, the first two victims Gacy had been suspected of killing based on evidence found in his house during the December 13th search by Joseph Kozenczak and his team. There was the photo processing receipt belonging to Robert Piest which Kozenczak claimed to have found in Gacy's kitchen bin. And John Szyc's Maine West graduation ring.
Maine West was also the high school attended by Joseph Kozenczak's son, who had been the same age as Robert Piest. After Robert Piest had been confirmed as a victim of Gacy's, his father Harold Piest started a charity in his name, the proceeds of which were all donated to the Maryville academy.
Marko Butkovich, the father of John Butkovich, had been employed as a Church janitor at one time by an assistant director of the Maryville academy named Rev. John Tilford, a former next-door neighbour of the Butkovich family who had personally known John Butkovich and presided over his funeral.
John Butkovich hadn't attended Maine West like Piest or Szyc, but it had been reported in 1979 he'd been friends with John Szyc and another one of the victim's named Gregory Godzik.
In 1986 a priest at the Maryville Academy named Robert Friese was charged for the sexual assault of a boy at the academy, in a incident originating from a complaint made to the academy's leadership in 1980, which claimed Robert Friese had been providing a group of boys there with drugs and alcohol, and had anal sex with one of them. The matter had been handled internally at the time by Maryville's director, Rev. John Smyth, who transferred Robert Friese to another position within the academy in 1982. John Tilford had been assistant director of Maryville at this time.
Then in 1987 similar accusations were made against a second Reverend at the academy. A Chicago Tribune reporter received an anonymous phone call from a 15-year-old boy, who claimed a Rev. Robert Mayer at the Maryville Academy had hosted parties for boys there where they were supplied with alcohol, shown porn films, and engaged in oral sex. The Des Plaine chief of police had contacted

Rev. John Smyth about the allegation, and it appears things were was handled internally and never became a police matter.

The interesting thing about this is that the police chief who contacted Rev. John Smyth had been none other than Joseph Kozenczak, who had since been promoted after making his career with the investigation into John Gacy. And it would appear Kozenczak had known Maryville academy director John Smyth will. His wife, Karen Kozenczak, described Reverend Smyth as a close friend in a 2010, and Joseph Kozenczak's funeral would be held at the Maryville Academy after his death in 2015.

John Smyth was personally accused of sexual abuse by former students of the Maryville Academy in 2019. These were then followed by further accusations made against his replacement Rev. David Ryan in 2020.

Perhaps there's something to this. I don't know. John Gacy was raised Catholic and was involved with Catholic organisations as an adult, such as the Catholic Inter-Club Council. But all of this is circumstantial evidence.

For citations of the information provided above, see the article: https://thehotstar.net/gacy.html

[110] Protection of Children Against Sexual Exploitation, Hearings before the Subcommittee to Investigate Juvenile Delinquency of the Committee on the Judiciary United States Senate, Ninety-fifth Congress, First Session. Page 205.

[111] 'Boys used in film for national sale', The Chicago Tribune, May 15 1977

[112] Hunt 6 men, 20 boys in crackdown, Chicago Tribune, May 16 1977

[113] 'Boys used in film for national sale', The Chicago Tribune, May 15 1977

[114] Chicago is center of national child pornography ring, Michael Sneed and George Bliss, Chicago Tribune, Chicago Illinois, May 16 1977

[115] Dentist arrested in child sex filming, Chicago Tribune, May 17 1977

[116] 'Chicago pair held, Porn suspects tied to state camp', Marilyn Wright, Traverse City Record-Eagle, May 18 1977

[117] 'Ex-director of state camp arraigned on porn charges', Traverse City Record-Eagle, May 20 1977

[118] 'Police say photos link area island, porn ring', Traverse City Record-Eagle, February 16, 1977

Hermes is also mentioned in relation to Francis Shelden in the North Fox Island case files on July 26 1976.
Michigan PD Supplementary Complaint Report 23-1728-76, July 26 1976, D/Sgt. Joel Gorzen.
[119] Michigan PD Supplementary Complaint Report 23-1728-76, July 15th 1976, D/Sgt. Joel Gorzen.
[120] Michigan PD Supplementary Complaint Report 23-1728-76, July 23 1976, D/Sgt. Joel Gorzen & Det Everett
[121] Michigan PD Supplementary Complaint Report 23-1728-76, July 26th 1976, D/Sgt. Joel Gorzen.
[122] 'North Fox: One man's rare dot on the universe', Detroit Free Press, Dec 28 1975
[123] 'Hunted millionaire quits school posts', Marilyn Wright, Traverse City Record-Eagle, Jan 31 1977 &
'Rescuing Bad Apples', Detroit Free Press, Oct 31 1973
[124] 'Millionaire sought by police has rich, prominent background', Marilyn Wright, Traverse City Record-Eagle, Dec 11 1976
[125] Michigan PD Supplementary Complaint Report 23-1728-76, July 26th 1976, D/Sgt. Joel Gorzen.
[126] Hearings Before The Subcommittee To Investigate Juvenile Delinquency Of The Committee On The Judiciary, United States Senate, Ninety-Fifth Congress, First Session.
[127] Michigan PD Supplementary Complaint Report 23-1728-76, July 26th 1976, D/Sgt. Joel Gorzen.
[128] Michigan PD Supplementary Complaint Report 23-1728-76, September 27th 1976, D/Sgt. Joel Gorzen.
[129] 'New Organization To Present Magic Shows With Meaning', The Times Herald, March 7 1970.
[130] Michigan PD Supplementary Complaint Report 23-1728-76, August 30 1976, D/Sgt. Joel Gorzen.
[131] Police link island to porno ring, Marilyn Wright, The Record-Eagle, Traverse City, December 11 1976
[132] 'Starchild a man of mystery', Marilyn Wright, Traverse City Record-Eagle, December 16 1977
[133] Boy Scout Organisational files on Malcolm McConahy, Plaintiff's exhibit, TS/MS/KS V. BSA et al. Cause No. 03-2-37274-9
[134] 'Porno ring uses church, tax laws', Traverse City Record-Eagle, April 4 1977
[135] 'Police link island to porno ring', Marilyn Wright, The Record-

Eagle, Traverse City, December 11 1976.

[136] 'Two Port Huron men sentenced to prison', The Times Herald September 14 1976

[137] 'Two Port Huron men sentenced to prison', The Times Herald September 14 1976
Photocopies of the diagram Richards drew, including a second page of notes with names, were included as evidence on pages 80 and 81 of the, Hearings Before Subcommittee on the Judiciary, House of Representatives, Ninety-Fifth Congress, First Session, On Sexual Exploitation of Children, May 23, 25, June 10, and September 20, 1977'

[138] Interview with Gerald Richards Jan 12 1977, Michigan PD Supplementary Report 23-1728-76, Jan 25 1977, D/Sgt. Joel Gorzen,
"Beyond the stage of Mail-o-Matic, you get to the larger operator's who sell 8 MM MOTION PICTURES of Pedophilia (& other sex). This is put out by a Company know as F&S that uses a PO box in San Francisco, Calif. (could be a forewarding service)."

[139] Interview with Gerald Richards Jan 12 1977, Michigan PD Supplementary Report 23-1728-76, Jan 25 1977, D/Sgt. Joel Gorzen. Hearings Before Subcommittee on the Judiciary, House of Representatives, Ninety-Fifth Congress, First Session, On Sexual Exploitation of Children, May 23, 25, June 10, and September 20, 1977',
"Senator Culver: Mr. Richards, did you know of Guy Strait in the child pornography business?
Mr. Richards: I know of him.
Senator Culver: Could you name any of his organizations?
Mr. Richards: The main one, the only one really that I have any knowledge of is a movie film business.
Senator Culver: What was the name of that, Mr. Richards, do you recall?
Mr. Richards: It has now been changed. It's now called F&F Distributors, and I don't remember what the old name was. I don't know if he used his own name or not."
On an index of the network diagram he drew, Gerald Richards labelled F&S Distributors with Guy Straits name. A scanned copy of this index along with the diagram can be found in the report on the Hearings Before Subcommittee on the Judiciary, House of Representatives, Ninety-Fifth Congress, First Session, On Sexual Exploitation of Children.

[140] Michigan PD Supplementary Complaint Report 23-1728-76, July 26th 1976, D/Sgt. Joel Gorzen,

"one of several magazines that dwells on boy-boy-man sex, SHELDEN writes articles for this magazine & personally knows editor/publisher. SHELDEN said[told Richards] the address is a box that re-mails correspondence. He believes it is printed & published in different cities in America. A second such magazine is 'HERMES' from California that is published by F&F Distributors."

[141] 'His only regret: I got caught', Chicago Tribune, May 17, 1977,
"Strait said he knows John Norman, who ran a national male prostitution ring employing young boys and helping put together 'a neater package' to attract customers. He also said he wrote an article for Hermes magazine, a Chicago-based journal publishing philosophy and sex stories of boy love."

[142] 'Mexican tots smuggled for sadists', Des Moines Register, May 24 1977

[143] 'Priest charged in sex crimes out on $10,000 bail', The Delta Democrat Times, November 12 1976.
'Porno ring uses church, tax laws', Marilyn Wright, Traverse City Record-Eagle, April 4 1977

[144] 'Boys Farm Branded National Porno Hub', Detroit Free Press, November 11 1976

[145] 'Starchild a man of mystery', Marilyn Wright, Traverse City Record-Eagle, December 16 1977,

[146] 'New warrant sought on Shelden', Marilyn Wright, Traverse City Record-Eagle, December 16 1976

[147] 'Tennessee boy farm linked to fake church', Traverse City Record-Eagle, April 5 1977

[148] "Scoutmaster, Aide, 3d Man Arrested As Sex Deviants, The Indianapolis Star, September 11 1976

[149] "Victimized Through Homosexual Ring", The Hays Daily News, September 12 1976

[150] "Boy Scout orgy leaders arrested", San Antonio Express, September 11 1976

[151] "Claims teen-agers exploited", The Daily Herald, November 11 1976.

[152] "7 Arrested In Plot To Rape Boys", The Amarillo Globe Times, October 6 1976

[153] "The California connection in youth pornography", The Des Moines Register, 24 May 1977

[154] Ibid

[155] "Dade Man Is Linked To Scout Sex Inquiry", The Miami Herald,

May 18 1977

[156] "How ruses lure victims to child pornographers", Chicago Tribune, May 17 1977

[157] 'Porno ring weaves international web', Traverse City Record-Eagle, January 14 1977

[158] "How ruses lure victims to child pornographers", Chicago Tribune, May 17 1977

[159] "South Boston man guilty in Boy Scout sex case", The Boston Globe, July 21 1977

[160] "How ruses lure victims to child pornographers", Chicago Tribune, May 17 1977

[161] "Man Claims Connick Fugitive's Gay Lover", The Town Talk, March 5 1980

[162] "DA Connick Denies Lover Accusations", The Daily Review March 6 1980

[163] "Reporters' data subpoenaed", The Times Shreveport, Louisiana, April 6 1980

[164] "Connick May Try Scout Sex Case", The Shreveport Journal, September 20 1980

[165] "Prosecutors Drop Case Against Scout Sex Suspect; Case Stale", The Daily Advertiser, July 23 1982

[166] NAMBLA News Fall 1981, Extracts from FBI files on NAMBLA, 1979-1986.

[167] "Boy Scout Leader given 75-year prison term", The Daily Herald, May 28 1977.

[168] Also talked about by detectives who investigated it during interviews in The Clown and the Candyman podcast, Ep.4: "Scouts Honor" – How the pedo mob infiltrated the Boy Scouts.

[169] "Homosexual Ring Co-Founder Says Several Politicians Were Customers", The Town Talk, November 26 1979

[170] 'Scouts Case Figures Ran Gay Tours', The Times-Picayune, New Orleans, November 25 1979

[171] Ibid

[172] "Legislators linked to 'callboy' service", The Roswell Daily Record, November 27 1979

[173] Interviews with detectives from The Clown and the Candyman podcast, Ep.4: "Scouts Honor" – How the pedo mob infiltrated the Boy Scouts.

[174] 'North Fox: One man's rare dot on the universe, Detroit Free

Press, Dec 28 1975
Campaign Ad for Donald J Berlage, Petoskey News Review, July 30 1976
'Charlevoix Assistant Prosecutor is Named', Petoskey News Review, December 18 1970

[175] Michigan PD Supplementary Report, St. Clair County, Complaint No. 23-1728-76, August 17 1976, Investigation note made by Tpr. David W. Lambourn

[176] Michigan PD Supplementary Report, St. Clair County, Complaint No. 23-1728-76, August 30 1976, Investigation note made by D/S Gorzen

[177] Michigan PD Supplementary Report, St. Clair County, Complaint No. 23-1728-76, September 10 1976, Investigation note made by D/S Gorzen

[178] Michigan PD Supplementary Report, St. Clair County, Complaint No. 23-1728-76, September 27 1976, Investigation note made by D/S Gorzen

[179] Ibid.

[180] Michigan PD Supplementary Report, St. Clair County, Complaint No. 23-1728-76, September 30 1976, Investigation note made by Sgt. Wolak

[181] Michigan PD Supplementary Report, St. Clair County, Complaint No. 23-1728-76, October 10 1976, Investigation note made by D/S Gorzen

[182] Letter sent by Peter E. Deegan, Office off the Prosecuting Attorney for the county of St. Clair, To ,United States Attorney, Eastern District of Michigan. February 8 1977, FBI FOIA# 1423617-001, https://vault.fbi.gov/francis-shelden/francis-shelden-part-01/view , page 10

[183] Shelden left a trail of shock, Marilyn Wright, Traverse City Record-Eagle, Traverse City, Michigan, Dec 14 1977
FBI Memo dated 12/29/77, FBI FOIA# 1423617-001, https://vault.fbi.gov/francis-shelden/francis-shelden-part-01/view , page 368

[184] Tazelaar was mentioned in the network diagram key written by Gerald Richards in September '76, Photocopies of this were included as evidence on pages 80 and 81 of, Hearings Before Subcommittee on the Judiciary, House of Representatives, Ninety-Fifth Congress, First Session, On Sexual Exploitation of Children, May 23, 25, June 10, and September 20, 1977'
Casenotes of Det. Corey Williams, 12-07-07 entry.

"I told [redacted] that I was investigating Josiah Tazelaar and his associates for the child killings and knew that he [redacted] had been involved with Tazelaar, Francis Sheldon & others at that time. [redacted] indicated to me that he wanted to help any way he can and is willing to meet with me, but stated that he has blocked a lot of that out of his mind from back then, but would do his best to remember. We got talking about Tazelaar and the camping trips that he & Jerry Richards would take the boys on, when stated that the guy I really want to talk to is [redacted] who [redacted] stated was the boy that introduced him to Joe Tazelaar & Jerry Richards. Jerry Richards was a close associate of Francis Sheldon. I asked Schuck if [redacted] is still around, to which he stated that he was and that he lives in [redacted] said that [redacted] was the boy that kind of arranged things as far as boys meeting with and going on trips with the pedophiles from Port Huron, like, Tazelaar, Richards, Sheldon & others"

[185] 'Detroit man arraigned for misconduct', 'The Times Herald, January 22 1977
'A highland park man, Josiah Tazelaar, 44, has been sentenced to 1 1/2 to 15 years in prison for sexual offenses involving children in a park over a three-day period' - The Herald Palladium, July 26, 1977
[186] Casenotes of Det. Corey Williams, 11-28-06 entry.
"Dave Robertson (MSP) was searching the OCCK tip-file that had been put on a disc, and found a tip called into MSP in 1977 by D/Sgt. Joel Gorzen (MSP St. Clair Post). The information in this tip, was provided by Detective Gorzen, who obtained this information while interviewing a subject he had arrested for child molestation, named Josiah Tazelaar. Tazelaar described Duffy as a b/m, 40's, that was a procurer of children and who would in turn supply these children to Francis Sheldon for the purpose of producing child pornography."
[187] Casenotes of Det. Corey Williams, 2-14-07 entry.
"In Gorzens report (MSP) in 77, Josiah's young boy lover [redacted] told MSP that he met Josiah Tazelaar through Gerry Gerald Richards in Port Huron. Gerald Richards was indicted along with Francis Sheldon (who fled the U.S to Amsterdam in 76-77) and was very close with Francis Sheldon"
[188] Casenotes of Det. Corey Williams, 1-4-07 entry.
"I went through the DPD homicide file today on Titus Jones Duffy and highlighted a couple of interesting things in the file. . .One thing for sure, is that it appears that Duffy left his home with someone he knew the day he was killed. The manner of death indicates a crime of passion as opposed to something like robbery or a hit."
[189] Casenotes of Det. Corey Williams, 8-7-07 entry.

"We have already established a loose connection between the two, with Duffy, who was a roommate with Ted Lamborgine in the mid 70's and who would bring young boys from southwest Detroit to Tazelaar's house in Highland Park for their pedophile party's. Tazelaar had also admitted to investigators that in the spring of 2007, that he knew Lamborgine through Duffy only after being cornered about this. How these pedophile parties were arranged, who attended, where they took place and what occurred was described by [redacted](Tazelaar's boy lover from Port Huron) to Gorzen in his 1977 report."

[190] Casenotes of Det. Corey Williams, 2-13-07 entry,
"I asked Bill what year Josiah came to the Detroit area from Muskegon and did he live with him & Ruth. Bill told me Josiah first came to this area approximately 1973-74 and lived with them for 1-2 years on Windemere. Bill said that approximately 1975-76, Josiah got an apartment on Stevens St. in Highland park and moved down there. . .I asked him if he remembers a little boy named Timothy King that was abducted from the drug store down the street and lived with his family a few blocks from here in this neighbourhood."

[191] Casenotes of Det. Corey Williams, 1-4-07 entry,
"Ralph was identified through information supplied to Det. Gorzen (MSP) in 1977, by Josiah Tazelaar. Tazelaar lived in the 6 Mile & Woodward (@ 88 Stevens) area at that time. Tazelaar supplied this information about Ralph to Detective Gorzen (MSP) back in 1976-77. Tazelaar confirmed Lawson's information about the young prostitute Ralph operating in that area at that time, stating that his name was Ralph Schonebeck."

Casenotes of Det. Corey Williams, 2-15-07 entry,
"After the meeting, I was reading some of the Schultz file from 1977 and observed that Kent Gilbert Schultz did in fact live behind the Methodist Church at Woodward Ave. & Church St. and was the caretaker of the church. . .An extensive investigation into Schultz was conducted by the taskforce in 1977. Eventually Schultz was interviewed, polygraphed (passed) and was cleared of involvement in the OCCK case. . .I was reading the Schultz file at home tonight and observed that the Task Force in 1977, interviewed a fourteen year old named Ralph [redacted], white male, born [redacted] 1963. . .During the interview [redacted] said that he has been a prostitute in the area since he was 9 years old. He also said that he has been Kent Schultz's Boy Lover for two years."

[192] Casenotes of Det. Corey Williams, 6-2-05 entry,
"McKinnon reiterated that if I can get Lawson talking he would be a wealth of information, stating that Lawson was connected to and kept files on

pedophiles in not only Detroit, but also places like Chicago, Indianapolis, New York…etc. I asked McKinnon about the David Schultz arrest, to which he said that when his crew arrested Schultz, they thought he was going to be the Oakland County Child Killer. McKinnon said that Lawson was the informant on the Schultz case. (Schultz was cleared in the OCCK case)"

[193] Casenotes of Det. Corey Williams, 9-15-06 entry,
"[redacted] went on to say that this sexual assault by Lawson took place by the pool table, in the basement of the Cass-Methodist Church in the Cass Corridor of Detroit. . .Cass-Methodist Church is where Lawson, Schuler & Tippett were Big Brothers to the boys in the Big Brother program at the church. The Big Brother program at Cass-Methodist Church was run by, two pastors at the church, Lewis Redmond & Felix Lorenz."
Casenotes of Det. Corey Williams, 8-29-05 entry,
"Also received the military records on Schuler and Lamborgine today, from the national archives. Along with this packet was the U.S Customs file on Robert Schuler. These files confirmed both their military service and Schuler's U.S Customs employment at the Ambassador Bridge in Detroit in the late 70's."

[194] Casenotes of Det. Corey Williams, 9-15-06 entry,
"The Big Brother program at Cass-Methodist Church was run by, two pastors at the church, Lewis Redmond & Felix Lorenz."
Casenotes of Det. Corey Williams, 9-13-06 entry,
"Coleman told me that he was introduced to Richard Lawson, Jim Tippett & Bob Schuler as Big Brothers by Pastor Felix Lorenz at the Cass-Methodist church in Detroit when [redacted] was approximately 10-11 years old."

[195] 'Staffers Got $30,000 Before Home Opened', Detroit Free Press, February 6 1972

[196] 'Minister's Son Dies in Shooting', Detroit Free Press May 7 1976

[197] Casenotes of Det. Corey Williams, 1-3-06 entry,
"[redacted] was close with Redmond's son Robert Redmond that ws shot and killed in Brian Reardon & Ricky Copley's apartment on 3rd near Alexandrine in May of 1976 over the rape of a kid named Steve [redacted] by Reardon & Copley. [redacted] was a friend of Robert Redmonds."

[198] 'Cass Church Hums with Life Each Day', Detroit Free Press July 14 1973

[199] Casenotes of Det. Corey Williams, 12-20-05 entry,
"I went an interviewed George McMahon about his involvement in the child pornography ring that was operating in the Cass Corridor in the late

70's. . George also said that he attended Wayne State University for approximately 20 years from the mid 60's until the early 80's, when he earned advanced degrees. George told detectives that he has been involved in running local community teen programs in the Cass area for many years and has also been involved with the Cass-methodist church. . .George admitted knowing Bob Moore and said that he knew that Bob was involved with young kids and that he thought that Bob was a pedophile."
Casenotes of Det. Corey Williams, 12-06-05 entry,
"Rev. Redmond's wife called me back later and said that her son did not remember anything like what I was describing, but that she had been thinking about it and remember that a guy named George McMahon owns a home in the area and has lived there for many years. I was familiar with this name as a guy Lawson named in a 1988 interview, as a guy that was involved in a pedophile pornography ring in the Cass Corridor area back in the 1970's. The report from this interview said that McMahon was supplying children to Bob Moore at that time to be filmed in this pornography."
Casenotes of Det. Corey Williams, 1-20-06 entry,
"I went over to George McMahon's today and showed him the report from the interview of Richard Lawson in 1988. . .Now that George McMahon has passed the polygraph, we tried to get him to open up about what Lawson said about McMahon also being a person who supplied kids to Bob Moore to be filmed, but that he was not involved with the kids missing from Oakland County. McMahon was uncooperative about this and continued to distance himself from Bob Moore and any involvement he had with Moore other than what he told us during the first interview."
[200] Casenotes of Det. Corey Williams, 11-14-07 entry,
[201] Casenotes of Det. Corey Williams, 11-14-07 entry,
"McKinnon stated that his crew was working alongside the Oakland County Task Force on this Schultz case and when they arrested Schultz, they were certain they had arrested the Oakland County Child Killer. McKinnon told me that Schultz was then cleared of involvement in the child killings after passing a state police polygraph."
[202] 'Man, 39. accused of sex with children', Lansing State Journal August 28 1984
[203] Casenotes of Det. Corey Williams, 10-20-08 entry,
"(Received the Huntington Beach PD reports today, on Greene's arrest in 1974, for multiple CSC's in Huntington, California) This police report, outlined the investigation into the incident that led to Greene being arrested, charged with 45-50 counts of Child Molestation, False imprisonment, attempted murder and then being sent to

a state mental hospital where he did only 6-12 months and was released."

[204] Flint Police Department application for arrest Warrant of Gregory Greene, complaint no 1892-77, January 25 1977

[205] OCCK Tip File #370, Gregory Woodard Greene, Received from Tom Waldren of Flint PD who Interviewed Gregory Greene January 25 1977.

"Suspect gave information on Subject Chris Busch as a suspect in this case. Turned out to be more of a suspect than informant."

Report on interview conducted with Christopher Busch,

"Officers advised him Greg Greene told these officers that he, Busch, had killed Stebbin's"

[206] Michigan PD Incident Report, Complaint No. 27-686-77, 24 February 1977,

[207] Narrative Report, Interview with Kenneth Bowman, January 26 1977, Complaint No. 7603-(remaining numbers cut off in scan copy of document)

[208] Busch Obituary, Detroit Free Press, 31 July 2002

[209] FBI report on Interview with Charles Nels Busch, 04/22/2008,

"CHRIS then returned to the United Stated and attended Wayne State University in Detroit for one year."

[210] Casenotes of Det. Corey Williams, 6-30-09 entry.

[211] Department of State Police Polygraph Examination Report of Christopher Busch by Ralph E. Cabot, January 28 1977, Regarding the murder of Mark Stebbins.

[212] Southfield PD City of Livonia narrative report, Complaint No. 7603079, Det. Lourn Doan interview of Christopher Busch, January 28 1977

Also mentioned in 'The Snow Killings' by Marney Rich Keenan, page 97

[213] Genesee County Jail Inmate Record, Complaint No. 30921, Inmate No. 77-00487, Christopher Busch released 1-31-77 2:05 PM

[214] 'Flint men accused of sex with boys', Lansing State Journal, February 18 1977

Busch, Greene, and the third man were named the following day in the article: '3 named in sex case', Lansing State Journal February 19 1977

[215] 'New sex charges filed in Oakland', Detroit Free Press March 1 1977

[216] Det. Corey Williams interview of James Gunnels
[217] The Snow Killings: Inside the Oakland County Child Killer Investigation, Marney Rich Keenan, p148
[218] Letter from Robert F. Leonard Prosecuting Attorney, Genesee County, to Benjamin Civiletti, Assistant U.S. Attorney General, March 4, 1977. Found in: Committee on the Judiciary hearing on Child Sexual Exploitation, May 23 & 25 1977
[219] Letter from Prosecuting Attorney Genesee County Michigan, Robert F. Leonard to David F. Tibbetts, April 6 1977
[220] Statement by Robert F. Leonard, Committee on the Judiciary hearing on Child Sexual Exploitation, May 23 & 25 1977
[221] 'Genesse prosecutor's staff questioned', The Times Herald, February 18 1978
'Leonard gets 5 years, Fine', The Herald-Palladium, February 26 1980
[222] Report on Operation Burial Ritual, Commenced May 9 1977 by OCCK Task Force.
[223] Case notes of Det. Corey Williams, entry 11-14-07,
"I called Dave Robertson and asked him when Schultz was polygraphed, to which he stated that he was polygraphed in December of 1977 by examiner Romatowski, an MSP examiner and cleared."
[224] Letter from F/Lt. Robert H. Robertson to Louis B. Sims, Chief U.S National Bureau Interpol, December 12 1977
[225] Mount Clemens Police Criminal Arrest Record, Complaint No. 262682, Criminal File No. 24572, Richard James McNamee.
[226] Bloomfield PD Narrative Report, November 20 1978,
[227] Oakland County Crime Scene casefiles on Christopher Busch suicide.
[228] 'Oakland child slayer squad will quit—without a suspect', Detroit Free Press November 21 1978
[229] 'Livonia cops make arrest in 1989 driveway slaying', Detroit Free Press February 23 2005
[230] Details of this smuggling ring can be found in Shane Liddick's "A Smuggler's Life", published in the April 2005 issue of San Diego magazine. Article is referenced in Det. Corey Williams case notes, 2-9-06 entry,
"Liddick wrote a story about Lawson's involvement in illegal alien smuggling over the U.S/Mexican border that was called 'A Smugglers Life' and was published in the April 2005 issue"

[231] Casenotes of Det. Corey Williams, 6-2-05 entry,
"He said that Richard is a full blown pedophile, was an excellent snitch and helped his crew arrest over 20 pedophiles working the Woodward and 6 Mile area at the time of the OCCK investigation, in an attempt to locate the child killer. . .McKinnon reiterated that if I can get Lawson talking he would be a wealth of information, stating that Lawson was connected to and kept files on pedophiles in not only Detroit, but also places like Chicago, Indianapolis, New York…etc."

[232] Casenotes of Det. Corey Williams, 12-13-05 entry,
"The only connection so far between Lawson and Francis Shelden's pedophile ring is that Lawson talked about Shelden financing the film of Timothy King, produced by Bob Moore. Lawson told detectives this during the interview in 1988, after he contacted Timothy King's father from the Macomb County jail, stating that he knew who killed his son. John and I agreed that the motive behind the kidnappings and killings was probably the money the suspects were getting for filming and selling the Snuff films of these children."

[233] Casenotes of Det. Corey Williams, entry 12-09-05,
"In the report that John Oulette (FBI) found from the interview of Lawson in 1988. Lawson had said that a wealthy pedophile named Shelden was the guy who financed the pornographic movies that Bob Moore was making in Detroit involving children."

[234] Casenotes of Det. Corey Williams, 2-15-06 entry,
"During the course of this lengthy interview with Lawson, it was determined that the only information Lawson might have that could assist the investigation is that he claims to have looked at two Polaroid photos of Timothy King alive, standing naked, and another adult male is standing in the photo with the King boy. Richard said that he was at Bob Moore's house at the time Ted Lamborgine showed him these photos, stating in a bragging kind of way, 'looks like the King kid.' Richard said that Bob Moore became upset when he noticed Ted showing Richard these photos."

[235] Casenotes of Det. Corey Williams, 2-16-06 entry,
"Lawson said he had an opportunity to think last night and that he remembered the name of the subject he called #1 in the 1988 interview report. Lawson also said that if the picture of Ted showed him was in fact of Timothy King, then he knows who the Oakland County Child Killer is and the guy in the photo with the King boy is the accomplice. Richard told me that he knows that guys name and that he is still alive today. Richard indicated that he was not going to reveal these two names to me yet"

[236] Casenotes of Det. Corey Williams, 12-1-05 entry,

"Lawson described a subject named Sheldon and three unnamed subjects as having been involved in a child-pornography ring in the Cass Corridor in the mid to late 70's. Lawson also stated that these subjects were also involved in the OCCK case. Lawson stated that the King boy was also possibly filmed by these subjects before he was killed. This report contained information from Lawson that mirrors the information that I have gathered over the past ten months in this case, minus the name. Lawson called these suspects numbers 1,2 & 3, and gave descriptions to detectives during this 1988 interview. These descriptions given by Lawson for # 2& 3, matched Bob Moore and Ted Lamborgine a.k.a Ted Orr. The subject called #1 by Lawson has not been identified."

[237] Casenotes of Det. Corey Williams, 11-27-06 entry,

"Lawson was frequenting poker games near the Wonderbread plant in Detroit in the mid to late 70's. Lawson was also frequenting this same poker game where they would share pedophile stories about kids. Faye confirmed this along with the 1988 report when Lawson called Timothy King's father at home and told him that he knows who killed his son. Lawson was pretty sure he knew, again, but couldn't prove it. In this report, Lawson told Detective Studt from Birmingham PD that he met the person he described in the report as #1 at a poker game. Lawson described these subjects as #1, 2 & 3 and told detectives that he believed these to be the people responsible for the killing of Timothy King and possibly the others. Lawson also told detectives in the 1988 report that #1 was high on cocaine one night at a poker game and told Lawson that he had seen a child porn movie with Timothy King in it."

[238] Casenotes of Det. Corey Williams, 2-7-07 entry,

"Approximately a year and a half ago, John Ouelett (FBI) forwarded a request to the FBI & Dutch police in Amsterdam to pursue a possible connection between a large distributor of child pornography in Amsterdam, according to Lawson, named Kim, Francis Sheldon and the possibility of a connection with the Oakland County Child Killings. Lawson had told authorities in 1988, when he was facing life in prison for child molestation, that he had travelled to Amsterdam in 1979 and had a conversation with this Kim. Lawson said that Kim named Francis Sheldon and #1 by name as having involvement in the abduction/murder of Timothy King. Lawson had mentioned in the 1988 report that Francis Duffield Sheldon (pedophile from the southwest Michigan area, was the person who was financing the child porn photos and films in the Detroit area and shipping them to Amsterdam for distribution to the eye of the chicken-hawk organization."

[239] Casenotes of Det. Corey Williams, 2-7-07 entry,

"Today, the FBI in Washington D.C., forwarded a response they received from the Dutch police in Brussels in regards to our request. In this response, the Dutch authorities, state that they compared all the photographs of our OCCK victims to photos and films they confiscated during a large child porn sting in Amsterdam in 1993, with negative results. However, they state that Kim was identified in the 1993 investigation as Kim Tam Ang, born 4-16-1933, a British national from Selangor, Malacca, living in Amsterdam. Ang was well known to Dutch police for child pornography and sexual abuse of minor boys in 1997. The Dutch police, also provided that Francis Duffield Shelden, w/m", born 9-5-28, from Wayne County, Michigan, U.S.A. died 7-9-96, was also named in their investigation. Ang & Sheldon were both mentioned in an investigation by the Danish police in 1993 concerning child pornography and sexual offenses against minors. This confirms Lawson's story."

[240] Casenotes of Det. Corey Williams, 2-14-07 entry,

"Another interesting possibility is that Josiah Tazelaar is the #1 subject that Lawson described to Barry King in the 1988 FBI report that we have been trying to identify. We had already known that #2 was Bob Moore and #3 was Ted from their descriptions in that report. #1 had told Lawson in the late 70's or early 80's, that he had seen the King boy in a child porn movie. According to Lawson, #1 was living in the Highland Park area at that time and was named by Kim (child porn magazine owner in Amsterdam) to Lawson in 79 when Lawson was in Amsterdam, as having been involved in the killing of Timothy King. We have already confirmed that Lawson did in fact travel to Amsterdam in 1979 and according to Louise Hodgson when interviewed in 1977, Josiah makes trips abroad (indicating out of the country). Josiah is Dutch and Amsterdam is the Child Porn Capital. This is also where Francis Sheldon fled to in 1976 while under indictment. Francis Sheldon was a millionaire and was involved in financing child porn just like Lawson had told me. Francis Sheldon's activities in Amsterdam and this Kim subject were both confirmed by the FBI stationed in Brussels. We had sent a lead to Brussels to check on this for us and received the positive response 2-7-07."

[241] Case notes of Det. Corey Williams, 2-14-07 entry,

"I was reading over the Francis Sheldon file tonight and observed a Kent Gilbert Schultz, born [redacted]-1944, who resides at [redacted] Church St. Highland Park, Michigan."

[242] Casenotes of Det. Corey Williams, 2-16-06 entry,

"Richard told me that he knows the guys name and that he is still alive today"

[243] Casenotes of Det. Corey Williams, 2-9-07 entry,
"I put the [redacted] Windemere address into the mapquest computer program, which revealed that the Tazelaars live and have lived in the same neighbourhood, approximately 3-6 blocks form the King family for many years."
[244] Casenotes of Det. Corey Williams, 12-01-05 entry,
"Lawson was awaiting trail[sic] on a four count CSC (child u13 case)...Lawson then asked for immunity on over 20 years of pedophilia by him. Lawson's CSC case was dismissed and this information was never followed up on."
[245] Casenotes of Det. Corey Williams, 2-8-07 entry
[246] Casenotes of Det. Corey Williams, 3-21-07 entry
Casenotes of Det. Corey Williams, 4-4-07 entry
[247] Casenotes of Det. Corey Williams, 7-31-06 entry,
"during the course of their interview with Ted, he admitted to having sex with several of the approximately 13 young boys (minors) named from the list that i had faxed to Detective Scharschmidt."
Casenotes of Det. Corey Williams, 8-24-05 entry,
"Lamborgine said that he was fairly close with Bob Moore but didn't really know Bob Schuler 'Big Bob' that well. Lamborgine said that this group of pedophiles gave him the name of 'Ted Orr' back in the 70's so he used it on the street. Lamborgine went on to say that Bob Moore had molested a lot of young boys in his day. Lamborgine said that he saw a photo album with hundreds of young boys' pictures that Moore had molested in the 70's...Ted went on to say that he and the others in his group did in fact participate in 'boys night out' which consisted of he and the others picking up young boys and molesting them."
[248] Casenotes of Det. Corey Williams, 3-28-07 entry
'Revisiting the Crimes', Detroit Free Press 17 June 2012
[249] Casenotes of Det. Corey Williams, 7-31-2007 entry
[250] Casenotes of Det. Corey Williams, 2-27-08 entry
[251] FBI report on Interview of Charles Busch, 4/25/2008
Casenotes of Det. Corey Williams, 4-28-08 entry,
"It is interesting that Charles Busch has conditions to supplying DNA as far as us notifying him prior to making any announcement (pres conference) on the results of the DNA. He also requested that prior to the Task Force making any announcement about Christopher Busch's DNA in the OCCK case, that Busch family members in Michigan be allowed to enter a witness protection type program. According to MacDonald's report, Charles Busch was adamant about these conditions being agreed to prior to

supplying his DNA."
[252] FBI report on Interview of Charles Busch, 4/22/2008
[253] *The Snow Killings: Inside the Oakland County Child Killer Investigation*, Marney Rich Keenan, p106
[254] OCCK Task Force tip file 102977
[255] Archive of website published by Barry King, www.afathersstoryocck.com/page/7/,
"Richard Lawson, a convicted murderer and pedophile activist in the Detroit Cass Avenue Corridor, wrote me a letter and asked for a meeting to discuss the OCCK case. I had met Lawson previously and had little respect for him. Dave Binkley of my law firm agreed to visit with him. Binkley was under instructions not to talk to him about anything other than the Christopher Busch involvement. Lawson advised Binkley that his associate Bobby Moore, used to take young boys to visit with H. Lee Busch, the father of Christopher Busch. Lawson has subsequently died and I am not aware as to whether or not the Task
Force followed up on this information."
[256] Casenotes of Det. Corey Williams, 4-7-06 entry,
"[redacted] also said that Moore prostituted him out when he was a young teenage boy, stating that Moore drove him to a home on a lake in Pontiac, Michigan and the older white man (Bill) that he had sex with, had a large boat docked in front of the house. [redacted] went on to say that the homeowner paid Moore the money and Moore in turn gave him some money for letting the homeowner perform oral sex on him. This matches information from Lawson, who had stated in earlier interviews that he and Moore took a young boy to a Chrysler executives home on the east side (possibly Warren) back in the mid to late 70's and the executive paid Moore to have sex with the boy. This also matches information from Tony Kawalcek(see his interview)."
[257] Catherine Broad Blog comment, https://catherinebroad.blog/2016/05/
""Hi Cathy, I was a teenager in Detroit at the time and my father had a stamp and coin store at Eastland Shopping Center. One of his customers was E. Harwood Rydholm, a big executive at Chrysler. Mr. Rydholm told my dad that the OCCK was the son of a powerful GM exec and that the police were protecting GM's reputation so he probably wouldn't be arrested. Mr. Rydholm passed away in 1987. The ghastly part is that Mr. Rydholm told my father this shortly after Kristine Mihelich went missing."
Also see *The Snow Killings: Inside the Oakland County Child Killer Investigation*, Marney Rich Keenan, page 243

[258] Copy of email received by Catherine Broad, www.catherine-broad.files.wordpress.com/2019/10/2019-10-28_114327.pdf
[259] Letter sent to Barry King, 02/07/2014, https://catherinebroad.blog/2020/12/13/when-i-heard-the-details-gm-executive-organized-ring-of-sexual-abuse-etc-my-blood-ran-cold/
[260] The Snow Killings: Inside the Oakland County Child Killer Investigation, Marney Rich Keenan, page 172
[261] FBI victims statement, File No. 31C-DE-NEW, Milford Michigan, 6/19/1992
[262] 'DU PONT TO BREAK FINAL G. M. TIES; 47-Year-Old Link Will End With a Last Distribution of 23 Million Shares', New York Times, November 17 1964
[263] 'Wall Street and The Rise Of Hitler', Antony C. Sutton, page 74
[264] Ibid, page 31
[265] 'Wallstreet and FDR', Antony C. Sutton, page 154
[266] 'Dupont's Up-and-Down History Shaped Biden's Views on Business
',Wall Street Journal, November 23 2020
[267] 'Biden: I Tried to 'Prostitute Myself' to Big Donors During First Senate Run', www.freebeacon.com/politics/biden-i-tried-to-prostitute-myself-to-big-donors-during-first-senate-run/
"I went to the big guys for the money," Biden said. "I was ready to prostitute myself in the manner in which I talk about it, but what happened was they said, 'Come back when you're 40, son.'"
"So I had to go out, I had to go out to a number of small contributors," he said"
[268] 'Beau Biden defends handling of du Pont heir sex case', delawareonline.com, April 3 2014
[269] 'A Project Veritas Employee Leaked Ashley Biden's Diary',The Intercept, September 7 2022
[270] 'Art Gallery Death a Mystery', Detroit Free Press, September 22 1977
'A guide to galleries around town', 'Detroit Free Press, May 24 1970
[271] Michigan Department of State Police Supplementary Complaint Report, no. 23-1728-76
[272] 'Porno ring uses church, tax laws', Traverse City Record Eagle, April 4 1977.
"Educational Foundation for Youth was more difficult to trace. The Secretary of State's office in Springfield, Ill. could find no record of its existence.

However, a clerk in Secretary of State's Chicago officer, where the foundation allegedly was located, said it was a non-profit arm of a profit making corporation. Described as an import-export business, the parent company was incorporated in 1962 and was involuntarily dissolved in 1975 for failure to pay state franchise taxes"

'Starchild a man of mystery', Traverse City Record Eagle, December 16 1977.

"It is known, however, that Starchild is linked to at least one Jamaican trust company. The Trust Co. of West Indies, Ltd. was incorporated by Starchild and a New Jersey attorney, Ralph Fucetola III. . .the trust company, and several other organizations now suspected by police of being fronts for child pornography operations. . .Fucetola said that the trust company incorporated by Starchild and him was set up as an offshore banking operation but was currently inactive. Some holdings of the trust company were to be funnelled to the Foundation for the Caribbean. Fucetola said. The plans were to solicit surplus books from U.S schools and businesses and ship them to underprivileged schools overseas."

[273] National Bank of Detroit, Plaintiff, v. Francis D. Shelden, et al., Defendants.the Trust Company of the Virgin Islands, Ltd., (no. 82-1905)and Peter J. Cipollini, (no. 82-1737), Defendants-appellants, v. L. Bennett Young and Detroit Bank and Trust Company, Second-successor Co- Trustees, Intervening Defendants-appellees, 730 F.2d 421 (6th Cir. 1984)

"On April 13, 1978, Shelden executed a document removing The Trust Company of the Virgin Islands as trustee and naming Edward Brongersma as successor trustee. This document was notarized in Amsterdam and complies in all respects with the provisions of the Trust Instrument. Brongersma accepted the appointment the same day. Shelden testified that Brongersma for many years had been "a Senator, a Dutch equivalent. He was a member of the Upper House of the Dutch Government; was chairman of the Judicial committee; was a lawyer, doctor of law."In his deposition, Antoon Kasdorp stated that he served the papers removing The Trust Company of the Virgin Islands upon Starchild in person April 20, 1978."

[274] 'Child Pornography' by Tim Tate (Methuen, 1990)

[275] Clean copy(images removed) of PAN volume one, http://exitinterview.biz/rarities/pan/n1/pan1.pdf

[276] 'Net tightens on child porn pedlars','The Sunday People, February 12 1984

'The evil men behind child sex empire', The Sunday People, June 16 1985

'Scandal of Britons who buy young boys for £3 a night', Sunday Times, August 3 1986
'Child Pornography' by Tim Tate (Methuen, 1990)
"Fully four months after Mahmood's article appeared in the Sunday Times, the Dutch police got round to raiding Stamford's luxury home in Baarn, a sleepy little village twenty-five miles outside Amsterdam"
[277] Spartacus guide for Gay Men 16th Edition April 1987, sourced from: http://brunoleaks.blogspot.com/2011/08/6teil-die-ganze-geschichte-vom.html
'Editor playing role of world's pimp on child sex charges', The Guardian, November 17 1994
Le Belge éditeur du guide pédophile «Spartacus» sera jugé en cour d'assises, Liberation, Sylvain Ephimenco, April 20 1995
[278] "Die grosse Angst: Berlin wird Europas Kinderporno-Hauptstadt", Berliner BZ, 13 May 1992, Von Uwe Steinschek.
Note: Authenticity of article and translation dependent on secondary source: http://brunoleaks.blogspot.com/2011/08/6teil-die-ganze-geschichte-vom.html
"The meanest criminal in our city went into hiding . The big fear: Berlin will become Europe's child porn capital. By Uwe Steinschek. Child porn is his dirty business - videos on which minors are abused: John D. Stamford (52), ex-priest from England. "He fled to Berlin," says a French scene expert, "he turned the city into the European porn metropolis.Chief Detective Kurt Richter from the vice squad: "It's possible that Stamford is hanging around in Berlin. But we don't know exactly where yet." Stamford describes himself as the "king" of dirty business . He fled to Berlin after the police confiscated 16 boxes of child pornography and 25,000 customer addresses from his villa near Amsterdam. Scotland Yard, the famous London police, has a terrible suspicion: Stamford filmed 20 boys dying after sex orgies in England. On these perverse films: after the children have been repeatedly raped by men, they have been strangled, suffocated, strangled. The videos were sold for around 1,500 marks per strip - to particularly good "customers"."The child porn scene is hard to crack," says Kurt Richter. "There are only a few victims who report it - shame plays a big role there. The number of unreported cases is high." The porn sharks take a close look at potential buyers. It's best to show your own "material" first. That identifies the "insider". Once the "security check" has been completed, the video tapes are sent via numbered lockers [meaning: normal postal boxes]. Kurt Richter: "Depending on their age, the porn victims are lured with money, sweets or toys." Example: A man from Reinickendorf lured the

children with money. He had posted notices on a residential street looking for boys who wanted to earn money by cleaning swimming pools. The 8 to 14 year olds had to undress and, following the man's instructions, play sex games in front of the camera - for 10 marks. The strips were sold for 135 to 260 marks. The matter blew up because a nine-year-old told his parents what had happened to him." [German to English Translation]

[279] 'En Belgique, l'ancien pasteur accusé d'incitation à la pédophilie se défend', Liberation, February 23 1995

"In addition, last week, a testimony of a former collaborator was read during the hearing according to which Stamford would have made a film showing how two young Filipinos would have been tortured and murdered by his care." [French to English Translation]

[280] 'Briton dies before child sex hearing', The Daily Telegraph, December 30 1995

Michigan Department of State Police Supplemental Incident Report No.070-0000355-76, May 2 1997.

[281] 'Paedophile Clarence Henry Howard-Osborne's files could have brought down government', Matthew Condon, The Courier-Mail, March 18 2016

[282] Ibid.

[283] Ibid.

[284] Ibid.

[285] '4 charged in London vice swoop', The Observer, August 8 1982

[286] 'Cover-up Bid In Vice Scandal', News of The World, August 8 1982

[287] 'Security Alert Over New Vice Scandal', Daily Express, August 7 1982

'VIPs on Vice Charges Soon?', The Sun, August 9 1982

[288] 'Vice police reopen file on boys', Daily Express, August 10 1982

[289] 'Attorney General to prove London brothel reports', Capital Gay, August 1982

[290] 'Elm Guest House couple walk free', Capital Gay, May 6 1983

[291] 'Police slash their Elm Guest House evidence', Capital Gay, April 22 1983

[292] 'Paedophile dossier', Scunthorpe Evening Telegraph, January 19 1984

[293] 'MP who handed VIP paedophile dossier to Leon Brittan was on triple killer's hit list', The Mirror, July 5 2014

'Fugitive May Have Used Car', Daily Mail, november 3 1983

[294] 'A RICHMOND children's home supplied young boys to a Barnes guest house for sexual and pornographic purposes, it was revealed at an inquest this week', Surrey Comet, August 10 1990
[295] 'Expose These Evil Child Sex VIPs', The Sport, August 23 1990
[296] 'Children's home boss facing historical sex abuse charges found dead', The Telegraph, January 16 2015
[297] 'Father Anthony McSweeney guilty of abuse at children's home', BBC, February 27 2015
[298] 'House of Porn: Ex-Cabinet Minister pictured with naked boys in sauna', Sunday Mirror, August 12 1990
'Child Sex:Top Tory named', The Sport, August 10 1990
[299] 'Social worker who accused Leon Brittan and other VIPs as being members of an alleged paedophile ring was convicted of fraud in 2011', Daily Mail, September 23 2015
[300] 'Cyril Smith named in Barnes abuse case', The Independent, January 27 2013
[301] Sir Cyril Smith 'visited alleged sex abuse guest house', BBC, September 13 2013
Met's paedophile unit seizes video of ex-minister at 'sex party', Exaro News, December 7 2013
[302] 'Child expert in porn inquiry', The Daily Telegraph, May 28 1992
[303] 'Edwardian house at heart of a long-simmering sex scandal', The Guardian, July 5 2014
[304] Photos of the Mary Moss notes were posted on The Needle Blog, www.theneedleblog.wordpress.com/richmond/the-mary-moss-elm-guest-house-documents-with-transcripts/
[305] 'Files reveal who turned Elm Guest House into paedo brothel', exaro news, February 2 2013 - www.exaro.news/files-reveal-who-turned-elm-guest-house-into-paedo-brothel,

"Papers seized by police name the man who helped turn a guest house into a paedophile brothel allegedly used by MPs and other VIPs. Exaro can reveal that the key figure who persuaded Carole Kasir, co-manager of the guest house, to create a haven for homosexual men to have sex with boys is Peter Glencross, who was part of an underground paedophile network called 'Spartacus'. The evidence, seen by Exaro, raises serious questions for the many MPs of all main political parties and other VIPs who, according to the papers, visited Elm Guest House in Barnes, south-west London. It comes as detectives interview victims, and prepare to make initial arrests and lay charges as part of 'Operation Fernbridge' – within weeks. The

Metropolitan Police Service is planning to hold a press conference soon afterwards to encourage more victims to come forward. Peter Spindler, the Met commander, is expected to be at the press conference, accompanied by Tom Watson, the campaigning MP, plus a representative of the NSPCC, the charity aimed at preventing cruelty to children. The Met last month launched a full criminal investigation into allegations that many prominent people, including politicians, abused boys in the early 1980's at the guest house. That move came after Exaro made a series of revelations about the case. In a joint investigation last weekend, Exaro and the Sunday People disclosed how a Conservative party campaign group "strongly recommended" the guest house to members in a newsletter. Papers relating to the guest house name its alleged VIP visitors. Detectives seized the papers in a raid last month. The papers suggest that two men persuaded Carole Kasir to change the guest house into a place for homosexual men in 1982. According to the files, they introduced her to Glencross, a South African based in Holland, one of whose roles was to create a network of venues for Spartacus members. Spartacus International, a gay guide, identified Glencross as its commercial manager. The Spartacus Club used it to attract members. A German company has since taken over Spartacus International, and transformed it into a respectable publisher of gay guides. Carole Kasir, who died at the age of 47 in 1990, may have been unaware of Glencross's connection with Spartacus. But the guest house placed advertisements in the gay Press that signalled it as a place for homosexuals who want to have sex with boys. The advertisements included the line: "10% Discount to Spartacus Club Members." Any Spartacus member, and many other paedophiles, would have understood the coded reference. Exaro revealed an example of these advertisements, from London's Capital Gay newspaper a fortnight ago, at the same time as tracking down the surviving co-manager of Elm Guest House, Haroon, or "Harry", Kasir, whose home has also been raided by police. He is refusing to comment. Spartacus Club and Spartacus International were then run from Amsterdam by John Stamford, a former Roman Catholic priest from Lancashire, who moved to Holland after being convicted in England of sending pornographic material through the post. The club was reported to have 25,000 British members. The group was named after the leader of the Roman slave revolt, who has long been a gay icon, especially after the scene in Stanley Kubrick's 1960 film in which the character of Crassus, a senator, is helped to bathe by his young slave, Antoninus. Stamford masqueraded as a libertarian gay, but championed the Paedophile Information Exchange, a network promoting sex with children. There is no trace of Glencross after 1989. Between 1979 and 1985, Stamford also published PAN, or Paedo Alert News, which described itself as a "magazine about boy-love." Spartacus was exposed by The Sunday Times in 1986. Undercover reporters were offered two boys in Manila, aged 8 and 14. Stamford was quoted as saying: "If you are discreet, I can guarantee you will get as many boys as you want in the Philippines. "Our chaps there will fix it up, and all it will cost you is a meal for the guides, and just the equivalent of a pound or so for the kid per night." Stamford died, aged 56, in prison of a heart attack in Belgium in 1995 just before he was due to stand trial on child sex charges."

[306] Photos of these can be found at:
www.theneedleblog.wordpress.com/2013/04/08/spartacus-invitation-to-elm-guest-house/
www.theneedleblog.wordpress.com/2013/04/08/another-letter-from-spartacus/

[307] 'Paedophile ring leader, Colin Peters, linked to Barnes scandal', The Independent, March 3 2013

[308] 'Father claims police covered up son's murder by Westminster paedophile ring', The Guardian, Josh Halliday, November 19 2014

[309] 'The Sadness Behind A Sant's Smile', Sunday Express, December 27 1981

[310] 'Vice police reopen file on boys', Daily Express, August 10 1982
'Lost Boys in Gay Probe', Daily Star, August 10 1982

[311] 'Paedophile ring allegations: police are failing us, murdered boy's father says', The Guardian, November 19 2014

[312] 'Paedophile ring allegations: police are failing us, murdered boy's father says', The Guardian, November 19 2014
'Notorious paedophile gang could have covered up 17 child murders and be linked to VIP guest house', Daily Mail, November 20 2014

[313] Independent Inquiry into Child Sexual Abuse, Witness Statement of Donald Hale, 29/12/18,
"It is also understood from a key police source that Australia intelligence officers carried out a thorough inquiry into his disappearance at the time, and examined the use of casual chauffeurs, who worked for, or visited the Commissioner's residence at Stoke Lodge, Kensington. The Met have no inferred that Martin could have been one of three young boys murdered by a VIP paedophile ring that included politicians and prominent people in the 1970's and 80's. All the murders are said to have occurred in a similar time period and are linked to several known paedophile venues at Dolphin Square, Elm Guest House, and an address in Kensington. . . Martin lived with his

family in the caretaker's cottage within the elegant grounds of the Commissioner's residence, which was visited at that time by a host of prominent officials. Regular attendees for civic functions were Prime Minister Margaret Thatcher ad her disgraced aides, including paedophile diplomat Sir Peter Hayman, the disgraced private secretary Sir Peter Morrison, and former Home Secretary Leon Brittan, now tainted with similar sex abuse claims. "

[314] Cops to quiz child killer Sidney Cooke as they reopen case of missing boy, Mirror, May 21 2016
The Independent Inquiry into Child Sexual Abuse, Witness Statement of Donald Hale, 29/12/18,
"Kevin told police it was common practise for the Commission to supplement its own regular drivers with casual drivers, or to hire an additional chauffeur firm from across the Thames. He said: 'At the same time as Martin's disappearance, a couple of paedophiles worked for the one car company that Australia House used as sub-contractors. Cooke and a few other infamous multi-murdering people worked for this company.'"

[315] 'A missing boy and the Australian high commission in London', The Australian, February 1 2015

[316] 'Westminster child abuse claims Elm Guest House', The Guardian, November 19 2014
'Elm Guest House paedophile network allegations', The Guardian, July 5 2014

[317] 'Police close probe into claims MP Cyril Smith was let go after being caught with child porn because of lack of evidence', Daily Mail, July 30 2015

[318] The Independent Inquiry into Child Sexual Abuse, Witness Statement of Donald Hale.

[319] ' Tory MP allegedly found with child porn in 1980s faced no charges, police told', The Telegraph, July 4 2014

[320] Man who tried to import video: 'I did not know what was inside', Exaro News, March 29 2014

[321] Customs and Excise Notice of Seizure under customs and Excise acts 1979 To R.H Tricker, London Gazette, 6 August 1982

[322] Customs seized video of child sex abuse and ex-cabinet minister, Exaro News, March 29 2014
"Tricker denies knowing what was contained in any of the material, which he says was in sealed packages. Senior managers at Customs and Excise then took over the case. They took no further action

against Tricker, and are understood to have passed the video cassette to the Security Service, MI5. No one was prosecuted. Customs and Excise later merged with the Inland Revenue to form HM Revenue & Customs (HMRC). Solanki has told friends that the former Conservative cabinet minister is seen on the video. The retired Customs officer identified the former cabinet member, but is so scared about the sensitive nature of the video that he refuses to say what the ex-minister is doing exactly."
Audio file set to blow lid off paedophile scandal at Westminster, Exaro News, july 19 2014
Transcript of Solanki interview, www.theneedleblog.wordpress.com
THE LONG STRANGE, SAGA OF LEON BRITTAN, Tim Tate, www.timtate.co.uk/blog/the-politician-the-paedophiles-the-police-press/
[323] 'Operation Midland: The story behind the Met's controversial VIP paedophile ring investigation', The Telegraph, 21 September 2015
[324] "Nine killed in child porn ring", The Guardian, July 28 1990
[325] 'Teenager confessed to filming snuff movie' , Maurice Chittenden, Sunday Times July 29 1990
[326] "Die grosse Angst: Berlin wird Europas Kinderporno-Hauptstadt", Berliner BZ, 13 May 1992, Von Uwe Steinschek.
Note: Authenticity of article and translation dependent on secondary source: www.brunoleaks.blogspot.com/2011/08/6teil-die-ganze-geschichte-vom.html,
"The meanest criminal in our city went into hiding . The big fear: Berlin will become Europe's child porn capital. By Uwe Steinschek. Child porn is his dirty business - videos on which minors are abused: John D. Stamford (52), ex-priest from England. "He fled to Berlin," says a French scene expert, "he turned the city into the European porn metropolis.Chief Detective Kurt Richter from the vice squad: "It's possible that Stamford is hanging around in Berlin. But we don't know exactly where yet." Stamford describes himself as the "king" of dirty business . He fled to Berlin after the police confiscated 16 boxes of child pornography and 25,000 customer addresses from his villa near Amsterdam. Scotland Yard, the famous London police, has a terrible suspicion: Stamford filmed 20 boys dying after sex orgies in England. On these perverse films: after the children have been repeatedly raped by men, they have been strangled, suffocated, strangled. The videos were sold for around 1,500 marks per strip - to particularly good "customers"."The child porn scene is hard to crack," says Kurt Richter. "There are only a few victims who report it - shame plays a big role there.

The number of unreported cases is high." The porn sharks take a close look at potential buyers. It's best to show your own "material" first. That identifies the "insider". Once the "security check" has been completed, the video tapes are sent via numbered lockers [meaning: normal postal boxes]. Kurt Richter: "Depending on their age, the porn victims are lured with money, sweets or toys." Example: A man from Reinickendorf lured the children with money. He had posted notices on a residential street looking for boys who wanted to earn money by cleaning swimming pools. The 8 to 14 year olds had to undress and, following the man's instructions, play sex games in front of the camera - for 10 marks. The strips were sold for 135 to 260 marks. The matter blew up because a nine-year-old told his parents what had happened to him."[German to English Translation]

[327] Ibid.

[328] 'Police failings put dozens of children at risk from notorious paedophile ring', Independent, March 3 2013

[329] 'When sex abuse can lead to murder', Nick Davies, The Guardian, November 27 2000

[330] 'Fugitive Briton linked to Dutch child porn hits at witch-hunt from Prague refuge', The Guardian, July 31 1998

[331] 'Britons killed boys in Dutch porn movies', The Guardian, April 5 1997

[332] '3000 names on Yard Paedophile register'', Andrew Culf, The Guardian, July 28 1990

[333] 'Britons killed boys in Dutch porn movies', The Guardian, April 5 1997

[334] 'Snared: Britain's most wanted paedophile flown back to face justice after 15 years on the run', Daily Mirror, November 19 2012
'The New Child Sex Capital: Radio 1 DJ's shame in Prague', Sunday Mirror, January 31 1999
'Fugitive Briton linked to Dutch child porn hits at witch-hunt from Prague refuge', The Guardian, July 31 1998

[335] 'Ex-DJ held on child sex charges, The Guardian, November 13 1997

[336] 'Gary Glitter quizzed over child porn on computer', The Evening Standard, November 19 1997

[337] 'All played out', The Guardian, May 4 1999

[338] Cleared of under-age sex then four months for child photographs', The Evening Standard, November 12 1999

[339] 'Glitter child abuse sentence cut', BBC, February 7 2007, news.b-

bc.co.uk/2/hi/asia-pacific/6337867.stm

[340] 'Hitman killed Jill Dando', The Guardian, June 15 2001

[341] 'Former Plymouth journalist Jill Dando knew of BBC paedophile ring, claims retired colleague', The Plymouth Herald, July 21 2014

[342] 'Ex-Radio 1 DJ jailed over sex with boys', The Daily Telegraph, march 16 2000

[343] 'Jonathan King gets 7 years for sex crimes', Evening Standard, November 21 2001

[344] 'Jonathan King arrested on child sex allegations', The Independent, November 24 2000

[345] 'He lured boys. He's a bully, Now he bleats', The Independent, April 3 2005

[346] '7 Years for Pop Pervert', Evening Standard, November 21 2001

[347] 'Czech court throws out plea to extradite Briton', The Guardian, November 28 2001.

[348] 'DJ Denning in dock over child abuse', The Evening Standard, June 2 2005

[349] 'More TV Stars Face Arrest', The Evening Standard, January 16 2003

[350] 'Jimmy Savile Toxic Legacy', Sunday Telegraph, October 7 2012

[351] 'Mark Thompson in spotlight at New York Times over Savile scandal', The Guardian, October 24 2012, www.theguardian.com/media/2012/oct/24/mark-thompson-jimmy-savile-new-york-times, It should be noted Mark Thompson denies this. You may believe him if you wish.

[352] 'Jimmy Savile crisis at the BBC', The Guardian, December 19 2012, www.theguardian.com/media/2012/dec/19/jimmy-savile-crisis-bbc-timeline

[353] 'BBC Worldwide chief tipped to leave in restructure', The Guardian, September 25 2012, www.theguardian.com/media/2012/sep/25/bbc-worldwide-chief

[354] 'New Times chief Mark Thompson leaves sex abuse scandal at BBC', The Guardian, October 16 2012, www.theguardian.com/media/2012/oct/16/new-york-times-mark-thompson-jimmy-savile-bbc

[355] 'Jimmy Savile: New victims say 'organised' paedophile ring operated at BBC', Evening Standard, October 24 2012, www.standard.co.uk/news/crime/jimmy-savile-new-victims-say-organised-paedophile-ring-operated-at-bbc-8224562.html

[356] 'Savile abused us, say eight more women', The Evening Standard, October 3 2012.
[357] 'Ex-Radio 1 DJ arrested over sex allegations', The Daily Telegraph, June 7 2013
[358] 'Former DJ Chris Denning jailed for 13 years over sexual abuse of 24 boys', The Guardian, December 17 2014
[359] 'BBC and victim apologise to Lord McAlpine after admitting abuse claims were a case of mistaken identity', The Independent, November 10 2012, https://www.independent.co.uk/news/uk/crime/bbc-and-victim-apologise-to-lord-mcalpine-after-admitting-abuse-claims-were-a-case-of-mistaken-identity-8301293.html
[360] 'Sir Cliff Richard: BBC pays £2m in final settlement after privacy case', BBC, https://www.bbc.com/news/entertainment-arts-49576940
[361] 'BBC faces questions on paedophile driver', The Daily Telegraph, October 30 2013
[362] 'BBC driver found dead on first day of trial was a prolific paedophile', The Independent, October 30 2013
[363] 'Jimmy Savile chauffeur Dave Smith was prolific paedophile with 22 convictions', The Telegraph, 29 October, https://www.telegraph.co.uk/news/uknews/crime/jimmy-savile/10410614/Jimmy-Savile-chauffeur-Dave-Smith-was-prolific-paedophile-with-22-convictions.html
[364] 'Ex-BBC driver David Smith found dead ahead of sex abuse trial', BBC, October 29 2013, https://www.bbc.com/news/uk-24722248
[365] 'David Smith Dead: Ex-BBC driver in Savile probe was paedophile with 22 sex crime conviction', Irish Mirror, October 29 2013, www.irishmirror.ie/news/david-smith-dead-ex-bbc-driver-2654033
[366] 'BBC tax boss admits off-books pay deals 'cut exposure' of Corporation to tax man', The Telegraph, October 5 2012, https://www.telegraph.co.uk/culture/tvandradio/bbc/9588877/BBC-complicit-in-tax-avoidance-for-household-names-say-MPs.html
[367] 'A missing boy and the Australian high commission in London', The Australian, February 1 2015, Jaquelin Magnay
https://www.theaustralian.com.au/nation/inquirer/news-story/b382b0173078c72bec915a7c5cd3d3b2,
Around that time it was reported that cellmate of a child murderer named Ronald Jebson claimed Jebson had boasted of working as chauffeur for a luxury limousine company hired out to prominent

persons in the 1970s. The cellmate claimed Jebson said the drivers were used to collect children and deliver them to pedophile parties, either from foster homes or from their own parents who were paid money.
www.dailystar.co.uk/news/latest-news/babes-child-killer-linked-westminster-18698802

[368] 'Jimmy Savile victim claims 5 more drivers linked to his abuse', Irish Mirror, https://www.irishmirror.ie/news/world-news/jimmy-savile-victim-claims-5-6654818

[369] 'Jimmy Savile Admits To Be Yorkshire Ripper', https://www.youtube.com/@SirJimmySavileOBEKCSG, uploaded December 28 2022, https://www.youtube.com/watch?v=D7Fhqavc_yM
I watched Savile say this on this video.

[370] 'Jimmy Savile was questioned by police investigating Yorkshire Ripper murders', The Guardian, November 7 2012, www.theguardian.com/uk/2012/nov/07/savile-questioned-yorkshire-ripper-police

[371] 'Detectives 'had a cast made of Savile's teeth' to check against bite-marks left on bodies of Yorkshire Ripper victims'

[372] Warwick Spinks arrest: Child sex attacker back in prison, BBC, November 16 2012

[373] The British paedophile who's still on the run, The Spectator, May 24 2013

[374] 02292-14 Spinks v The Sun, IPSO Ruling, www.ipso.co.uk/rulings-and-resolution-statements/ruling/?id=02292-14

[375] 'A terraced street in suburbia that shrouded a guilty secret', Nick Davies, The Guardian, November 25 2000
'When sex abuse can lead to murder', Nick Davies, The Guardian, November 27 2000

[376] Deduction was used from the following sources to reach this conclusion.
'Nur die kleinen Fische'(Only the small fish), Der Spiegel, August 2 1998,
"So far, investigators have not been able to find anything criminal at Gero-Video Productions GmbH in Düsseldorf, one of the largest distributors of homosexual pornography in Europe. Several investigations were closed. Uwe Tomek, owner of the company since the end of 1994, presents himself as a clean man. Without legal pressure, he emphasizes, he took around 340 porn videos "with younger models" off the market. Films with »just over

14 years old« are no longer in the range.
The discoveries in Zandvoort have nevertheless brought Gero-Video into the spotlight. The alleged child molester Robby van der Plancken, who is incarcerated in Italy because he is said to have shot his partner Gerrit Jan Ulrich, can be seen in at least five Gero strips. Tomek: "Before my time, the films were bought by a Dutch production company in 1993." To his knowledge, there was no personal contact whatsoever between Gero-Video and van der Plancken."[German to English Translation]
Paedophilia is easy 2: how a paedophile murder inquiry fell apart, The Guardian, November 27 2000,
"There have been successful paedophilia operations between British and European police. Scotland Yard detectives recently have twice arrested wanted men and extradited them to Holland for trial on child-sex offences. The Bristol detectives, following the activities of Tucker and Gay, led German police to raid a video distributor in Dusseldorf."

[377] This information comes from a document of dubious origin, originally uploaded at www.boublog.nl/2012/11/08/een-wondelijke-link-naar-het-rolodex-onderzoek/. It is seemingly a dossier provided by an alleged bookkeeper of child trafficker Karel Maasdam named Richard Samson. Those familiar with the cases dealt with in this book would know much of the information checks out and helpfully fills in blanks. None the less, its authenticity is questionable.

[378] 'Britons killed boys in Dutch porn movies', The Guardian, April 5 1997

[379] 'Paedophile networks traffick young boys across Europe', Nick Davies, Previously unpublished, October 1 1998 Researched on commission from the New Yorker.

[380] Ibid.

[381] Ibid.

[382] Dutch Joris Demmink Affair Reveals Heroin, Cocaine and Pedophile Entrapment Affairs; Orange Royal Family Similarly Linked to Child Abuse and Mafia Networks, Joël v.d. Reijden, ISGP-Studies, October 31 2014, www.isgp-studies.com/joris-demmink-and-prince-bernhard-s-alleged-westerflier-cult

[383] 'Dutch Joris Demmink Affair Reveals Heroin, Cocaine and Pedophile Entrapment Affairs', Joel Reijden, october 31 2014, www.isgp-studies.com/joris-demmink-and-prince-bernhard-s-alleged-westerflier-cult

[384] Dutch Joris Demmink Affair Reveals Heroin, Cocaine and Pe-

dophile Entrapment Affairs; Orange Royal Family Similarly Linked to Child Abuse and Mafia Networks, Joël v.d. Reijden, ISGP-Studies, October 31 2014, www.isgp-studies.com/joris-demmink-and-prince-bernhard-s-alleged-westerflier-cult

[385] Els Borst gedood met 41 messteken(Els Borst killed with 41 stabs), NOS Nieuws, September 1 2015

[386] Dutch ex-minister Els Borst found dead, The Guardian, February 12 2014

Ex-Justice chief to be investigated for child abuse, NLTimes, 21 January 2014

[387] Tomas Ross RTL7 interview on Joris Demmink, Els Borst

[388] 'Demmink and officers named in sex case', nu.nl, March 5 2014, www.nu.nl/binnenland/3718379/demmink-en-officieren-genoemd-in-zedenzaak.html

[389] Listening To Victims of Child Sex Trafficking, Commission on Security & Cooperation in Europe: U.S. Helsinki Commission, October 4 2012.

[390] 'Zaak-Demmink lijkt op een spektakel met guillotine'('Demmink case looks like a guillotine spectacle'), NRC, March 22 2014

[391] Paedophile networks traffick young boys across Europe, Nick Davies, Previously unpublished, October 1 1998, Researched on commission from the New Yorker.

[392] 'Demmink en officieren genoemd in zedenzaak, NU, March 5 2014

[393] 'Zaak-Demmink lijkt op een spektakel met guillotine'('Demmink case looks like a guillotine spectacle'), NRC, March 22 2014

[394] Dutch Joris Demmink Affair Reveals Heroin, Cocaine and Pedophile Entrapment Affairs; Orange Royal Family Similarly Linked to Child Abuse and Mafia Networks, Joël v.d. Reijden, ISGP-Studies, October 31 2014, www.isgp-studies.com/joris-demmink-and-prince-bernhard-s-alleged-westerflier-cult

[395] Forced child prostitution case: Netherlands elite royalty under microscope, NL Times, April 18 2016

[396] 'Politicians and officials named in court as 'boy brothel' case begins', Dutch News, April 18 2016

[397] 'Politicians and officials named in court as 'boy brothel' case begins', Dutch News, April 18 2016

[398] Morkhoven gaat kinderpornofoto's overhandigen aan Nederlandse politie("Morkhoven will hand over child pornography

photos to Dutch police"), DeMorgen, July 18 1998

[399] Cassette vidéo de l'émission Faits Divers de la RTBF de septembre 1998 : Réseaux pédophiles
Segments from the interview between Marcel Vervloesem and Robbie Vander Plancken also aired on the more widely available french documentary entitled, 'Zandvoort, the file of shame - Karl Zero Absolute'.

[400] 'No kind of Hero', Tim Hulse, The Independent, September 13 1998

[401] 'The Crusader', Ian Traynor, The Independent, July 22 1998

[402] Ibid.

[403] 'Raid uncovers huge child porn ring', The Guardian, July 17 1998

[404] 'No kind of Hero', Tim Hulse, The Independent, September 13 1998

[405] 'The Crusader', Ian Traynor, The Independent, July 22 1998

[406] 'Raid uncovers huge child porn ring', The Guardian, July 17 1998

[407] 'Mechanisch brutal'('Mechanically brutal'), Der Spiegel, July 19 1998

[408] 'Zaak-Morkhoven: ontdekster komt om in ongeval'('Morkhoven case: discoverer dies in accident'), De Morgen, 17 november 1998

[409] 'Overlijden Gina Pardaens intrigeert Zwitserse justitie'('Death of Gina Pardaens intrigues Swiss justice'), De Morgen, 23 november 1998
Dossier filed by Morkhoven Workgroup with 20 CD ROMS from the Zandvoort child crime network, March 4, 2001, fondationprincessedecroy.eu/07-ZANDVOORT_PLAINTE-au-procureur-bourlet-deposee-avec-les-CD-ROMS.htm

[410] 'Die Spur der Kinderschänder - Dutroux und die toten Zeugen', Piet Eekman, ZDF Network, broadcasted in 2001.
"Before her death, she tells friends about a video tape in which a girl is being murdered during a sex party. She believed one of the perpetrators to be an acquaintance of Nihoul."

[411] Marcel Vervloesem P.V No. 8.257/01, 10.04.2001, Police Federale S.J.A, www.fondationprincessedecroy.eu/001-PV_bebe_-porno_zandvoort_2001___fr__a.htm,
"In February 2001, I came into contact with Robert Warmerdam, who claimed to have frequented the small SM world of Amsterdam for about 15 years. He taught me the following. He told me that he regularly visited the G-force. He claimed that a certain Gerda Lamere operated the bar. The

owner is said to be American. One of the good clients was a certain Marc Dutroux, who had meetings at the G-force on regular dates with a certain Nordholt, who was an official in the Amsterdam police, as well as with a certain Peter De Groot, who worked in a clinical laboratory. Warmerdam claimed that he had often been at table with them and that Dutroux had said that he expected problems, and that he was going to go to prison for a short time. . .Still according to Warmerdam's statements, and when questioned by me on this subject, Dutroux knew how to express himself in Dutch. I am not informed with certainty that Dutroux knows how to speak Dutch. However, I think not. To your question how I judge the information given by Warmerdam, I have to answer you this: I am convinced that Warmerdam has a lot of information and information, in short, that he knows a lot. But he doesn't know how to put them in chronological order, and sometimes he confuses the information. The only serious error that I said I found in his statements is the language - Dutch - spoken by Dutroux. I consider it a useful source of usable information. Warmerdam claimed that he met robby van der Plancken in Amsterdam and then at G-force and he also met him in rotterdam."

[412] 'The ring of child molesters surrounding Marc Dutroux reached as far as Berlin', Berlin Morgenpost, August 3 2004,
"There are numerous indications of the existence of child molester rings. Statements from perpetrators and victims as well as shocking photos and films of abused, raped and tortured children. 20 CD-ROMs with such material are attached to the file. They are currently being evaluated by the public prosecutor's office in Turnhout, Belgium. Belgian private investigator Marcel Vervloesem compiled the dossier for Dutroux prosecutor Bourlet. The 51-year-old was heard by Bourlet's investigators several times."

[413] Zandvoort Cdroms Kinderporno affaire dokumentation, 2001, Documents concerning Vervloesem Marcel and the Zandvoortaffaire; Vervloesem in prison at Bruges, released June 1 2009, www.wikileaks.org/wiki/Zandvoort_CDroms_Kinderporno_affaire_dokumentation,_2001

[414] 'Justice A false network hunter: Vervloesem was a pedophile', Le Soir, July 7 2008,
" A self-proclaimed defender of pedophiles through his ASBL "Morkhoven", Marcel Vervloesem, 55, was sentenced by the Antwerp Court of Appeal to four years in prison for sexual abuse of three minors, publication of child pornography and scam posters. This sentence could have been heavier, the man, now recognized as a pedophile, has indeed benefited from the prescrip-

tion for several other acts of morals against children. This conviction puts an end to what appears to be a huge deception, born in the wake of the Dutroux affair. The name of Marcel Vervloesem had appeared in the media in 1998 when he claimed to have found in a Dutch pedophile from Zandvoort, a CD-ROM containing 88,000 photos of children in a situation of abuse. Vervloesem refused to communicate the images stolen from the Dutchman. These images, seized by the Belgian justice system, were transmitted to the Dutch. Quickly, it appeared that they were only old pedophile photos recovered from the internet. Among these photos were images of Asian children as well as photos from private collections, that, for example, of a German butcher adept at sadomasochism between adults. "

[415] Marcel Vervloesem P.V No. 8.257/01, 10.04.2001, Police Federale S.J.A. www.fondationprincessedecroy.eu/001-PV_bebe_-porno_zandvoort_2001___fr__a.htm

[416] Dutroux dossier summary, 1235 pages, 2005, page 357 via www.wikileaks.org/wiki/Belgium:_Dutroux_dossier_summary,_1235_pages,_2005,
"INFORMATION - ROXANNE Continuation PV 10.600 of 19/11/96 of PJ BXL ROXANNE = PELLERIN Didier (07/08/59 in PARIS) = transsexual Several files in his charge for FALSE and USE OF FALSE - INCENTIVE TO THE DEBAUCH _ CONSIDERATION OF MORES _ Sadomasochistic prostitute Clos Chambon 07 in GANSHOREN She sells her production of K7 via REX PRODUCT and ROX FILM PRODUCT companies from the NETHERLANDS (DEN HAAG) Some K7s are very hard The K7s produced by ROXANNE are systematically seized A BSR BXL report of 02/10/96 indicates that NIHOUL could have lent itself to Sado-maso shoots at ROXANNE Every month: a buffet evening at her place = initiation to sado-maso ROXANNE already heard: PV 41.425 of 18/10/96 DECOCKERE was secretary at ROXANNE An anonymous witness would have seen at ROXANNE photos of children chained or handcuffs These photos appear in a press-book ROXANNE would have pointed out that the trade in pedophile K7 is very lucrative in BELGIUM but dangerous She would have indicated an address in LUXEMBOURG: Avenue Petrus in KIRSCHEN The testimony is not entirely reliable" [Flemish to French to English Translation]

[417] Marcel Vervloesem P.V No. 8.257/01, 10.04.2001, Police Federale S.J.A. http://fondationprincessedecroy.eu/001-PV_bebe_-porno_zandvoort_2001___fr__a.htm,
"Then, we did the same research about Admiral de Ruyterweg 111. It seemed to be SM practices from the Roxanne film production. On the act

was the name of a Didier Pellerin. There seemed to be a second firm in Brussels owned by this same Pellerin. Based on information from various informal contacts, it appeared that Pellerin had been, among others, the employer of Marleen Decokere. Which Marleen Decokere was, again according to this same information, a contact of Nihoul, which also emerged from the press archives." [French to English Translation]

[418] Message from provider to client among the Zandvoort materials received by the Morkhoven Workgroup, copied onto the Foundation Princess of Croy website, www.fondationprincessedecroy.eu/06-childtrade-price_of_children-GB.htm,

"Exact copy of the original document

Hello my dear friend. Here is a new list of girls we can offer you. I hope you are satisfied with offer. We have new girl age 4 to 17. Choose from list you see down.

1) Marija, age 5, you can do only blowjob, no sex, only masturbate, cum on her face, no swallow, no fuck, you can film her playing with older boys. price us-dollars 100.

2) Petra, age 14, you can do everything with her, she is doing blowjob, fuck, fuck in asshole, swollow cum, maximum 2 man at a time. you can film her, you can show her, face on film. she is fucking with her dad also, you can film this (price us-dollars 100). price for fuck us-dollars 150, fuck with 2 man us-dollars 250.

3) Pjotr, boy age 8, is doing blowjob, you can film him with other boy play and fuck. no fuck with too long cock. he swollow cum also pissing game. for more cash (us-dollars 300) his father travel with you in austria and stay 3-4 days with you. price for fuck or piss game us-dollars 150.

4) Melija, age 7, is fucking, and doing blowjob. she swollows cum. only one man can do with her at a time. you fuck good with her, no force, because she is new girl. you can have her and sister Petra, age 5.Petra no fuck, only blowjob, no swollow cum. you can cum on face. she is virgine. if you want fuck her special price us-dollars 400. only fuck with care. fuck with Melija cost us-dollars 150.

5) Anika, age 10, ungarian girl. she is fucking and blowjob. if you fuck her you order 2 weeks ago. has to come from ungaria with mother. You can cum on face, in pussy or swollow cum. cost us-dollars 200. mother go to your country for us-dollars 300.

6) a very special offer: baby for masturbation. you can lick baby pussy and blowjob possible. NO FUCK. you can cum on pussy and in face. swollow cum is possible. price us-dollars 300.

7) new offer: only filming a fuck. you bring camera and make film. no

fuck."
[419] 'Sex abuse scandal crèches criticised for staffing levels, organised sleepovers', Dutch News, December 14 2010
'Grote kindermisbruikzaak Amsterdam'('Large child abuse case Amsterdam'), RTL Nieuws, December 13 2010
[420] Marcel Vervloesem P.V No. 8.257/01, 10.04.2001, Police Federale S.J.A. www.fondationprincessedecroy.eu/001-PV_bebe_-porno_zandvoort_2001___fr__a.htm,
"The foregoing has driven us to investigate the g-force. It turned out to indeed belong to an American, the name John Edward Mullaney. This person is associated with various other large businesses, such as the Adonis company, which appears in the list of Norbert De Rijck from Temse. His name is associated with Korper and Korver, for example, which in turn are associated with John Stanford and Spartacus. He is also related to Alex Groaner and Karel Van Maasdam (Alex Prive). In connection with what I declare, I provide you with a copy of my file entitled "Part I and II - G. Forse - Robert J.W" (see attachments numbered 1 to 245)"[English Translations of French]
[421] 'The ring of child molesters surrounding Marc Dutroux reached as far as Berlin', Berlin Morgenpost, August 3 2004,
"Vervloesem had already reported on April 10, 2001 that he had met a certain Robert Jan W. three months earlier. This man had been active in the SM scene in Amsterdam for 15 years and was a regular visitor to the "G-Force" club. The statements of the Dutch witness are reproduced in the interrogation. The man assured that Dutroux had been to the establishment again and again, the file says. There is talk of two apartments in Amsterdam to which children are said to have been delivered. Visitors - this witness assures us - were also Marc Dutroux and a man named Robby van der P. This means that the connection to Germany is occupied. Because this same Robby van der P. is the central figure in the network reaching to Berlin. He assured this newspaper in Amsterdam that he had seen several Berlin boys in Dutch children's brothels. He himself was often in the German capital and lured children to Rotterdam and Amsterdam with brothel owners. And in 1993 he witnessed the abduction of the then twelve-year-old Tempelhof boy Manuel Schadwald to the Netherlands. " [German to English translation]
[422] 'Paedophile networks trafficks young boys across Europe', Nick Davies, Previously unpublished, October 1 1998, Researched on commission from the New Yorker, https://www.nickdavies.net/1998/10/01/paedophile-network-trafficks-young-boys-across-

europe/
"Serving drinks at the Festival Bar, Ricky the transvestite said quite simply that he remembered the German boy coming in. In an unbroadcast section of his interview with Dutch TV, I found that Robbie van der Plancken had claimed that some time after being taken from Berlin by Lothar Glandorf, Manuel had been sold to the Englishman Warwick Spinks in Amsterdam. These English paedophiles had been the core investors in the Amsterdam branch of the industry."

[423] 'The ring of child molesters surrounding Marc Dutroux reached as far as Berlin', Berlin Morgenpost, August 3 2004

[424] 'The ring of child molesters surrounding Marc Dutroux reached as far as Berlin', Berlin Morgenpost, August 3 2004,
"And Robert Jan W. also describes scenes from this film. The investigation file from the Neufchâteau public prosecutor's office states that the video was filmed in a bungalow near Amsterdam. The then 13-year-old boy from Germany initially refused to satisfy the perverse desires of several men. But he was then forced to do so and suffocated. This statement is also available to the public prosecutor in Haarlem, Netherlands." [German to English translation]

[425] 'Die verlorenen Kinder'('The Lost Children'), Welt, July 12 2015

[426] "Vater des vermißten Manuel Schadwald freigelassen / Rainer Wolf flog zurück nach Irland("Father of missing Manuel Schadwald released / Rainer Wolf flew back to Ireland"), Berliner Zeitung, July 28 1998,
"Rumors had circulated over the weekend that Rainer Wolf had been involved in kidnapping his son to a Dutch brothel. Justice spokesman Matthias Rebentisch only confirmed that a witness connected the name of Rainer Wolf with the "Pinocchio" bar. The Schöneberg pub is considered by the police to be a meeting place for rent boys and their customers. The accusations against Wolf are based on the statements of Berliner Peter Goetjes, who described himself as a child trafficker. Rainer Wolf feels defamed: "It's a dirty campaign against me when statements by child traffickers are suddenly taken as serious." Someone wants to use this to obstruct the investigation into my son's disappearance, said Wolf." [German to English Translation]

[427] 'Kinderpornographie: Stasi erpresste Politiker'('Child pornography: Stasi blackmailed politicians'), Berlin Morgenposter, February 9 2002

[428] 'Kinderpornographie: Stasi erpresste Politiker'('Child pornography: Stasi blackmailed politicians'), Berlin Morgenposter, February 9

2002

[429] 'Neue Spur im Fall Manuel Schadwald'('New lead in the Manuel Schadwald case'), Welt, July 11 2015

[430] 'Justice A false network hunter: Vervloesem was a pedophile', Le Soir, July 7 2008,

" A self-proclaimed defender of pedophiles through his ASBL "Morkhoven", Marcel Vervloesem, 55, was sentenced by the Antwerp Court of Appeal to four years in prison for sexual abuse of three minors, publication of child pornography and scam posters. This sentence could have been heavier, the man, now recognized as a pedophile, has indeed benefited from the prescription for several other acts of morals against children. This conviction puts an end to what appears to be a huge deception, born in the wake of the Dutroux affair. The name of Marcel Vervloesem had appeared in the media in 1998 when he claimed to have found in a Dutch pedophile from Zandvoort, a CD-ROM containing 88,000 photos of children in a situation of abuse. Vervloesem refused to communicate the images stolen from the Dutchman. These images, seized by the Belgian justice system, were transmitted to the Dutch. Quickly, it appeared that they were only old pedophile photos recovered from the internet. Among these photos were images of Asian children as well as photos from private collections, that, for example, of a German butcher adept at sadomasochism between adults. " [French to English translation]

[431] diversmorkhoven.wordpress.com/2014/11/09/werkgroep-morkhoven-voert-onderzoek-naar-verdwenen-duitse-jongen-2/

[432] 'Nur die kleinen Fische'(Only the small fish), Der Spiegel, August 2 1998

[433] 'Dutch Joris Demmink Affair Reveals Heroin, Cocaine and Pedophile Entrapment Affairs', Joel Reijden, October 31 2014, www.is-gp-studies.com/joris-demmink-and-prince-bernhard-s-alleged-westerflier-cult

[434] 'Prosecutor in Pedophile Case Kills Himself : Belgian Official's Death Puts Top Cases On Hold', New York Times, July 16 1999.

[435] 'Belgium's silent heart of darkness', The Observer, May 5 2002.

[436] 'What became of Alexandre Gosselin', DeMorgen, February 5 2004

[437] 'Belgium's silent heart of darkness', The Guardian, May 5 2002.

[438] Belgium Pedophilia Scandal /Did Authorities Cover Up Its Scope?: Book Revives Fear of Grand Conspiracy, New York Times, December 16 1999.

[439] ACCIDENTS DE LA ROUTE("Road Accidents, Two Dead, Includ-

[440] 'Elisabeth Brichet : quatorze ans d'enquête, de doutes et de suspicions'("Elisabeth Brichet: fourteen years of investigation, doubts and suspicions"), Roland Planchar, La Libre, June 29 2004

[441] 'Belgium's silent heart of darkness', The Guardian, May 5 2002.

[442] 'Prosecutor in Pedophile Case Kills Himself : Belgian Official's Death Puts Top Cases On Hold', New York Times, July 16 1999.

[443] www.isgp-studies.com/Belgian_X_dossiers_alleged_assassinations

[444] 'Crying out loud', Timothy W Ryback, The Independent, March 15 1997
'House of Horror stuns Belgium', The Guardian, August 19 1996

[445] 'Crying out loud', Timothy W Ryback, The Independent, March 15 1997

[446] 'Belgians seek police advice in Europe', The Guardian, August 21 1996

[447] 'Fears grow of new paedophile horror', The Daily Telegraph, January 23 1997

[448] 'Meisjes verdwijnen niet zomaar' by Fred Vandenbussche, published by Kosmos/Z&K Publishers in 1996. Translation provided by, https://isgp-studies.com/belgian-x-dossiers-of-the-dutroux-affair

[449] 'Dutroux m'aurait tuée'('Dutroux would have killed me'), DH Net, May 3 2004

[450] 'Dutroux trial jurors visit horror house', The Guardian, April 28 2004

[451] 'De X-Dossiers' by Marie-Jeanne Van Heeswyck, Annemie Bulté and Douglas De Coninck, 1999, p. 72,
"On December 6, 1995 Marc Dutroux is arrested. He stays in the prison of Jamioulx until March 20. It is the time of the house searches of BOB officers Rene Michaux in the Marcinelle home. He hears children's voices there, but ignores them. He confiscates a video there on December 13, 1995, marked 'Perdu de Vue, Marc'. He also finds chains, locks and keys - apparently stuff with whom he chained down An and Eefje. A speculum, a small bottle of vaginal cream, chloroform... More than three years after the facts it also turns out that Michaux confiscated a videotape on which Dutroux had taped himself working on his basement and raping a Czech girl.", English translation via https://isgp-studies.com/belgian-x-dossiers-of-the-dutroux-affair#15

[452] 'I knew my son couldn't be trusted, mom says', Miami Herald,

November 17 1996
[453] 'Two Dutroux victims buried alive', Sydney Morning Herald, March 11 2004
[454] 'THE SECRET OF DUTROUX'S ACCOUNTS SLOWLY RAISED DUTROUX'S ACCOUNTS PATIENTLY DECORTED', Le Soir, September 23 1996,
"The Flemish television channel VTM has just revealed: we now have a lot of information on Marc Dutroux's bank accounts. Two hundred thousand francs... eight hundred thousand... one million one hundred... Large movements seem to characterize these accounts and it even seems possible to link these payments to several disappearances of children. Will we finally have proof that Dutroux stole and sold his victims? It's far too premature, we are told in Neufchâteau. The account movements revealed in the press are accurate, but we do not yet know who paid this money into Dutroux's accounts and the connection with kidnappings is only a theory. The ("coded") data provided by the banks are in fact innumerable: Dutroux, his wife Martin and his accomplice Lelièvre had more than ten accounts in Belgium and abroad. They are examined over a period of ten years and the operations number in the thousands. . .However, investigators have already been able to establish that some of the "large sums" paid to Dutroux correspond to bank loans, such as the sum of 1.1 million advanced for the purchase of the Sars-la-Buissière property." [French to English translation]
[455] 'HORROR FOR JULIE AND MELISSA, FRAGILE HOPE FOR AN AND EEFJE CHRONICLE OF TERROR THE RIGHT TRACK A COP'S LIFE', Le Soir, August 19 1996,
"Under the shovel of a digger, the mutilated bodies of Julie, Mélissa and an accomplice of the pervert slowly appeared in the setting sun. . .Not all tapes have been viewed yet. But we found, in one of Dutroux's "hides", video equipment and a computer connected to each other. Perhaps an electronic "editing bench" used to make carefully edited videocassettes" [French to English Translation]
[456] DUTROUX: ON S'ACHEMINE VERS UN DESSAISISSEMENT("Dutroux: We are moving towards a divestment"), Le Soir, October 11 1996
[457] 'King Forced to Step In / Pedophile Scandal Just One of Many : Belgium's Confidence Crisis Is Deepening', New York Times, September 12 1996,
"The police have so far dug up the bodies of four girls from properties owned by Mr. Dutroux, a convicted child rapist. But at least eight children

still are missing. And on the videotapes of sexual abuse and torture found during the searches, investigators reportedly have seen 12 children as yet unidentified, according to the newspaper Le Soir."

[458] 'Child sex case adds outrage to scandals rocking Belgium', Chicago Tribune, October 27 1996,

"Lizin said Dutroux was not a true pedophile, as he has been portrayed. He had a record of dealing in stolen cars, selling arms to hoodlums and trafficking in prostitution. 'When he discovered that men paid a lot more for little girls for prostitution, he started kidnapping them,' she said. When Dutroux finally was arrested, police found in his house video films of him raping little girls. They said he did this so he could sell the films to pedophiles."

[459] 'A DOCUMENT THAT SUPPORTS THE LINK BETWEEN THE DUTROUX AFFAIR AND THAT OF THE FALSE BULGARIAN VISAS', kairospresse.be, January 22 2022, www.kairospresse.be/en/a-document-that-supports-the-link-between-the-dutroux-affair-and-that-of-the-false-bulgarian-visas/,

"On November 28, 1985, three weeks after his release, Bernard Weinstein arrived in Belgium. Mireille flies to his rescue. On December 1st, he is hired in the SPRL Video Promotion, which belongs to the brother of Schulman, Joseph (« Marc »). The company, established in a disused Acec warehouse at 167 Marconi Street in Forest, is mainly involved in copying videocassettes. Video Promotion transformed a part of the dilapidated building into a film studio. « Weinstein worked there as a video copier on the night shift, » recalls Joseph Schulman, who for the rest doesn't remember much, ten years later. 'He was a withdrawn man, always alone, with an absolute lack of interest in anything to do with sex', says the former manager, who knows what he's talking about, having frequented the Brussels partying scene in the 1970s. Schulman still says his companies never made pornography, but he doesn't know if Weinstein did any off-duty work for his own account"

[460] 'De X-Dossiers' by Marie-Jeanne Van Heeswyck, Annemie Bulté and Douglas De Coninck, 1999.

[461] 'Crying out loud', Timothy W Ryback, The Independent, March 15 1997

[462] PV 100.223 Interview of Lelievre, Dutroux dossier summary, 1235 pages, 2005, via https://wikileaks.org/wiki/Belgium:_Dutroux_-dossier_summary,_1235_pages,_2005, page 886

"LELIEVRE'S HEARING 19/08 Confirms previous declaration Route from BERTIRX to MARCINELLE He took out LAETITIA wrapped in a blanket Neighbors saw him - said he was drunk DUTROUX always said he

had orders DUTROUX says he is not the only one to do it He left and came back shortly after. DUTROUX wore his pants but was shirtless On 10/08 he called NIHOUL for an unemployment problem and to go with it him to the police He went to NIHOUL with JEAN-CLAUDE 12/08 DUTROUX told him that the work was done He understood that AETITIA had been delivered He didn't know there was a cache in MARCINELLE" [Flemish to French to English Translation]

PV 100.241 Interview of Lelievre, Dutroux dossier summary, 1235 pages, 2005, via https://wikileaks.org/wiki/Belgium:_Dutroux_-dossier_summary,_1235_pages,_2005, page 887
"LELIEVRE'S HEARING 22/08 During the kidnapping of SABINE DUTROUX shouted at her to put the bike in the van. The bike was later abandoned in the parking lot of a supermarket. DUTROUX had returned AN and EEF without precaution SABINE had to put herself in a military style chest When SABINE was kidnapped: blue jeans - gray t-shirt - blue sweater and black cap A scenario had been established to make SABINE believe that her parents did not want to pay a ransom and that the chief wanted to kill her DUTROUX had to play the protector He barely knew anything to say because SABINE was crying. It was DUTROUX who said almost everything DUTROUX told him that she was the daughter of a gendarme DUTROUX said he conditioned girls to be docile and submitted for clients" [Flemish to French to English Translation]

[463] 'Dutroux says he procured girls for Belgian network', The Guardian, January 22 2002,
"Marc Dutroux, the Belgian electrician accused of kidnapping, raping and murdering four young girls in the mid-1990s, has claimed that he did not act alone but was part of a wider paedophile network. . .'A network with all kinds of criminal activities really does exist,' Dutroux told VTM, a Flemish TV station. "I maintained regular contacts with the people who made up this network. But the authorities don't want to look into it."

[464] 'Images of King Albert II with an underage girl': Michel Nihoul, relic of the old corrupt Belgium, is no more', Demorgen, October 23 2019

[465] 'Four Girls Abducted, Raped, Murdered. A Country on Trial.', New York Times, February 23 1997.

[466] 'Belgium flounders in grief and guilt', The Tennessean, February 1 1997,
"Among Dutroux's cronies rounded up in the wake of the discoveries have been Jean-Michel Nihoul, a low-level political fixer known to have contacts

with national politicians who is thought to have been dealing in amateur videotapes showing child pornography, and Inspector Georges Zicot, the police officer in charge of vehicle crime in Charleroi."

[467] 'Four Girls Abducted, Raped, Murdered. A Country on Trial.', New York Times, February 23 1997

[468] 'Policeman linked to paedophile network', The Age, August 27 1996,

"The prosecutor said Chief Detective Zicot's connection to the paedophile case was through Bernard Weinstein, an accomplice of Dutroux. 'Dutroux has admitted killing Weinstein after a disagreement between the accomplices in an affair of truck theft' Mr Bourlet said."

[469] 'Another policeman is questioned in child-abuse case', Chicago Tribune, September 12 1996

[470] 'Belgian fury at paedophile case sacking', The Guardian, October 15 1996

[471] 'Judge accused of cover-up in Cools murder case', The Independent, September 12 1996

[472] 'Rotton to the core', Sydney Morning Herald, September 17 1996
'Child killings spark soul searching in Belgium', The Commercial Appeal, September 3 1996

[473] 'Belgium's silent heart of darkness', The Observer, May 5 2002

[474] 'Belgium erupts in protests', Chicago Tribune, October 16 1996

[475] 'Belgium Pedophilia Scandal /Did Authorities Cover Up Its Scope?: Book Revives Fear of Grand Conspiracy', New York Times, December 16 1999

[476] 'Belgium backs its king', The Guardian, October 12 2001,

"Belgium sued a French publisher on behalf of its king yesterday for putting out a book suggesting that he may have been connected to a paedophile scandal in the 70s and 80s. The state asked a Paris court to order the publishing house Flammarion to insert King Albert's denial in all unsold copies of the book. A ruling is expected next Thursday."

[477] Im Netz der Dossiers'("In the network of dossiers"), Der Spiegel, October 14 2001

[478] Wikileaks April 17 2009 release of: Dutroux dossier summary, 1235 pages, 2005
'WikiLeaks slammed over publishing dossier including Belgian pedophile killer Marc Dutroux', The Australian, August 27 2010
'10 days in Sweden: the full allegations against Julian Assange', The Guardian, December 18 2010

An international arrest warrant for Julian Assange was issued on November 17 2010 by the Swedish Prosecutor's Office, which marked the beginning of the end for him. If it can be assume Assange was targeted for a wikileaks release prior to this date that only leaves a few possibilities. In April 2010 wikileaks released the collateral murder video. Wikileaks had also published the X-Dossier in Feb 2009, but this hadn't actually been discovered until August 2010.

"The recent publication of secret documents on Wikileaks is causing trouble in Belgium: Sensitive investigative files from the case of the convicted child molester Marc Dutroux have been uploaded to the disclosure portal. Liège Attorney General Cédric Visart de Bocarmé told Belgian broadcaster RTBF on Wednesday that he was "unhappy because the documents come from trial files that are still classified" - Enthüllungen sorgen für Ärger, Suddeutsche Zeitung, August 25 2010

At the end of August 2010 Assange was first questioned by Swedish police regarding his rape accusation. The very first criminal investigation brought against him. These charges stemmed from complaints made by two women on August 20 together. Woman A had arranged for Assange to visit Sweden and he had stayed at her flat where they had sex. Woman A then introduced Assange to woman B, who invited him to stay at her flat where they had sex. Both women then reported rapes of identical detail.

[479] 'The last hours of Pasolini', The Guardian, November 3 1975

[480] 'Berlusconi to stant trial on sex charge', The Guardian, February 16 2011

See section from this article entitled 'Previous prosecutions How tycoon became most persecuted man in history' for the following excerpt,

"In 1990, he was declared guilty of false testimony over his membership of Propaganda 2, a Right-wing masonic lodge that was described as a 'state within a state' and counted among its members industrialists, politicians, military leaders and journalists."

[481] 'E LA TRIESTE CHE CONTA HA AIUTATO MONCINI'("AND THE TRIESTE THAT COUNTS HAS HELPED MONCINI "), la Repubblica, August 12 1988,

"At the time he was a prominent figure in the Friulian capital. Rich, Rotarian, president of the province's Automobile Club, former vice-president of Triestina football team, and owner of a tire shop in the centre. He had good political connections and had been a Freemason (the man was on

the P2 lists)." [Italian to English Translation]

[482] 'Belgium's silent heart of darkness', The Observer, May 5 2002

[483] 1998, Regina Louf, 'Zwijgen is voor daders - De getuigenis van X1' ('Silence is for perpetrators - The testimony of X1'), p. 55-58

[484] 1998, Regina Louf, 'Zwijgen is voor daders - De getuigenis van X1' ('Silence is for perpetrators - The testimony of X1') p. 58

[485] 'Belgium's silent heart of darkness', The Observer, May 5 2002

[486] 'A DOCUMENT THAT SUPPORTS THE LINK BETWEEN THE DUTROUX AFFAIR AND THAT OF THE FALSE BULGARIAN VISAS', kairospresse.be, January 22 2022, www.kairospresse.be/en/a-document-that-supports-the-link-between-the-dutroux-affair-and-that-of-the-false-bulgarian-visas/,

"On November 28, 1985, three weeks after his release, Bernard Weinstein arrived in Belgium. Mireille flies to his rescue. On December 1st, he is hired in the SPRL Video Promotion, which belongs to the brother of Schulman, Joseph (« Marc »). The company, established in a disused Acec warehouse at 167 Marconi Street in Forest, is mainly involved in copying videocassettes. Video Promotion transformed a part of the dilapidated building into a film studio. « Weinstein worked there as a video copier on the night shift, » recalls Joseph Schulman, who for the rest doesn't remember much, ten years later. 'He was a withdrawn man, always alone, with an absolute lack of interest in anything to do with sex', says the former manager, who knows what he's talking about, having frequented the Brussels partying scene in the 1970s. Schulman still says his companies never made pornography, but he doesn't know if Weinstein did any off-duty work for his own account"

[487] 116.019, 28/10/96 Findings death of "CLO", Dutroux dossier summary, 1235 pages, 2005, via https://wikileaks.org/wiki/Belgium:_Dutroux_dossier_summary,_1235_pages,_2005, page 406

"28/10/96 CLO would be worn between June and December 83 HUPEZ VANDEBOGAERT comes unexpectedly to pick up X1 and the driving blindfolded to a house where she is locked in a room on the ground floor with CLO who is about to give birth. X1 helps CLO give birth and a boy is born alive. X1 cut the cord and puts the child on CLO's stomach. They came to pick up the child while X1 takes care of CLO. CLO dies and VANDENBOGAERT forces X1 to leave. LIPPENS, VANDERELST and 2 strangers go with X1 to a restaurant Chinese in BRUGES. They are joined by an assistant commissioner from KNOKKE and a French-speaking man in his forties named GUY. After the restaurant, they all go to KNOKKE at the grandmother of X1 (Cécile) where they are expected by the

grandmother. X1 is raped by LIPPENS then by VANDERELST. X1 struggles and at 5 (2 others in addition to LIPPENS, VANDERELST and the commissioner hold her and rape her. CLO is identified as: DELLAERT Carine (01/04/66)" [Flemish to French to English]
116.018, 25/10/96 - Fourth audition of X1, Dutroux dossier summary, 1235 pages, 2005, via https://wikileaks.org/wiki/Belgium:_Dutroux_dossier_summary,_1235_pages,_2005, page 408
"Three or four months after his first delivery (November or December 83), Tony came to pick up X1 in GAND (blindfolded). Arrived in a house not very far from Ghent, (description of the places). Presence of three or four people in the living room (Tony, LIPPEN and VANDERELST + two other people). X1 in the same room as CLO - Childbirth of CLO. CLO bleeds a lot. X1 is alone and no one helps CLO. Birth of CLO's baby (a boy). X1 cuts the cord. They come to get CLO's baby. This one dies (losing a lot of blood). X1 had to accompany the men (sans Tony) in VANDERELST's car. Arrival in a Chinese restaurant in the center of BRUGGE with LIPPENS, VANDERELST, the two accompanying persons and two new arrivals (including the deputy commissioner of KNOKKE). Deputy Commissioner had previously raped X1 during parties at the SWALLOW. Leaving the restaurant: appointment with the grandmother (Cécile). XI in the commissioner's car must perform oral sex while driving. X1 is violated by everyone present. (LIPPEN, VANDERELST, and the others... X1 is hit). Presentation of photos to X1: recognizes CLO, points to several girls also raped. Precision: simple orgies = in the living room. The others so as not to stain with blood: garage or kitchen. Orgy also at X1's father's employer. XI, also cites De Hanne, UCO, his own mother, NIHOUL's wife. X1 also specifies the presence of BOUTY when she was raped by NIHOUL at JETTE rue Dupré n°51. BOUTY had an active part in parties and liked to upset children. (putting objects in the children's orifices...knives, screwdrivers, ... which hurt the children). BOUTY had the role of executioner. X1 = NIEMAND. BOUTY dressed in leather, latex during special evenings. The other participants too. Use of crosses, various signs...(drawing done by X1). Introducing a photo of a young girl that X1 has seen at several "parties" before, it clarifies that THEY KILLED HER. Daughter brought by Tony (and possibly CLO) to a house in GHENT. (at CLO). X1 claims to have had to participate in the "killing of this young girl". Put knife and chisel, broken bottle in her vagina. Slashed everywhere with a razor. Presence of Tony, the old man from Dekascoop, his son (the oldest), the lawyer VANDERELST. The girl was raped. X1 was forced to act (being raped and injured as well) X1 stabbed the girl to death. Stage presence X1, this girl, CLO and another girl named in a photo by X1. X1 is

then raped, along with CLO and the other girl. X1 falls asleep and is taken home by Tony (always with his MERCEDES). X1 is bleeding profusely. The girl killed = Véronique. X1 had heard the first name from CLO." [Flemish to French to English]

[488] 'The girl who gave birth in secret', Demorgen, January 8 1998

[489] *150.073 21/1/97 - NITIAL BR*, Dutroux dossier summary, 1235 pages, 2005, via https://wikileaks.org/wiki/Belgium:_Dutroux_-dossier_summary,_1235_pages,_2005, page 1038,

"21.66.150073/97 FALSE IN PRIVATE WRITE Following hearing X1 of 25/10/96 PV 117.986/96 file 109/96 JI LANGLOIS Victim DUBRULLE Véronique (16/02/66) According to the witness, she was the victim of a sado-maso party She was raped and killed in 1983 It is possible that the whole party was filmed (snuff-movie) Official death = 04/09/83 natural death C3 issued by doctors DE SCHRIJVER L. and DE WAELE L. of the St-Vincent de GENT hospital The body is buried in the cemetery of DRONGEN parc 3 tomb 915" [Flemish to French to English]

116.020, 28/10/96 - Finding RAPE and MURDER ON DUBRULLE VERONIQUE, Dutroux dossier summary, 1235 pages, 2005, via https://wikileaks.org/wiki/Belgium:_Dutroux_dossier_summary,_1235_pages,_2005, page 409

" Identification of those present: 1° Minors: - Veronique DUBRULLE born in GAND on 16.02.66 declared dead in GAND on September 04, 1983. last. Address: TerRivieren 18 in 9031 GHENT. - X1 - DUPONT Sandra. Wife DE VIDTS Johan born in GHENT on May 24, 1972 linked to GHENT Veronicastraat 18. - her friend Clo DELAERT = Carine (deceased identified above). 2° Majors: -DELLAERT Emile (11.05.40) last address GHENT Kanteklaarstraat n°5. - NIHOUL Michel - BOUTY Annie. - VAN DEN BOGAERT Antoine (26.01.42) linked to ANTWERP Turnhoutsebaan 81/10. - BERT Albert (09.10.27) says the old man from Decascoop. last address COURTRAI Wikingerhof n°7. - BERT Joost (18.04.56) says the old man's eldest son. dlinked to COURTRAI Wikingerhof n°11. (managing director of DECSCOOP). - VANDERELST Michel (10.06.46) linked to LINKEBEEK Hellebeekstraat n°347. DUBRULLE Véronique was declared dead on 04.09.83 in GAND. CLO is present during the events although reported missing since 30.08.92 she dies after giving birth between June and December 1983. The facts rape and murder (murder) of DUBRULLE Véronique takes place at Clo DELLAERT Emile Clo's father was present. - Verifications concerning: exact location of the places. official circumstances of the death of Véronique DUBRULLE. Identification of Sabrina (another girl present at a similar evening) Identification and

possible location of the Mercedes used at the time by VANDEN BOGAERT." [Flemish to French to English]

[490] 'Ik soigneer de mensen graag. Het moet in orde zijn'("I like to look after people. It must be alright"), De Morgen, October 6 2007

[491] 'Het meisje dat in het geheim beviel'('The girl who gave birth in secret'), De Morgen, January 8 1998

[492] 'Is dit Katrien De Cuyper?'('Is this Katrien De Cuyper?'), De Morgen, June 22 1999

[493] De X-Dossiers by Van Heeswyck, Annemie Bulte, and Douglas De Connick, 1999, p.165-166, Dutch to English translation provided by Joel van der Reijden in article 'Beyond The Dutroux Affair: The Reality of Protected Child Abuse and Snuff Networks', First published July 25 2007, last hosted at www.isgp-studies.com/belgian-x-dossiers-of-the-dutroux-affair

[494] 1998, Regina Louf, 'Zwijgen is voor daders - De getuigenis van X1' ('Silence is for perpetrators - The testimony of X1') p.129

[495] 150.889, 24/03/97, FAX TRANSLATION of X1 of 03/18/97 - Factory - CLO, Dutroux dossier summary, 1235 pages, 2005, via https://wikileaks.org/wiki/Belgium:_Dutroux_dossier_summary,_1235_pages,_2005, page 480
"DUMONT went with black PORSCHE, white MERCEDES 500SEL One day her mother went to pick her up from school in a CHEVY and took her to DECASCOOP where DUMONT arrived and took her to ASCO She had to suck DUMONT in the car At ASCO he left her in the car and someone else went to pick her up (NIHOUL) Present: NIHOUL - DUMONT - Chris - VANDER ELST - BONVOISIN - Martin - MARTENS - WATHELET - VDB - guard dog and others and as children MIEKE (Marie-Thérèse), SANDRA (10 years old) and another (09 years old) already seen in the circuits When they talked about business the women did not attend except sometimes BOUTY" [Flemish to French to English]
'Images of King Albert II with an underage girl': Michel Nihoul, relic of the old corrupt Belgium, is no more', Demorgen, October 23 2019,
"Nihoul took care of the electoral campaigns of the later Brussels minister Jean-Louis Thys and Jean-Paul Dumont in the late 1970s, and also describes meetings with former Prime Minister Paul Vanden Boeynants in his autobiography, published in 1998."

[496] 100.165/97 26/11/96, ANONYMOUS STATEMENT, Dutroux dossier summary, 1235 pages, 2005, via https://wikileaks.org/wiki/Belgium:_Dutroux_dossier_summary,_1235_pages,_2005, page 936

" The declarant knew DUMONT Jean-Paul well between 1984-89 DUMONT was the right arm of VANDENBOEYNANTS DUMONT offered the declarant sexual relations but refused DUMONT asked him to accompany him on special evenings in a castle from Namur = refusal DUMONT asked him to find young people aged 10-12 = refusal DUMONT frequented the ANDRE café at the time - the MOK MA ZWET restaurant and the CIRCUS dance hall ANDRE and the MOK MA ZWET run by thugs also linked to MOZART One day after closing of the CIRCUS and under the direction of DUMONT the last customers and the owners went to a villa to which DUMONT had the keys Villa 05 minutes by car from the CIRCUS Swimming pool - naked swimming DUMONT was the lawyer for people involved in the CRIES case including DESSY DESSY = pedophile DESSThere is a villa near RIXENSART where miners live DESSY pays a lot for pedophile tapes (torture) and/or for children He was part of the SPARTACUS homosexual network This is the brother of Georges DESSY Georges DESSY is authorized representative of the BBL - he is a homosexual fetishist and practices urolagnia DESSY Georges' fetish booty is hidden in a garage near his home" [Flemish to French to English]

[497] 'Les égouts du royaume. Les secrets des scandales belges' by Andre Rogge, published in 1996, ISBN-10:2226088768, translation and excerpt provided by user at, www.bendevannijvel.com/forum/viewtopic.php?id=720

[498] 'Cour d'appel de Bruxelles'("Brussels Court of Appeal"), Le Soir, October 28 1988,

"Jean-Claude Weber, then detained in France for similar acts, was sentenced to the maximum, ten years. Philippe Carpentier, the head of CRIES, the organization that the court had said was nothing more than an instrument of child prostitution, was sentenced to nine years. Michel Felu, the former internee for pedophilia, the man who took advantage of Jos Verbeeck's solicitude by organizing porno photo sessions in the cellars of Unicef-Brussels, received eight years, as did Claude Drieghe, the filmmaker of the group. Repeat offenders Christian Jacque and Pierre Delporte were sentenced to six years, Michel Decré who organized special evenings at his home received five years, Doctor Michel Mesureur four years. " [French to English Translation]

[499] 'Unicef Man On Child Sex Charges', The Guardian, June 19 1987

[500] 'THE DISAPPEARANCE IN PARIS OF THE PASTOR OF HOMOSEXUALS JOSEPH DOUCE TO CHRIST THE LIBERATOR, NOTHING TO SAY', Le Soir, August 8 1990,

"In anticipation of a debate scheduled for September on pedophilia and

child prostitution networks, Françoise Vandemoortele had in fact reconnected with Pastor Doucé. She had informed him that representatives of the Protestant Churches of Belgium believed that Joseph Doucé was abusing his title of pastor (of the Baptist Church). Joseph Doucé had sent him the contact details of Dutch specialists in pedophilia issues, notably the senator and former lawyer Edward Brongersma, and the psychologist Frits Bernard, author of several works. He also spoke about Philippe Carpentier, founder of CRIES (the research and information center on childhood and sexuality), sentenced two years ago to a correctional facility in Brussels) and a CRIES correspondent in Paris, a defrocked priest who was arrested as part of an investigation into the kidnapping of a child, of whom we spoke at the time of the Brussels investigation into the pedophilia network linked to CRIES."

Information provided by Serge Heylens notes close relationship between Douce and Carpentier, X-Dossier summary, 1235 pages, 2005, published by Wikileaks in 2009, https://wikileaks.org/wiki/Belgium:_Dutroux_dossier_summary,_1235_pages,_2005, page 1031

[501] 'ENQUETE SUR LA DISPARITION A PARIS DU BELGE JOSEPH DOUCE (CITE VOICI TROIS ANS DANS L'AFFAIRE DU CRIES)'(" INVESTIGATION INTO THE DISAPPEARANCE IN PARIS OF THE BELGIAN JOSEPH DOUCE (QUOTED THREE YEARS AGO IN THE CRIES CASE) "), Le Soir, August 2 1990,

"Quoted three years ago on the sidelines of the investigation into the pedophilia network linked to CRIES (the Center for Research and Information on Childhood and Sexuality, several members of which were convicted in Brussels for pedophilia), Joseph Doucé, who was in contact with the founder of CRIES, had specified that his association, accessible only to adults, took care of the pastoral and psychological aspects of sexual minorities (homosexuals, transsexuals, pedophiles) without having any commercial activity." [French to English]

[502] 'All tracks of the affair of pastor homosexual', Le Soir, September 4 1990,

"For lack of other leads, the newspaper puts forward, among other hypotheses, that of embezzlement which could explain his disappearance (some give Joseph Doucé the reputation of a "pastor on commission"), or the existence of a blackmailer, or again his contacts with an association with Nazi ideology, "Gaie France", led by Michel Caignet, a former member of the Fane, dissolved, then the FNE (European Nationalist Groups)." [French to English Translation]

[503] ("Passive Pedophiles Facing Justice In Paris"), Le Soir, 13 Sep-

tember 1996,

"Around a hundred defendants for "receiving objects originating from the corruption of minors aged 15 and under" (a criminal qualification never used until now) will soon answer, before a Parisian court, for the possession of video cassettes showing very young children gagged, tortured and raped. The investigation began in the fall of 1995 with the discovery of a network of cassettes devoted to pedophilia, organized between the United States and Europe, and leading - for France - to a former far-right activist. from the Paris region. The latter distributed the "material" throughout France through classified ads in specialized newspapers. To do this, he contacted a company in Val-de-Marne which, in addition to inserting this very particular advertisement, was responsible for taking orders and sending "confidential" packages to customers lured by the advertisements. published. The cassettes were branded Toro Bravo. The police found a batch of 250 at the home of the French "wholesaler". He was helped by a photographer sidekick. During their arrest, various clues found in the premises they occupied led investigators to suspect that the pornographic tapes had been made in Colombia. In fact, having gone to Bogota last November, the French police were able to locate the filming locations - where children sometimes aged 8 to 10 years old appear. The original documents, which had been used to make the cassettes, and which contained scenes of unbearable violence, were seized on site. As soon as this evidence was gathered, a police operation was decided and executed in France itself. Immediately, the Val-de-Marne company was searched, before the alert could be given by possible accomplices. Parcels found there and a computer file of "customers" were seized." [French to English]

[504] 'Le réseau «Ado 71» comparaît cette semaine à Mâcon La France juge 61 pédophiles'("The "Ado 71" network appears this week in Mâcon France judges 61 pedophiles"), Le Soir, March 14 2000,

"In 1996, during operation "Toro Bravo" (named after a Colombian film production company), they got their hands on a large client file at the home of a professor in Cluny, near Mâcon. Operation "Ado 71" (71 is the department number) allowed them to seize several hundred pornographic tapes featuring children, some showing rapes where the perpetrators were with their faces uncovered. A thousand pamphlets of a pedophile nature were also found. . .Never in France has such a raid been organized in pedophile circles. This spectacular dragnet had also sparked a wave of controversy. Five men in police custody had committed suicide! The president of the Human Rights League was particularly concerned about the conditions in which the searches took place, the violation of the pre-

sumption of innocence and that of the secrecy of the investigation." [French to English]
'Pédophiles: des violeurs parmi les voyeurs. Un suspect, chez qui la police avait trouvé des cassettes, s'est pendu.'("Pedophiles: rapists among voyeurs. A suspect, in whom the police had found cassettes, hanged himself"), Liberation, Franck Johannes, June 20 1997
"A postal inspector, heard all day Tuesday by the gendarmerie in the case of trafficking in pedophile tapes, was found hanged yesterday morning at his home, in Saint-Martin-d'Hères, in the suburbs of Grenoble. His name appeared in the network's file and investigators carried out "two incidental seizures" at his home, but he had not been indicted as part of the raid organized since Tuesday by a Mâcon judge. Already on Saturday, in a completely different matter, the director of a school in Châteaurenard (Loiret) committed suicide in a river after being indicted the day before for "sexual assault on a minor" [French to English]

[505] 'Priest charged with child pornography', Sun Herald Mississippi, July 5 1990,
"A 77-year-old priest has been charged with taking pornographic pictures of children in the town in central France where he served for 42 years, court and church officials said Wednesday. The British-born priest, Nicolas Glenncross, was charged Saturday by a Paris judge with inciting minors into lewd behavior. He has been jailed pending further court proceedings."
Alternative Source: Nazisme et homosexualités, imbrications historiques et retour du refoulé, Thierry Meyssan, June 1 1997, https://www.voltairenet.org/article7502.html

[506] According to the genealogy profile of the Glencross family managed by an 'Emma Jane Glencross' on geni.com, Peter Glencross(https://www.geni.com/people/Peter-Glencross/6000000024683905610) was the son of John Christopher Glencross(https://www.geni.com/people/John-Glencross/6000000024681089134), who was the brother of Nicolas Henry Petrock Glencross(https://www.geni.com/people/Nicholas-Glencross/6000000024681066186), the priest in question. Birth and death dates match ones provided in separate sources.

[507] 'Les Mondes de François Mitterrand' by Hubert Vedrine (Fayard 2016),
"In short, François Mitterrand, who never stopped pushing in front of new generation voters and building up a reserve of political leaders, had planned my candidacy for the municipal elections in the east of the constituency, in Saint-Léger-des -Vignes, on a list of young socialists. Afterwards, if I had

succeeded in the first part of the program which was incumbent on me, he would ensure that I was designated by the departmental assembly of activists as a substitute, since representing the other part of the constituency. But how, I asked him, could I be a candidate in a town where I knew no one? He was going to take care of it, he told me, by putting me in contact with friends, the Maringes, who would in turn put me in touch with the priest of Saint-Léger-des-Vignes, Father Glencross, an Englishman . original stranded in Nivernais since the war, adored by its parishioners and very close to the leaders of the young socialist team, Robert Billoué and Guy Leblanc. So it was done." [French to English Translation]

[508] L'enquête sulfureuse de Bernard Violet sur l'assassinat du pasteur Doucé, Remi Darne, L'Humanite, March 18 1994,

"The hundred of my interlocutors, friends or enemies of the pastor - including Senator Henri Caillavet - are unanimous in recognizing that, although Pastor Doucé proudly and publicly claimed his homosexuality, he was never a pedophile. He was simply their lawyer. To answer the question precisely, it is correct that in 1989 the juvenile brigade uncovered a vast trafficking of photos of children in which we find the neo-Nazi Caignet and two accomplices: Bernard Alapetite and Jean-Manuel Vuillaume, who present themselves as photographers and art editors. Among those charged: educators, summer camp leaders, senior civil servants, and even a priest. Who is?[the priest]...Nicolas Glencross, parish priest, since 1948, of a small parish in Nièvre, Saint-Léger-des-Vignes. In the region, everyone knows that the door to the presbytery he had built, on Route de la Machine, always remains open. Certainly, we often see many young men and women there, but we cannot think of anything bad. His hobby: drawing. "I have a pencil in my eyes, I like to capture what is fleeting," he told the investigating judge, Catherine Scholastique. Every year, he brings children back from his trips to India, Peru and Sri Lanka. In short, he took between 20,000 and 30,000 photos of children in the space of forty years! The boys were most often found naked, in academic or suggestive poses. Minors received 50 francs per session. Imprisoned in Fresnes in 1990, at the age of seventy-seven, he ended up dying in December 1991. " [French to English]

[509] 'Priest charged with child pornography', Sun Herald Mississippi, July 5 1990,

"A 77-year-old priest has been charged with taking pornographic pictures of children in the town in central France where he served for 42 years, court and church officials said Wednesday. The British-born priest, Nicolas Glenncross, was charged Saturday by a Paris judge with inciting minors into lewd behavior. He has been jailed pending further court proceedings."

[510] 'ENQUETE SUR LA DISPARITION A PARIS DU BELGE JOSEPH DOUCE (CITE VOICI TROIS ANS DANS L'AFFAIRE DU CRIES)'("INVESTIGATION INTO THE DISAPPEARANCE IN PARIS OF THE BELGIAN JOSEPH DOUCE (QUOTED THREE YEARS AGO IN THE CRIES CASE) "), Le Soir, August 2 1990,

"Already in June, three men claiming to be police officers had taken an interest in Pastor Doucé and had already paid him a late visit. He had alerted the "Rescue Police". For a month, "general intelligence" police officers had on various occasions gone to the "Autre cultures" bookstore, specializing in homosexual issues and located a few steps from his home. Incidents had taken place with several customers. They sought to discover possible links with pedophile networks, in particular with a network based in Holland." [French to English]

[511] 'LE PASTEUR DOUCE RESTE INTROUVABLE:DES INDICES RECHERCHES EN BELGIQUE,CHEZ LA MERE DU PASTEUR?'("PASTOR DOUCE REMAINS NOT FOUND: CLUES SEARCHED IN BELGIUM, AT THE PASTOR'S MOTHER?"), Le Soir, August 14 1990,

"Yesterday, French investigators tried to collect testimonies in order to establish the possible presence of the pastor after July 19. The agents of the Criminal Brigade could, in the coming days, also go to the Netherlands, where the pastor regularly made business trips." [French to English]

[512] 'WORRYING REVELATIONS ON THE INVESTIGATIONS OF INSPECTOR DUFOURG THE SWEET CASE WEIGHS ON THE PARISIAN RG', Le Soir, October 22 1990

[513] 'THE DISAPPEARANCE IN PARIS OF THE PASTOR OF HOMO-SEXUALS JOSEPH DOUCE TO CHRIST THE LIBERATOR, NOTHING TO SAY', Le Soir, August 8 1990,

"In its Thursday delivery, "France Soir" specifies that Pastor Doucé was to participate in the "Screen Witness" scheduled for September and was preparing to give names of people controlling the child trade. Françoise Vandemoortele denies it: the pastor was not invited to the show and had no revelation to make. His Dutch correspondents also believe that there is no commercial network there, but rather prostitution of young people, from the age of sixteen. There is therefore apparently no reason to establish a link between possible revelations that Pastor Doucé was about to make and his disappearance. Joseph Doucé had also planned to spend the entire month of August in Paris, where he was preparing another book." [French to English]

[514] 'EST-CE LE CORPS DU PASTEUR EN FORET DE RAMBOUIL-

LET ? DE L'AFFAIRE DOUCE A L'AFFAIRE DUFOURG'("IS THIS THE BODY OF THE PASTOR IN THE RAMBOUILLET FOREST? FROM THE SWEET AFFAIR TO THE DUFOURG AFFAIR"), Le Soir, October 26 1990,
"We thus move from the Doucé affair to the Dufourg affair, which is causing a stir in police circles. A request for a parliamentary commission of inquiry into General Intelligence was introduced by RPR deputies Jacques Toubon and Jean-Louis Debré. Having learned from Dufourg's revelations that the RG had robbed the headquarters of SOS Racism in 1987, Harlem Désir protested to the Minister of the Interior Pierre Joxe. We also learned that the RG placed illegal wiretaps (but countersigned by the Prime Minister's office) at the bookstore run by the pastor." [French to English]

[515] 'THE DISAPPEARANCE IN PARIS OF THE PASTOR OF HOMOSEXUALS JOSEPH DOUCE TO CHRIST THE LIBERATOR, NOTHING TO SAY', Le Soir, August 8 1990,
"In anticipation of a debate scheduled for September on pedophilia and child prostitution networks, Françoise Vandemoortele had in fact reconnected with Pastor Doucé. She had informed him that representatives of the Protestant Churches of Belgium believed that Joseph Doucé was abusing his title of pastor (of the Baptist Church). Joseph Doucé had sent him the contact details of Dutch specialists in pedophilia issues, notably the senator and former lawyer Edward Brongersma, and the psychologist Frits Bernard, author of several works. He also spoke about Philippe Carpentier, founder of CRIES (the research and information center on childhood and sexuality), sentenced two years ago to a correctional facility in Brussels) and a CRIES correspondent in Paris, a defrocked priest who was arrested as part of an investigation into the kidnapping of a child, of whom we spoke at the time of the Brussels investigation into the pedophilia network linked to CRIES." [French to English]

[516] 'Even hardened police admit to their shock', Huddersfield Daily Examiner, January 5 1988.

[517] 'Child Pornography:An Investigation' Tim Tate, 1990
"The April 1986 issue of BLW contained a glowing tribute to Frank Torey for his advice and support. The editor of that issue was listed as Martyn Simons. Simons had previously edited PAN magazine using the name Roger E. Hunt. Neither was his real name. Simons, aka Hunt, was born Roger Lawrence on 25 February 1946. . .He left Spartacus in January 1986 after a row with the organisation's leader, John Stamford. He went on to edit PAN and BLW. Just over a year later he met up with a Swiss paedophile named Beat Meier; together the two men packed a car and, on 24

January, drove it on to the midday Ostend-to-Dover ferry."
[518] 'Child Pornography:An Investigation' Tim Tate, 1990
"Staunton ordered a search of Meier's car. In it he found a treasure trove of child-pornography videos and magazines. This was not altogether surprising: Meier had been editor of Libido, a particularly nasty Zurich-based child-sex magazine."
[519] Monsters and Men, Bob Long & Bob McLachlan, 2002, page 80
"The information was consistent with the character of Beat Meier, who, when arrested, was found in possession of photographs of a femle baby, no more than eight months old, being tortured with a speculum."
[520] 'Pedophile set for deportation', Huddersfield Daily Examiner, January 5 1988
[521] 'Even hardened police admit to their shock', Huddersfield Daily Examiner, January 5 1988.
[522] 'UN porn hunt grows', Daily Mirror, June 20 1987
[523] Monsters and Men, Bob Long & Bob McLachlan, 2002
[524] 'Unicef Man On Child Sex Charges', The Guardian, June 19 1987
[525] 'Un empleado de Unicef y un funcionario belga implicados en una red de pornografía infantil'("A Unicef employee and a Belgian official implicated in a child pornography ring"), Ignatius Chairman, El Pais, March 12 1987,
"The identity of another of those involved surprised the police, however, because Michel Decré not only had no judicial record but also held a job that required inspiring great trust, being in charge of translating the information and documents communicated. by the Trevi group, through which the ministries of the Interior and Justice of the 12 member countries of the European Community (EC) coordinate the fight against terrorism and drug trafficking." [Spanish to English]
[526] 'Justice Plus de 15 m3 de documents saisis Les archives des pédophiles'("Justice More than 15 m3 of documents seized Pedophile archives"), Le Soir, October 2 2001.
[527] 'BREVE FAITS DIVERS'("BRIEF MISCELLANEOUS FACTS"), Le Soir, November 22 2001,
"The Liège indictment chamber ordered, a few days ago, the release of the four men who had been arrested in Namur on October 1 in a case of possession of pedophile images. The investigation, which is continuing, revealed exchanges between them of large collections of images of children. A search also led to the seizure of 15 m3 of documents. Two of these men were well-known figures: Jacques Delbouille, 61, from Hantes-Wihéries, a former gravedigger with nebulous behavior, and Michel Decré, 50, from Brussels,

sentenced to 7 years in prison in connection with the Cries case. The indictment chamber this time followed the release order taken by the council chamber of the Namur court." [French to English]
'Justice Plus de 15 m3 de documents saisis Les archives des pédophiles'("Justice More than 15 m3 of documents seized Pedophile archives"), Le Soir, October 2 2001,
"Delbouille, whose criminal record only reveals one conviction for rebellion against gendarmes, was placed in preventive detention for five days in connection with the Cries affair, this child prostitution network dismantled in March 1987 and which had splashed the Belgian committee of Unicef. The Cries scandal is also closely associated with one of the four other people arrested in Namur. Michel Decré, 50, from Brussels, was sentenced by the Brussels Court of Appeal to 7 years in prison. He was one of the organizers of "special evenings" where child prostitutes from Cries appeared." [French to English]

[528] This is a rather bizarre piece of information I cannot verify, but Le Soir appear to have sourced it from the dossier of information the Morkhoven Workgroup, see website: fondationprincessedecroy.eu/007-Coral___nl.htm

[529] 1999, Marie-Jeanne Van Heeswyck, Annemie Bulté, and Douglas De Coninck, 'De X-dossiers', p. 277

"At the very beginning of the Dutroux investigation the gendarmerie of Charleroi did a house search at the abandoned cabin of Bernard Weinstein in Jumet. In between the piles of junk which were dragged outside there, a note was found, folded in four, with a few typed sentences: 'Bernard, don't forget that the feast is nearing and that the high priestess expects her present, Anubis.' In the official report of the search there's not sign to be found of this rather wondrous message. It is clear that the detectives only did their 'discovery' several days or weeks later. Anubis, that is also the ritual name of 'grandmaster' Francis Desmet. That name is everything but secret: Anubis and Nahema-Nephthys, aka Dominique Kindermans, published a book several years before, Le prince de ce monde (The Prince of the World), a 'manual for Western demonology and dictionary of demons'. A book that they sign with their ritual names, complete with pictures and biographies. According to the detectives, the high priestess can be no one else than the partner of Anubis, Dominique Kindermans. And the gift she expects, what else can it be than a child - a child to sacrifice?"

[530] 'LUCIFER,LE PORTEUR DE LUMIERE,RAYONNE SUR LE BASSIN CAROLO'("LUCIFER, THE BEARER OF LIGHT, RADI-

ATES ON THE CAROLO BASIN"), Le Soir, October 26 1993

[531] 'Warrants issued for cult leaders', The Guardian, October 8 1994

[532] LE POLICIER D'ABRASAX : "PAS ILLEGAL"("THE ABRASAX POLICEMAN: "NOT ILLEGAL"), Le Soir, January 9 1997,

"A municipal police officer from Charleroi-Centre has actually been a member and treasurer, for several years, of the Abrasax institute in Forchies-la-Marche. In recent hours, he met at length with his chief commissioner and took stock of the teachings and "small rituals" that he received and practiced within the institute. His partner, also a police officer, was briefly part of the sect in 1992. Furthermore, a contract agent, who left the police in 1994, was also part of the sect. These two have never, according to Dominique Kindermans, of the Abrasax institute, followed anything other than the first cycle of their courses, namely the Satanist cycle, that of the Belgian Church of Satan." [French to English]

[533] ("DID JOURNALISTS COMPROMISE ABRASAX'S SEARCH?"), Le Soir, January 11 1997,

"Has one of our colleagues committed an indelicacy likely to compromise the result of the search on December 21 at the headquarters of the Abrasax institute, in Forchies-la-Marche? It was in particular our colleagues from "La Libre Belgique" who mentioned this fact in their Thursday editions, reporting that the investigators had, in fact, learned that the two senior officials of Abrasax had received, in the week preceding the searches, the visit from a journalist who had informed them that the supreme grand master Anubis, Francis De-smedt in the civil registry, was cited in one of the files put under investigation in Neufchâteau." [French to English]

[534] 118.477 21/12/96 DECKER SEARCH at MULTIDIFFUSION SA Chaussée de Charleroi 71 in St-GILLES, X-Dossier summary, 1235 pages, 2005, published by Wikileaks in 2009, https://wikileaks.org/wiki/Belgium:_Dutroux_dossier_summary,_1235_pages,_2005, page 121

"At the request of Neufcahateau cell following PV 5.341 of 10/21/96 from PJ ARLON (hearing of VASSAUX Willy regarding VAN GHYSEGEM Armand) On site: closed premises and for rent Search by consent on 12/24/96 with SACRE Michel (real estate agency responsible for rentals) It was indeed an esoteric bookstore... Documents with NEW AGE letterhead (accounting) List of people and telephones and addresses Companion of VAN GHIJSEGEM = GOLTFUS Fabienne NOUVEL AGE is bankrupt: curator Anne DESMETH Seized documents will be used by the Neufchâteau Cell Copies of the lists seized in the annex" [Flemish to French to English]

[535] Police Statement 5.341 21/12/1996 CELL CHARL MORIAME - INTERVIEW of Willy VASSAUX, X-Dossier summary, 1235 pages, 2005, published by Wikileaks in 2009, https://wikileaks.org/wiki/Belgium:_Dutroux_dossier_summary,_1235_pages,_2005,
"Employed on 01/03/1994 by VAN GHYSEGHEM Armand for company SA
MULTIDIFFUSION
Dismissed in 06/1995
VAN GHYSEGHEM told him that regularly made love to little girls who were locked up in iron cages
He spoke about 5 year old girls
VAN GHYSEGHEM goes regularly to THAILAND
He was physically threatened by VAN GHYSEGHEM, just as Milka LINGURSKI
- he mentioned the name of criminal of CHARLEROI: Jean RENSON
VAN GHYSEGHEM is linked to ABRASAX and hangs out with ANUBIS and NAHEMA
Maurice JOSTEN explained to him that during a black mass at ABRASAX a man died
VAN OVERSTRAETE (lawyer of VAN GHYSEGHEM) is a member of ABRASAX
VAN GHYSEGHEM was protected by Charles PICQUE (Ed: a notable Belgian politician)
Jacques LEJEUNE and VAN CAUWENBERGHE (Ed: Mayor of Charleroi) are involved in pedophilia (learnt from Jacquelin JUIN - RTBF)
They were also involved in drug trafficking coming form Turkey via the airport of GOSSELIES (Ed: Charleroi airport)
VAN GHYSEGHEM had been seen in BANGKOK discussing with pimps
VAN GHYSEGHEM was at the centre of trafficking young girls from THAILAND to BELGIUM and HAMBURG
The cleaning lady of VAN GHYSEGHEM is scared to talk
VAN GHYSEGHEM is sometimes called ABA VANGH
VAN GHYSEGHEM attended orgies with DESSY who inherited the Forges de
Clabecq"
Police Statement 5.205 09/01/1997 PJ ARLON DAVIN - INTERVIEW of
LINGURSKI Milka (18/02/1961), X-Dossier summary, 1235 pages, 2005, published by Wikileaks in 2009, https://wikileaks.org/wiki/

Belgium:_Dutroux_dossier_summary,_1235_pages,_2005,
"She had been employed by VAN GHYSEGHEM from 04/1994 to 05/1995
She had stopped because of she was physically assaulted by VAN GHY-SEGHEM
He had a lot of money but was incompetent as a book publisher
He was very interested in young children
He boasted of his 'exploits' in ASIA
Someone named CHARLIER said that he had met VAN GHYSEGHEM in THAILAND
He said he was protected and that no criminal charges were ever laid against him
VAN GHYSEGHEM had proposed to go with her to ABRASAX but she had declined
DESSY was probably the mistress of VAN GHYSEGHEM, she gave him a lot
of money
She had heard vague rumeurs of a black mass at ABRASAX at which a man had died"
Police Statement 5.053 14/01/1997 PJ ARLON DAVIN - INTERVIEW of
SCRAUWEN Lilian (03/12/1946), X-Dossier summary, 1235 pages, 2005, published by Wikileaks in 2009, https://wikileaks.org/wiki/Belgium:_Dutroux_dossier_summary,_1235_pages,_2005,
"Teacher at St Peter's College in UCCLE
Since 1988 she copywriter for VAN GHYSEGHEM
She refused to contribute to the PRINCE OF THIS WORLD project (ed: a book on black magic) because the text and illustrations were too 'daring'
She participated in a black mass at Abrasax.
Very young children were brought by their parents and took communion in the name of Satan.
KINDERMAN Dominique = Very intelligent and very dishonest.
VAN GHYSEGHEM gave her videos containing an account of his life, in order to produce a book
He spoke of his sex life and acts of pedophilia in ASIA
No crimes in BELGIUM
Does not have a copy of the videos; had an argument with VAN GHY-SEGHEM"
[536] 3.011 30/12/96 PJ ARLON MASSON, X-Dossier summary, 1235 pages, 2005, published by Wikileaks in 2009, https://wikileaks.org/wiki/Belgium:_Dutroux_dossier_summary,_1235_pages,_2005,

"IDENTIFICATIONS following hearing of VASAUX Willy LINGURSKI Milka - 02/18/61 VAN GHYSEGEM Armand - 05/09/40 GOLTFUS Fabienne -01/11/71 JOOSTEN Maurice - 03/09/38 HOYOIS Jacqueline - 06/04/33 DESSY Suzanne - 02/08/27"

[537] RAPPOR T 14/11/96 BSR PHIL GROENNE, X-Dossier summary, 1235 pages, 2005, published by Wikileaks in 2009, https://wikileaks.org/wiki/Belgium:_Dutroux_dossier_summary,_1235_pages,_2005,

"ANONYMOUS INFO The witness operated a nightclub in BXL In 84 he was worried in a drug case and took DUMONT JP as his lawyer DUMONT defended him poorly because he refused homosexual relations with DUMONT DUMONT = personal friend of VANDEN BOEYNANTS DUMONT also asked him to find young people aged 10-12 DUMONT also suggested that he participate in "special" evenings in a castle near NAMUR Between 1984-89 DUMONT has good relations with Georges DESSY, retired manager of a BBL agency, as well as with his brother DUMONT is a leader of pedophile networks"

100.165/97 26/11/96 ROELANS – ANONYMOUS DECLARATION, X-Dossier summary, 1235 pages, 2005, published by Wikileaks in 2009, https://wikileaks.org/wiki/Belgium:_Dutroux_dossier_summary,_1235_pages,_2005,

"The witness knew DUMONT very well between 1984-89
DUMONT was the right hand of VANDEN BOEYNANTS
DUMONT proposed sexual relations to the witness. Refused
DUMONT asked him to accompany him to special parties in a château of Namur. Refused.
DUMONT asked him to find children aged 10-12 years. Refused.
DUMONT frequented at the time the café ANDRE – the restaurant MOK MA ZWET and the CIRCUS discotheque.
ANDRE and the MOK MA ZWET was run by gangsters who also had links to the MOZART.
One day after the CIRCUS was closed, and under DUMONT's direction, the last clients and bosses went to a villa to which DUMONT had the keys. Villa 5 minutes away in the car from the CIRCUS
Swimming pool – nude bathing
DUMONT was the lawyer of individuals implicated in the CRIES file, including DESSY
DESSY is a paedophile

DESSY has a villa near RIXENSART where minors live.
DESSY pays a lot of money for paedophile cassettes (tortures) and/or children
He is a member of the homosexual network SPARTACUS
He is the brother of Georges DESSY
Georges DESSY is a senior figure at BBL - he is a homosexual fetishist who practices urology.
The collection of DESSY Georges is hidden in a garage near his home"

[538] 'Zwijgen is voor daders - De getuigenis van X1', Regina Louf, 1998

[539] History of the Royal Zoute Golf Club, Clubs website as of August 2023,
https://www.rzgc.be/club/history-of-the-club

[540] 114.037 34 29/09, HEARING of X1, X-Dossier summary, 1235 pages, 2005, published by Wikileaks in 2009.
Continuation PV 117.154 of 10/13/96 (hearing of X1), X-Dossier summary, 1235 pages, 2005, published by Wikileaks in 2009.)

[541] 150.027 01/02/97 FOURTH INTERVIEW with CANNOODT Nathalie, X-Dossier summary, 1235 pages, 2005, published by Wikileaks in 2009 ,

"FOURTH INTERVIEW with CANNOODT Nathalie She refuses an audiotaped interview Her father was a sex maniac He had asked his mother to participate in orgies and/or swinging His dad had a photo lab the kids couldn't go to - he didn't take pictures. In the evening his father repaired TVs After the separation she remembers that the day after her return from a visit to her father she cried all day but she no longer knows why. Her parents and those of X1 knew each other before they went to the same school She finds TONY dirty and disgusting She only remembers 2-3 things about her - she forgot the rest

His sister had to sleep next to his father but she does not know more She must have been the victim of serious facts She refuses any physical contact She has been followed by a shrink for 07 years

For a long time she feels that something has happened with her (Nathalie) but does not know what She does not like to be filmed or photographed or to look at herself in a mirror She has periods of depression where she takes refuge alone in a room She wishes that her daughter does not have the same youth as her When she sees her daughter naked in her bathtub she has sexual urges During her auditions she always wants to cry without knowing why Following her first interview, she contacted her mother and explained the situation to her, asking for photos of her youth. Since then she no longer has contact with her mother, which seems abnormal. She asks to see a shrink before a new interview"

PV 150.434 01/03/97, INTERVIEW with CANNOODT,
"Father = sexually obsessed - he forced his mother to have sex with a friend while he was busy with the friend's wife (JEAN-PAUL and AGNES) JEAN-PAUL and AGNES = sexually obsessed - they have two children JEAN_PAUL showed photos of the sex of his pregnant wife CANNOODT's father was aggressive during sex (from AGNES) A 15-year-old girl came to her parents to learn Dutch - she left in a hurry In a campsite she rode naked on a bicycle with one of her father's friends (NICOLE) who was also naked Recent talks with his mother: Her father was violent during sex He was sexually greedy - change of position, partners, younger and younger girls - swinging He spent the night in his 10-12 year old sister's bed (single bed) His father once burned his sister in the arm with a cigarette. Divorce at the request of his sister because his father went too far Her father had a photo lab but she never saw him take a picture When he went to the lab his mother had to go with him He decided to steal the dog that the three children adored The father had no love-respect for the older sister (PATRICIA) PATRICIA was forced by her father to go with him and her friend NICOLE on vacation to GREECE"

[542] PV 150.459 25/02/97 ANALYSIS and FINDINGS following STORME HEARING of 02/14/97, X-Dossier summary, 1235 pages, 2005, published by Wikileaks in 2009,

"Educated from 01 to 12 months in French by a nurse at WESTKAPPELE Her parents didn't know how to take care of her (no time) The parents' Tea-Room has collapsed and the maternal grandfather did not know how to help The tea-room still exists (MERRIDOR) and his parents own the building His mother became the concierge of a Zeedijk building in DUINBERGEN His father is a salesman at BUTCH in KNOKKE STORME went to the Kindergarten in DUINBERGEN Weekends with his grandparents Communication problems in kindergarten The grandmother and the mother considered her responsible for their misfortunes Grandmother bewitched by the devil wanted to initiate it and if she spoke about it she would undergo what her grandmother showed her in the satanic books At the age of six his parents moved to KNOKKE Kustlaan 60 Primary studies at the Heilig Hart School From the age of 4, his father took him to SLUIS where he bought porn books and vibrators. At SLUIS she saw porn with children Her mother masturbated in front of the TV in front of her and in front of her father Her father walked around the house naked Around the

age of 10 X1 sends the police to her house saying that there are a lot of porn magazines at her house as well as photos of her parents having sex She was X1's best friend She regularly went to X1's grandmother - Description of the house When there were customers she could not go upstairs and had to be discreet and silent When customers went there, they had no luggage - always men Customers = regulars Grandma tough on X1 - was seen threatening X1 with a gun Few memories of X1's parents She saw few children at the grandmother's house She was assaulted at ANTWERPEN Zoo by a stranger during a school trip (4°) Her teacher did not believe her and punished her Premiere Moderne in St-Bernardus 2° and 3° sewing and tailoring at OLV ONBEVLEKT 4° 5° and 6° at St-LUC in GENT (last year in kot) At 18 she meets her future husband and gets married at 21 Bad relationship with his parents Remained 06 years without seeing her mother She only saw her father once in a while She loved her father very much but not her mother The mother was jealous of her daughters who monopolized her husband His parents have no friends Parents = STORME Roland (23/01/33) and VANNIEUWENHUYSE Jenny (25/03/32) Grandparents = VANNIEUWENHUYSE Raoul (dcd) and DONCHE Maria (15/06/10)"

150.816 20/03/97 FINDINGS STORME HEARING of 04/02/97 STORM Flash of 01/30/97,
"A fact of pedophilia at the grandmother of X1 in a room with two beds (PV 150.088/97 page 23) It was dark, a man threw her on the bed and made her kneel He made her suck him and swallow the cum before letting her out She told X1 she couldn't go on like this She thinks it was not the first time she suffered such acts She does not know who taught her but remembers that she was taught to use only her mouth She doesn't know who sent her to the bedroom The grandmother never hit her or defended her When she wanted to go down the grandmother waited in the corridor and she knew what she had to do She does not remember other places where she was abused She remembers biting the sheets when the man hurt her by taking her in the anus If the man was happy then she had to suck him She has never had an injury but refuses that her husband takes her in this position She was happy to then find X1 in the garden She remembers making love to a man with X1"

[543] 151.441 04/06/97 HEARING OF DESIMPELAERE L + MULLIE G, X-Dossier summary, 1235 pages, 2005, published by Wikileaks in 2009. (Original document is a French translation of Dutch, which had been translated into English using the Google translation utility)

* * *

"151.441 04/06/97 HEARING OF DESIMPELAERE L + MULLIE G - DESIMPELAERE specifies that STORME Chantal was indeed mistreated in her youth and that she did not have a normal education. - DESIMPELAERE confirms the rumors concerning THE NAVY tea-room operated by Chantal's parents. It seems that this establishment was closed at the time for acts of morals (sexual orgies, taking pornographic photos). - DESIMPELAERE and MULLIE specify that Chantal has also had couple problems since her marriage and this is explained by the difficulties that have arisen since her youth. – They both contacted Chantal's father following the problems that arose during the weekend of May 17-19 (PINKSTEREN). Chantal's father has been made aware of the existence of a judicial inquiry and its scope. He would have expressed himself by saying that his daughter has always lived with problems, that she should be interned. About the NAVY, it is according to him old stories of more than 20 years. - DESIMPELAERE says he warned Chantal's father that this investigation originated with a former friend of Chantal (friend of the BRITANNIA hotel). - DESIMPELAERE declares that following an interview with his daughter STORME Roland would have told him that in fact the girlfriend was not that of the BRITANNIA hotel but indeed that of the TINNEL hotel. He added that this former girlfriend would be the granddaughter of a police commissioner from GHENT. Roland would have declared that his wife would have let Chantal play at the villa of this friend's grandmother once or twice. - DESIMPELAERE adds that on 21.05.97, Roland STORME visited Chantal following her suicide attempt. He reportedly told his daughter that all these current problems were caused by the setting up of the 0800 green line by Mr CONNEROTTE. - MULLIE adds that Chantal never spoke of sexual abuse before the intervention of our services but that she remembers that in her time, Chantal had spoken of the existence of pornographic photos being taken. It would only be after our hearings that Chantal confessed to having been sexually abused."

[544] PV 118.575 14/12/96 IDENTIFICATION CANNOODT Nathalie (25/09/68) by X4, X-Dossier summary, 1235 pages, 2005, published by Wikileaks in 2009,

"Presentation of photo albums X4 recognizes a girl who played in pedophile films + photos The girl in question taught X4 a card game The recognized daughter is CANNOODT Nathalie"

118.576 14/12/96 IDENTIFICATION STORME Chantale (18/01/68) by X4

"Presentation of photo albums X4 recognizes a girl who starred in pedophile films + photos X4 did "embarrassing" things with this girl The

recognized girl is STORME Chantale"

[545] PV 116.799 06/11/96, DESIGNATION OF LOCATIONS by X2 in KNOKKE, X-Dossier summary, 1235 pages, 2005, published by Wikileaks in 2009,

"DESIGNATION OF LOCATIONS by X2 in KNOKKE First contact with X2 on 06/11/96 X2 explains a period of her life when she participated in orgies (1985-1990) Facts take place in KNOKKE villas Similarities to places denoted by X1 On-site visit with X2 - X2 guides the verbalizers Hotel CROMWELL - no longer exists in KNOKKE "SCARSDALE" Blinckaertlaan 19 in the Koningbos Restaurant UYLENSPIEGEL Apartment Zoutelaan 80 House Binnenhof 9 or 11 or 13 (not sure) Elizabethlaan 62 Zeedijk 841 "LEKKERBEK" Eikenlaan or BOSLAAN 43 X1 had also designated the SCARSDALE villa and the Binnenhof houses Hotel TINEL and the house of X1's grandmother are located opposite Elizabethlaan 62"

[546] 150.567 04/03/97, X-Dossier summary, 1235 pages, 2005, published by Wikileaks in 2009,

"DENTIFICATION OF PERSONS QUOTED by X2 LIPPENS Léopold (20/11/41) DENIS Patrick (28/12/??) VAN ROSSEM Jean-Pierre (29/05/45) by BONVOISIN Benoit (14/03/39) DUMONT Jean-Paul (07/04/52) HUBERT Benoit (05/03/58) LEROY Claude (27/06/40) MARNETTE Georges (14/12/46) ZIMMER Yves (03/02/49) CEUPPENS Georges (22/01/48) BOUHOUCHE Madani (14/06/52) VANDER ZWALMEN Albert (30/07/37) LIPPENS Maurice (09/05/43) CLAREBOETS Luc (11/06/49) CRUCIFIX Alain (18 /02/51) PELOS, Jean-Paul (29/11/48)"

[547] 118.383 13/12/96 HEARING OF X2 - Karel VAN MIERT, X-Dossier summary, 1235 pages, 2005, published by Wikileaks in 2009

"She frequented the PLATOS, Porte de Namur Generally meal at BOUM-BOUM oyu at HILTON and late evening at PLATOS After midnight: orgies with sometimes consenting minors aged 14-15 During an orgy she made love with Karel VAN MIERT During this report he strangles her until she almost collapses"

[548] 'Suspicion over bid to rescue steel-maker', Politico, July 3 1996,

"EUROPEAN Commission clearance of a38-million-ecu bail-out of loss-making Belgian steel-maker Forges de Clabecq appears doomed to fail."

[549] 118.379 12/12/96, Interview of X2, X-Dossier summary, 1235 pages, 2005, published by Wikileaks in 2009,

"DENIS Patrick (lover of X2) is also threatened with death SIMON Marc would also have suffered such threats as well as his wife and daughter DEPRETRE sent love letters to X2 - she gave these letters to CASTIAUX

X2 went regularly to DOLO where she met BOUHOUCHE X2 also meets BOUHOUCHE's wife at the HILTON during a meeting between GOL - MOUREAUX Philippe - MARTENS Wilfried, VDB, DE CLERCK Willy - NIHOUL Jean-Michel - DELVOYE and KAREL X2 did not attend the meeting - she was waiting at the bar BOUHOUCHE was never heard on the DOLO, the HILTON and the people he knew"

[550] 114.037 29/09, Interview of X1, X-Dossier summary, 1235 pages, 2005, published by Wikileaks in 2009.

[551] HEARING of X2 on 03/27/97, X-Dossier summary, 1235 pages, 2005, published by Wikileaks in 2009.

"She went 5-6 times. In a huge wood - hunts. She had to go. She never witnessed anything. Participating: the most violent of the KNOKKE gang including the LIPPENS brothers. In CHIMAY she heard shouting and shooting but she does not know what, she has never seen game. There's also a LEVY she's already talked about. It was around CHIMAY castle - description of the castle she already knew before. The wood is walled up It was the cries of children maybe 10 years old (??)

She thinks there were 4-5 children. The screams stop dead. She stayed with LEVY and at that moment the LIPPENS brothers left with 1-2 other people including the "game warden". The participants were all in KNOKKE and EINDHOVEN

She never saw the children. The screams were horrible and indescribable

She didn't hear the shot. LEVY was very nervous as if he shouldn't have been there. When the screams stopped she, LEVY and the others had to leave quickly as if they were disturbing. LEVY was very disturbed. There was also a pretty strong woman, dark hair 40 years old - jeans sweater boots and other people from KNOKKE-EINDHOVEN. It takes place on a weekend afternoon, first half 88

She goes and comes back with LEVY (MERCEDES) - before the hunt: meal near VIRELLES. Description MERCEDES by LEVY. The wood is 05 minutes from the place of CHIMAY. Initially the cries were not loud, rather cries of pain then much louder cries for a few seconds and a sudden stop. In FAULX there were also cries but they did not stop. She has never seen a girl come back whole vde at Léopold LIPPENS. When the screaming stopped LEVY stopped making love to her and went back to the car very quickly with her - he drove very fast while swearing

[552] Frederick M. Alger Jr. obituary, Daily News, January 7 1967,

"An early backer of Dwight D. Eisenhower, Algier was named Ambassador to Belgium and held the post from 1952 until 1956."

[553] 'Baudouin gets the Congo treatment', Even Standard, London, July 2 1955
[554] 151.829 02/06/97, AUDITION OF X3 (ROYAL FAMILY PART), X-Dossier summary, 1235 pages, 2005, published by Wikileaks in 2009,

"Participants in the evenings: CHARLES Prince of Belgium Prince of LIEGE King BAUDOUIN 1° Prince of LIEGE (Young) Prince CHARLES - Victim SOLANGE (enucleated by X3 during a social evening). X3 victim from 03 to 12 years old (rape-orgies-torture-zoophilia-prostitution) From 03 to 08 years old: rape by his parents and friends of his parents Large, less well-off family She or her sister was delivered to the winner of the bridge games organized at her house Initially: touching but then more and more violent until partial removal of the clitoris Participants: COPPENS Roger, ADRIAANSSEN Henri, SMET François and his wife Jeanne, doctor VANDEN EYNDE René who fixed it after the sessions Deflowered by her father then raped by the men present Around 07-08 years: partial removal of the clitoris by COPPENS in the presence of the other cities Food of the children poisoned so that one of them is sick During a party, the game consisted of introducing all kinds of objects into her vagina and other natural orifices (carrot, poker) Rape by VANDEN EYNDE in his house in OOSTDUINKERKE - very painful report After 12 years she was introduced into a pedophilia network with three types of parties. Photo evenings Her mother made her as attractive as possible for the men who came to see the children She spread her sex. Evening shows Her mother drugged her (medicines) to put her to sleep (injection or oral route - PHENERGAN??) Her father drove her to a meeting place She was taken care of with other children in a black MERCEDES, leather interior with two seats facing each other Also picked up in pink American car with white roof driven by CHARLY Fairly long journey with yellow lights Always luxurious houses editor's note: she will talk about the two distinct "houses": the one where the shows took place and the one where the hunts took place Son picked her up from the meeting place and brought her back to the house where VANDEN EYNDE treated her On the spot the car stopped on a flower bed in front of the house House surrounded by a park Two supervisors on site: RALF and WALTER The children were brought in a natural stone turret with wooden door There was probably a floor in the turret an underground started from the turret towards cellars Underground without light - earth and slope In the cellars there were cells where the children were locked up waiting their turn There were also cells for dogs (Dobermans) The corridor overlooked a theater In the turret: bodies of dead

children in various stages of decomposition (sometimes dismembered and/or missing pieces) and carcasses of dogs Spectators: always the same but difficult to identify - around fifty She recognized the regent CHARLES, King BAUDOUIN and King ALBERT and two others whom she calls CHARLY and POLO She thinks she recognized Willy CLAES and doctor VANDEN EYNDE Dogs obedient to RALF and WALTER Dogs drugged to be excited Shows = orgies, killing children and dogs, ... Theater with strong smell of dog excrement Dogs loose in the garden GILLES (12 years old??) was emasculated by POLO The other children had to drink his blood She thinks she saw him cut out again in the dead room. Girls slashed with razor blades X3's sex lips were partially cut out and fed to the dogs Hunt prepared by CHARLY and POLO Present: Charles-Ferdinand NOTHOMB (???) On another place Big white house with upstairs and stables Park with round pond and fountain emerging from a character Children were let loose naked and when caught they were raped The hunt ended in torture in the playhouse A girl's big lips were sliced and fed to the dogs. Deflowering of a 7-9 year old girl by a dog Exciting product on girl's sex The other children must have licked the blood - Around the age of 10 she had to initiate other children editor's note: she says however that it happens after her 12 years. A baby devoured by dogs Childbirth of a teenager by caesarean section Baby ripped from belly and given to dogs by POLO She saw the dismembered mother again in the dead room. She saw the dead dogs in this room. She must have eaten human flesh cut from the corpses in the death room. She must have eaten pieces of children (fingers) served in gelatin Good taste - slightly sweet This caused a huge feeling of hunger and thirst Drinking blood relieved the feeling of thirst Childbirth of a single woman From birth the baby was devoured by dogs After birth: rape of the mother by POLO ert CHARLY The remains of the child must have been eaten by the children present POLO kills dogs and hollows them out like butchered pigs. A game involved having children stick knitting needles into the vagina of a girl tied to a board The girl died and was raped by RALF, POLO, CHARLY, WALTER and ALBERT. She even had to cut the throat of a girl with a knife given by POLO She was then cut up and the inside of the body was given to the dogs After the murder she was raped The next day she attended a barbecue. She talks about another murder she committed on a 3-5 year old girl under the threat that it would be her brother who would be killed She opened the sex girl to the sternum with a box cutter She gave the inside of the body to the dog someone cut off their head the child was devoured by the dogs. Murder of a young pubescent woman opened by VANDEN EYNDE She had to give the girl's guts to the dogs who were then put down The baby was crying in his mother's womb

She sewed up the belly with the baby inside. Quartering of CEDRIC (6-8 years old) because he had refused to cut his throat It was BAUDOUIN who saved her from the throat. She also had to eat dog feces 4-5 year old boy whose penis was sewn to the purse. She had to cut off the vulva of a female dog called RITA. A girl whose vagina lips were sewn before being raped We also sewed threads to the lips of her sex to spread them. social evenings Same process as for arriving at evening shows Luxurious house with perimeter wall and gate then unlit winding path There were stables Flowerbeds with flowers Entrance hall = cream and blue tiles - red fabrics on the steps Marble walls with a painting by BAUDOUIN as a teenager She spent a whole night with BAUDOUIN - blowjob and sodomy Presence of servant She recalls a night when she was slathered in crème fraîche before being brought to table on a tray She was licked and raped In this house there were many servants the evening ended in an orgy Description of parts At the end of another evening a child of 08 years old (??) was emasculated The children present buried the boy in a flowerbed She remembers a child who was decapitated then cut up and fried before being eaten She remembers children hanging from hooks in the kitchen A certain Solange was enucleated by her and an old lady with a spoon Shortly before her 12th birthday she was placed as a prostitute in a bar It was CHARLY who put it there It stopped after he was raped by his uncle On this occasion, his penis had remained stuck and he freed himself by hitting his head against the ground. She was hospitalized for 15 days in OOSTENDE it was her parents who delivered her to the network She was continually threatened with death for her and her loved ones She gives diagrams of the places mentioned"

[555] 'Belgium Pedophilia Scandal /Did Authorities Cover Up Its Scope?: Book Revives Fear of Grand Conspiracy', New York Times, December 16 1999

[556] 'Belgium's silent heart of darkness', The Observer, May 5 2002

[557] 'Procès Dutroux-bis: Michel Nihoul inculpé, non lieu en vue'('Dutroux-bis trial: Michel Nihoul indicted, no place in sight'), La Libre, May 3 2010

'Beelden van koning Albert II met minderjarig meisje': Michel Nihoul, relict van het oude corrupte België, is niet meer', DeMorgen, Douglas De Coninck, October 23 2019

[558] 'Sybil was wellicht valse constructie'("Sybil' may have been false construction'), De Morgen, August 19 1998

[559] 100.250 24/08/96, DIAKOSTA HEARING , X-Dossier summary, 1235 pages, 2005, published by Wikileaks in 2009,

"During his second trip with DUTROUX he was interested in a gypsy at a gas pump
He is presented with a photo taken from a K7 (naked girl lying on a bed)
This is YANKA MAKOVA
EMILIA told him that EVA was hypnotized by DUTROUX
EVA believes she was raped (summer 94)"
[560] 101.037 L68 MAR 16/08, SEARCH MARTIN Michelle - rue de RUBIGNIES 43-45 Assistance to the BSR THUIN, X-Dossier summary, 1235 pages, 2005, published by Wikileaks in 2009,
"Seizure :
hypnosis equipment
DEMA INTERNATIONAL envelope
plastic bag with pieces of rope
swifts
surgical retractors
ALVITYL (50 dragees)
OESTROGEL
vaginal probes
vaseline jar
Tazille 42 black jeans
ARGENTA bank card 01128523 account 979
3848463-90 (DUTROUX) a Walloon Region keyring
document written in a foreign language and
translation and mention "DAMIEN??"
doc Urbain FLORIS tel 41.43.77
BRION garage business card tel 30.60.90 sémadigit 018/56.54.01 with last call
075/62.85.47 dirty plaster
two padlocks with three keys
plastic bag with dozens of keys and
keychain"

112.553 24/08, X-Dossier summary, 1235 pages, 2005, published by Wikileaks in 2009,
"DUTIES TO BE PERFORMED FOLLOWING FIRST TRI IN NEUFCHATEAU 24/08 PERQUI rue de Rubignies
Letter from DUTROUX to JI LORENT authorizing MARTIN to reside on Rt. de Philippeville during his detention
Has the move been made?
Note that JULIE and MELISSA must have been at the address at that time

Links between hypnosis equipment and abduction of OOSTENDE PERQUI rue des Hayettes - DIAKOSTA
Lock of hair to send to INC"

[561] 'Girls believed Dutroux was protecting them, says judge', The Age, Melbourne Australia, March 5 2004

[562] PV 100.241 Interview of Lelievre, Dutroux dossier summary, 1235 pages, 2005

[563] PV 100.225 HEARING of Michel LELIEVRE, X-Dossier summary, 1235 pages, 2005, published by Wikileaks in 2009.

[564] FBI FOI/PA# 1364377-1, Letter from George Estabrooks to J. Edgar Hoover, dated June 10 1959, released document obtained from theblckvault.com

[565] Project MKUltra, The CIA's Program Of Research in Behavioral Modification,US Senate Select Committee on Intelligence, Ninety-Fifth Congress, August 3 1977, page 391

[566] MKULTRA Subproject 136 Proposal, 30 May 1961, Experimental Analysis of Extrasensory Perception, approved by the Chief, Technical Services Division/Research Branch, Central Intelligence Agency, 23 August 1961

[567] British Journal of Psychiatry (1995), Correspondance, 167, 263-270

[568] FBI FOI/PA# 1364377-1, 'Hypnosis in Juvenile Delinquency', Proposal dated September 1959 to September 1961George Estabrooks, released document obtained from theblckvault.com

[569] Florida Offense report 87-3990, 02/08/87, p. 132 fbi 1of4. https://vault.fbi.gov/the-finders/the-finders-part-01-of-04/view

[570] Florida Offense report 87-3990, 02/08/87, p. 134 fbi 1of4 https://vault.fbi.gov/the-finders/the-finders-part-01-of-04/view

[571] Case note of FBI Case (7-1685), Released in FIO/PA# 1412188-000 (TheFinders FBI Vault release 1of4 - as of August 2023), p. 55 & p.56 https://vault.fbi.gov/the-finders/the-finders-part-01-of-04/view

[572] Tallahassee PD Offense Report 87-3990, 02/08/87, Released in FIO/PA# 1412188-000 (TheFinders FBI Vault release 1of4 - as of August 2023), p.136 https://vault.fbi.gov/the-finders/the-finders-part-01-of-04/view

[573] Memo Dated 02/07/87 by U.S Customs Special Agent Ramon J. Martinez

[574] Ibid

[575] FBI case note, Released in FIO/PA# 1412188-000 (TheFinders FBI Vault release 4of4 - as of August 2023) p.176

[576] Memo Dated 02/07/87 by U.S Customs Special Agent Ramon J. Martinez
[577] FBI case note, Released in FIO/PA# 1412188-000 (TheFinders FBI Vault release 4of4 - as of August 2023) p.176
[578] Memo Dated 02/07/87 by U.S Customs Special Agent Ramon J. Martinez
[579] Metropolitan Police Department Investigation Report, Case No. 87-225, 2/19/87, Released in FIO/PA# 1412188-000 (TheFinders FBI Vault release 1of4 - as of August 2023) p.67 & p.68 https://vault.fbi.gov/the-finders/the-finders-part-01-of-04/view,

"At Approximately 1530 hrs, 2/18/87, Det [redacted] spoke with S/A [redacted] reference any contact the members of the Finders may have had with the Agency[CIA - author's note], S/A [redacted] was guarded but frank in his responses. He confirmed that [redacted] Isabells, now deceased, was an employee of the agency from 1950 until 1971. When asked if our investigation was 'treading on anyone's toes out there', [redacted] replied 'sort of'. . He acknowledged that they have had someone working on the case since it first broke on the news media. He also stated that the agency is aware that during the period 1969-1971 [redacted] travelled to Moscow. North Korea. and North Vietnam. [redacted] S/A [redacted] Stated that he would contact Det [redacted] on 2/19/87 to arrange to come to this office for further discussion. As of 1430hrs, 2/19/87, he has not contacted this office.

As a practical matter, what is not being said is as important as what S/A [redacted] has said. [redacted] acknowledged that we are treading on their toes and that they have had someone working on the case since Feb 5 when it broke. They apparently have a vested interest in [redacted] and/or group. They have not contacted any of the investigating agencies while they have been working on the case. They are also aware that [redacted] traveled to prohibited countries during a period of hostilities that could only have been arranged by them. Finally, he stated that [redacted]. This could explain a lot about the groups funding, which we have been unable to document to this point. [redacted]. Did not know that the person he turned the information over to in Europe was a source of this office and is not aware that the Source brought the Disc back to this office. [redacted] actually transferred the disc in London. Det [redacted] then turned the Disc over to WFO(?)/FBI, Counter Intelligence office for analyzation. We have not been apprised of the results of that alaysis[sic], nor do we expect to be.

Regardless of what type operation they may be engaged in, there will be no justification for the way the children have been treated, and the matter will be addressed in Family Division, Superior Court."

[580] Ibid.

[581] 'FBI dropping investigation of Washington commune', Chicago Tribune, February 13 1987

[582] 'The Devil You Say', Joseph Laitin, Washington Post, February 15 1987

[583] 'CIA tied to cult accused of abuse', Washington Times, Paul M. Rodriguez, December 17 1993.

[584] https://apnews.com/article/4c5cd8141e930159ea3e4f0492a41ade (there's not date or headline for article),

'The Justice Department said Friday it is investigating allegations the CIA used a "front company" run by a commune to train agency employees and that the CIA blocked investigation of the group.'

[585] 'Handy Andy', Jeffrey B. Roth, The Gettysburg Times, November 29 1986

[586] 'Keep your eyes peeled for 4', THe Indianapolis News, March 9 1987

[587] "Hearing set for accused child pornographer", The Gettysburg Times, August 5 1987

[588] 'Illinois inmate attempts suicide by biting himself', The Des Moines Register, August 3 1987

Milton Keynes UK
Ingram Content Group UK Ltd.
UKHW020107041123
431801UK00010B/75

9 780645 953800